Consciousness as Complex Event

Consciousness as Complex Event: Towards a New Physicalism provides a new approach to the study of consciousness. The author argues that what makes phenomenal experiences mysterious is that these experiences are extremely complex brain events. The text provides an accessible introduction to descriptive complexity (also known as Kolmogorov Complexity) and then applies this to show that the most influential arguments against physicalism about consciousness are unsound. The text also offers an accessible review of the current debates about consciousness and introduces a rigorous new conception of physicalism. It concludes with a positive program for the future study of phenomenal experience. It is readable and compact and will be of interest to philosophers and cognitive scientists, and of value to advanced students of philosophy.

Key Features

- Provides a new approach to the study of consciousness, using information theory.
- Offers a valuable discussion of physicalism, of use in other disciplines.
- Contains an introduction to the main literature and arguments in the debate about consciousness.
- Includes an accessible overview of how to apply descriptive complexity to philosophical problems.

Craig DeLancey is Professor of Philosophy at the State University of New York. He is the author of *Passionate Engines: What Emotions Reveal about Mind and Artificial Intelligence* (2001) and *A Concise Introduction to Logic* (2017).

Consciousness as Complex Event
Towards a New Physicalism

Craig DeLancey

Routledge
Taylor & Francis Group

NEW YORK AND LONDON

First published 2023
by Routledge
605 Third Avenue, New York, NY 10158

and by Routledge
4 Park Square, Milton Park, Abingdon, Oxon, OX14 4RN

Routledge is an imprint of the Taylor & Francis Group, an informa business

Library of Congress Cataloging-in-Publication Data
A catalog record for this book has been requested

ISBN: 978-1-032-33450-9 (hbk)
ISBN: 978-1-032-34131-6 (pbk)
ISBN: 978-1-003-32068-5 (ebk)

DOI: 10.4324/9781003320685

Typeset in Times New Roman
by Apex CoVantage, LLC

For Aletheia and Lorena

Contents

Mortal, that thou mayest understand aright,
I humanize my sayings to thine ear,
Making comparisons of earthly things,
Or thou mightst better listen to the wind,
Whose language is to thee a barren noise,
Though it blows legend-laden thro' the trees.

—Keats

Preface

0.1 Key Claims of the Text

This book defends a theory about consciousness. My concern is with the qualitative nature of consciousness and, in particular, with a class of phenomenal experiences that I call the "paradigmatically mysterious phenomenal experiences." By this, I mean the kinds of phenomenal experiences that philosophers typically cite as mysterious. The theory rests on three claims.

1. Paradigmatically mysterious phenomenal experiences have constitutive properties that are extremely complex.
2. Our current theories, and our current observations, about phenomenal experiences do not include all the information required to explain those experiences. These theories and observations are much less complex than the properties that constitute the phenomenal quality of paradigmatically mysterious phenomenal experiences.
3. Our judgments about a paradigmatically mysterious phenomenal experience, and our memories of that experience, cannot include all the information required to explain that experience. Rather, our judgments and memories typically include sufficient information to distinguish the kind of experience from relevant other kinds of experiences.

These claims require significant clarification, but if correct, they show that our theories and beliefs are not sufficient to enable accurate judgments about what is possible with respect to phenomenal experiences. As a result, the contemporary arguments against physicalism about phenomenal experience all fail.

The notion of complexity used here will be explained at some length in the text, drawing upon that branch of logic variously known as descriptive complexity or Kolmogorov complexity, and which is closely related to minimal description length (MDL) theory.

These are empirical claims, and ultimately their defense must rest upon further corroboration. However, I give a number of reasons to believe that each is true. Furthermore, one reason to pursue the theory is because of its productivity and utility. Most of my work in this book is to explore the implications of these claims and show how they can solve a number of outstanding philosophical puzzles. These claims provide us with an alternative explanation for the plausibility of the canonical arguments against physicalism (the knowledge, modal, gap, and zombie arguments, and applications of what I call the "superfunctionality claim"). These canonical arguments against physicalism with respect to consciousness would each appear sound, or at least plausible, if phenomenal experiences were very complex physical events. But this should raise serious doubts about the current anti-physicalist projects that characterize many of the contemporary debates about consciousness. If these canonical arguments would appear sound either when the experience was not physical, or when the experience was very complex, then we have an alternative explanation that deserves careful consideration.

These claims have other implications that I explore. These include that phenomenal experiences that are not descriptively complex will, at least in some cases, not be treated as mysterious. I argue that this is often so. Also, if both physicalism about consciousness and the complexity of consciousness claim are true, then paradigmatically mysterious phenomenal experience will require large neural events. The current anti-physicalist theories are incapable of explaining why there is a correlation between information demands and phenomenal experience, a very serious flaw with their approach.

I make no claims that this theory is sufficient to fully explain consciousness. That is why I call it a theory "about," rather than a theory "of," consciousness. Instead, I claim that the theory is true and that it has beneficial consequences. Also, the theory is very general and should be of use to, and consistent with, very many other theories of consciousness. Even anti-physicalists may find the theory of use.

We tend to think of experiences as units, as single entities. The favored term in analytic philosophy for experiences, "qualia," implies that there are atoms of consciousness to be had for each kind of experience. But my claim is that a proper explanation of a paradigmatically mysterious phenomenal experience would require a very great deal of information. And because of their complexity, they appear mysterious. But this is consistent with physicalism about consciousness, and given the productivity of science and the vagueness of the alternatives, continuing with physicalist research programs is currently our best bet for explaining consciousness. However, having said that, my version of physicalism is falsifiable and might be falsified; this takes some explaining and is addressed in Chapter 3 of this book.

These are merely a few claims to defend, but to make them rigorous requires a significant amount of clarification, argument, and application. The good news is that following the course of the arguments is, I hope, rather easy to do.

I will be throughout this book primarily concerned with consciousness understood as phenomenal quality or phenomenal character.[1] I do grant that there is a separate problem of consciousness as subjective awareness, and I will have some things to say about subjectivity in what follows, but that is not my primary target of explanation. I will mostly get by with the assumption that if we can form memories about an experience or report on the experience, then this is sufficient evidence that we are subjectively conscious of the experience. I recognize that subjective awareness is not conceptually identical to reportability—or, at least, I grant that it need not be. But my arguments will not require that I get more specific. As for other problems of consciousness that the reader may value, I can only say that I cannot in this book, without making it untenably large, try to address all such problems. Nor am I capable of doing so. Hopefully, the reader will be charitable in understanding what I am trying to accomplish and will forgive me if I do not directly address here her favorite problem of consciousness. I do predict, however, that my theory about consciousness is likely to provide you with insights into your favorite problem.

0.2 Overview and Partial Abstract

Most philosophy readers, I suspect, rarely read a philosophy book straight through. I am sympathetic: all those pages of arguments and distinctions! In the interest of making this book more accessible to jumping about, I present here, along with an overview of the chapters, an abridged version of some of my principal arguments. There is much more in this book, but this abstract at least might act as one possible set of salient signposts.

Chapter 1 introduces the central claims of the text, using several tales (I fear calling them "thought experiments," since they are more parodies than experiments). I then introduce the concept of descriptive complexity and its definition in Kolmogorov complexity. Several clarifications are needed for the arguments that follow: an account of what is presumably being measured and called "complex," some answers to common misunderstandings, and a distinction between theories and the inputs to those theories or between general properties and particulars. These latter distinctions are often overlooked in metaphysics and the philosophy of science, so the clarification is of some independent philosophical value. With the notion of descriptive complexity explained, I can state more formally the key premise of my arguments: the claim that paradigmatically mysterious phenomenal experiences are descriptively complex. I also introduce three principles that are central to my argument, which I call the modal judgment constraint principle (that the accuracy of our modal judgments depends on the completeness of our information), the contingent information principle (that many of the phenomena we aim to explain are not going to be explained by theorems of our theories alone but rather will require the addition of contingent—that is, historical—information), and the incompressibility cost principle (that, even if our theory alone explains a phenomenon, it requires additional information to reliably identify an explanation of a phenomenon more complex than the theory).

Chapter 2 defends some minimal claims about the status of our everyday phenomenological talk, our best current theories of consciousness, and our capabilities with respect to paradigmatically mysterious phenomenal experiences. I argue that our current descriptions and theories of consciousness are inadequate for the task of explaining a paradigmatically mysterious phenomenal experience because these descriptions and theories are too simple. I also argue that the capacity of our theoretical abilities is less than the information that would be required to explain the relevant phenomenal experiences.

Putting Chapters 1 and 2 together, we get the central argument. There is an objective measure of descriptive complexity, which applies to descriptions and theories. Paradigmatically mysterious phenomenal experiences include necessary properties that are very descriptively complex. Our descriptions of, and our theories of, paradigmatically mysterious phenomenal experiences are all less complex than some of the necessary properties of our paradigmatically mysterious phenomenal experiences. Furthermore, the capacity of our ability to reason about questions like metaphysical possibility is less than the complexity of some necessary properties of our paradigmatically mysterious phenomenal experiences.

We can now combine these observations with the three principles introduced in Chapter 1. The modal judgment constraint principle tells us that our judgments about what is possible with respect to these phenomena (and therefore our judgments about things like theoretical dependence) are unreliable. The contingent information principle tells us that it is naïve to presume that our scientific theories will alone explain such phenomena, in the absence of other information. And the incompressibility cost principle tells us that we can expect to need information as complex as the phenomena in question to be able to reliably explain them. Each of these observations is alone sufficient to explain why phenomenal experiences appear inexplicably mysterious. As a result, physicalism remains a good bet with respect to phenomenal experience. But this raises the questions of what physicalism is and whether we can directly reply to the influential arguments against physicalism with respect to consciousness.

Chapter 3 addresses the first issue: how should we understand "physicalism"? Some traditional forms of physicalism have received a series of effective refutations in recent years. I offer a revised conception of physicalism that will escape the problems of most theories of physicalism but still allow us to formulate the classical arguments against physicalism with respect to phenomenal experiences and related metaphysical questions. This is the view that I call *strong physicalism*. By "strong," what I mean is that this version of physicalism is easily falsifiable. My arguments in the chapters that follow could all be rephrased, likely without loss of applicability, using your favorite alternative notion of physicalism; thus, if you do not accept strong physicalism, you may still accept my other arguments. However, I think it is important to call attention to the fact that the dominant conceptions of physicalism are untenable. Also, physicalism is typically a deeply vague and confusing notion. Clarifying how the term is used in this book can only help clarify all the arguments that follow that rely on a notion of physicalism. Because strong physicalism has the benefit that it is falsifiable, anti-physicalists should be pleased by my formulation.

There is an added benefit to this discussion also. The notion of descriptive complexity introduces a neglected variable into our discussions of ontology: namely, it is typical to assume in philosophy that a failure of reduction entails that we must add new fundamental kinds to our explanations. But there is another possibility: incompressibly complex arrangements and interactions of our given ontology are also possible, and these can be unpredictable and even indescribable from the perspective of our current theory, such that explaining the phenomenon will require *new and additional theory and observations* (of complexity equal to or greater than this unexplained phenomenon) but might not require the posit of new basic ontological kinds. Consciousness is plausibly such a phenomenon.

Chapter 4 turns to answering the important arguments against physicalism with respect to phenomenal experience. Obviously, there are many such arguments and it would be impractical to respond to all or even many of them; however, five arguments have been most influential. I review the knowledge, modal, conceivability, and gap arguments, along with applications of the super-functionality claim. I show that, if the relevant phenomenal experiences are complex, each of these arguments would appear compelling, but each could be either question-begging or unsound.

In Chapter 5, I take up a prediction: if paradigmatically mysterious phenomenal experiences are complex events, and they are mysterious *because* they are complex, then we can predict that there might be (relatively) less complex phenomenal events of which we are aware and yet which we do not treat as mysterious. This prediction proves true. The thought experiments that are the center of the canonical arguments are all absurd when considering certain kinds of experiences. There is a surprising related matter: some philosophers have tried to *deny* that there is a phenomenal experience in these simpler cases. Metaphysical epicycles are added to theories of subjectivity and to theories of phenomenal experience solely to accommodate this bias in the sampling of phenomena. Here there are two systematic biases. The first is the attempt to split subjective awareness from phenomenal quality, to allow awareness without quality. The second bias is that scholars have focused all attention on the complex cases of phenomenal experiences and ignored the simpler cases. Only the most complex kinds of phenomenal experiences are ever used as examples, and the simple events are ignored or treated to eliminativism. These criticisms support a positive claim: to make progress in understanding consciousness, we will need to start with the simpler cases.

In the conclusion, I make some observations about the nature of phenomenal experience and the poetry of complexity.

0.3 Provenience

This book is the (somewhat delayed) outcome of a eureka moment I had in graduate school. I had two such moments. The first came when, during a course in neuropsychology, I discovered that our best scientific understanding of emotion was baldly inconsistent with the dominant philosophical theories of emotion. More interesting still was the subsequent discovery that our best understanding of emotion was inconsistent with many leading theories of the mind. I set to work writing a book, *Passionate Engines,* a portion of which I submitted as my thesis, and the whole of which I submitted to Oxford University Press (DeLancey 2002). The second eureka moment, and the one relevant to this book, came when I studied machine theory.

Computer scientists have a well-established set of tools to measure the costs of doing various kinds of computational work. For example, time complexity measures how many steps an algorithm requires, and space complexity measures how much memory an algorithm requires. Without these measures, the production and application of algorithms would be a very impractical business, for many in-principle solutions to problems are really no solutions at all: sometimes the easiest "solution" to find is the solution that would take billions of years to complete or require trillions and trillions of bits of memory. A third complexity measure, descriptive complexity or Kolmogorov complexity, I found enormously exciting. I saw immediately that not only was this clear and powerful branch of logic able to objectively describe things that many philosophers had declared indescribable or subjective (most notably, simplicity), but it—and the measures of time and space complexity—also made immediately obvious that many influential claims (one is tempted to say, dogmas) of analytic philosophy were refutable.

It is often observed that philosophy in the English-speaking world took a linguistic turn in the twentieth century. That's as may be, but analytic philosophy also took a logical-possibility turn in the second half of the twentieth century— and we're still on that bender. The most influential arguments in the philosophy of mind and the philosophy of language are arguments about what is logically possible, argued with complete indifference to basic considerations about practicality (and, sometimes, even an indifference to considerations about the limitations revealed by undecidability and incompleteness results). Thus:

- I have heard philosophers say that Quine has "shown" that reference is inscrutable—and yet Quine's argument for this inscrutability of reference requires that any two representational structures that could in principle produce the same behaviors are equally correct (equally likely interpretations of an agent's semantic network). This holds even if one of the two structures is so complex that it could not be represented if the whole universe were converted into one computer dedicated to embodying that structure. I hope it's simply obvious that claim is ridiculous if one thinks that there is such a thing as meaning (I recognize that, as a skeptic about meaning, Quine would be undisturbed by this—but Quine's inscrutability of reference is used by many who are not skeptics about meaning, and Quine himself seemed to believe the inscrutability argument bolsters his meaning skepticism, rather than being—as it really is—a consequence of his peculiarly costly understanding of meaning). Once we recognize that time and space are costs that matter, the inscrutability argument fails. Only a small class of interpretations is appropriate.

- Many philosophers believe that Kripke (or rather Kripkenstein) has "shown" that there is a real problem with determining and following rules, but his rule-following paradox requires that there are rules which would take 100 billion years to compute, or which would require all the matter in the universe to represent, that are equally good interpretations of my past behavior when adding two numbers, as is the addition algorithm I actually use (see DeLancey 2007b). Such a belief strikes me as a kind of argumentative nihilism. (Not to mention that Kripke's claim—essential to his skeptical argument—that simplicity is subjective is, simply, false.)

- Many philosophers still claim that Davidson has "shown" that there can be no psychophysical laws, or at least that he has "shown" that anomalous monism is a conservative and viable ontological option in the philosophy of mind, but Davidson's anomalous monism entails that you and I will be doing something significantly different when performing the same calculation—and indeed, I should be doing something significantly different when performing the same calculation on different occasions. This requires that the human brain be vastly inefficient, adopting different (and eventually immensely impractical) implementations for the same task. Why Nature would hit on a strategy of seeking unique and ever more costly implementations, rather than just settling upon efficient ones, is never explained; but perhaps Nature has read "Mental Events" and found it convincing.

- Conceivability is taken to be a guide to metaphysical truths that shape the entire universe, and, worse yet, it has become common practice in contemporary philosophy of mind not just to declare what the metaphysician can conceive but also to lay claim to insights into what an ideal reasoner, or a godlike intelligence, can conceive. My mind simply doesn't have the room to consciously represent the complexity of, say, the interactions of the microorganisms in a test tube of water dipped from the small wetland near my home. And, we have many proofs that various complex phenomena are *in principle* unpredictable. So why believe that our fancies about what an omniscient or ideally reasoning being would know is any guide to the potentially complex laws of a more mature science or metaphysics?

Such a diatribe can continue *ad nauseum,* but I hope my point is made. What many philosophers of mind and language have willfully neglected is the simple fact that *thought is work.* Davidson said there are no psychophysical laws but he was wrong; this is one such law. And, once we recognize that thought is work, then all the limitations that work must satisfy must apply to thought. This psychophysical law has many law-like corollaries: a thought that is actually occurring in the wild cannot be using an algorithm that takes a huge number of steps or a vast amount of energy or space; a thought cannot occur without using, and wasting, some energy; an organism that uses more efficient means to solve a reoccurring mental problem may earn a fitness benefit; the logical limits that apply to algorithms in mathematics must apply to algorithms of thought; and so on. There are no problems in the philosophy of mind that will not benefit from careful consideration of these kinds of questions and measures.

This book is more modest than these grand observations: it focuses on one kind or aspect of thought, the qualitative nature of phenomenal experience. Even if one is a strong dualist about phenomenal experience, it must be the case that the causal correlates of phenomenal experience are work. Furthermore, our considerations of phenomenology, our considerations of intuitions about consciousness, and our considerations of arguments about consciousness are work. My task here is in part to show some of the implications of taking these facts into account.

My principal conclusions are consistent with the arguments that some other philosophers have made in recent years. Daniel Dennett, for example, has argued that questions about the conceivability of laws and phenomena, and the usual suspects among the thought experiments, begin with presumptions that the phenomena are simple:

> But if what it is like to see triangles can be adequately conveyed in a few dozen words, and what it is like to see Paris by moonlight in May can be adequately conveyed in a few thousand words (an empirical estimate based on the variable success of actual attempts by novelists), are we really so sure that what it is like to see red or blue can't be conveyed to one who has never seen colors in a few million or billion words? What is it about the experience of red, or blue, that makes this task impossible? (And don't just say: they're *ineffable*.)

> (Dennett 2005: 115)

Similarly, Daniel Stoljar (2006) has offered an "epistemic view" of the problem of consciousness, in which the leading arguments against physicalism are (mis)taken as plausible because of our own ignorance. Alva Noe has argued that a red experience, for example, seems ineffable because it is complex; its quality is "a matter of its looking such as to enable one to discriminate it in a *very* broad range of different ways, it is to experience it as possessing a complicated network of potential saliencies" (2004: 149). Pete Mandik (2010) has argued that an essential feature of physicalism about the qualitative experience is the recognition that qualitative experience is complex or at least has structure. Kenneth Williford has views sympathetic to those in this book: "Behind phenomenal space there is a vastly complicated machine that introspection and experience can only give us hints of" (Williford et al. 2012: 334). There are interesting parallels (and important differences) between my view and the debate about "overflow" of conscious experience (see Block and MacDonald

2008). Integrated Information Theory, developed by Giulio Tononi and his team (e.g., Masafumi et al. 2014), is a theory of consciousness that has as a consequence that phenomenal experiences are very complex. No doubt there are other similar developments.

The novelty of this book is that it offers a rigorous explanation of why the phenomenon in question may be complex and hard to convey and otherwise about which it may be difficult sometimes to draw correct conclusions. My approach also has the added benefit that it provides positive and testable predictions. But, most importantly, I consider it some corroboration to have arrived by my own route among auspicious company. I hope it is a sign of some convergence on a successful theory that we find similar views developing from very different starting places, and also that I am able to offer a technical description and explanation of phenomena that others have observed.

Acknowledgments

Part of the research and writing that went into this book occurred while I was a fellow at the Center for the Philosophy of Science at the University of Pittsburgh. I am grateful to the Center for their support and to the other fellows for their conversation. Part of the research and writing of this book was also completed while I was a junior fellow of the National Endowment for the Humanities. I am grateful to the N.E.H. for their support. The rest of the work of writing the book was undertaken during a one-semester sabbatical and also during two summer research projects, and I thank the State University of New York at Oswego for providing me with time and support for those. Thanks also to Oswego's Research Foundation.

Special thanks to Lorena Ferrero DeLancey and Aletheia DeLancey. Thanks to Joe Fornieri for his friendship and encouragement. Thanks to Gage McGill, who proofread, and offered advice on, an earlier version of the text. I am grateful to, and indebted to, three anonymous reviewers for Routledge.

Versions of parts of Chapter 1 and 4 of this book appeared in a different form in *Erkenntnis* (as "Phenomenal Experience and the Measure of Information," 2007, 66 (3): 329–352), *Philosophical Studies* (as "Consciousness and the Superfunctionality Claim," 2012, 161 (3): 433–451), and *Ratio* (as "The Modal Arguments and the Complexity of Consciousness," 2013, 26 (1): 35–50). I thank each journal for letting me use the material here.

Note

1. And when I talk of "phenomenal consciousness" or "phenomenal experience," I mean what Josh Weisberg calls the "moderate reading" of these terms—that is, I do not intend to rule out functional properties for experience. See Weisberg (2011a: 438).

1 Complexity in Mind

1.1 Overview

This chapter has two purposes. First, it introduces the notion of descriptive complexity, establishing that there is a rigorous and objective measure of complexity that will be used in this book. I also review how the measure is to be applied. Second, I give an overview of some consequences of this complexity; these consequences are essential to the arguments of this book.

But I begin with some illustrative parodies.

1.2 Three Tales

Consider the following tale:[1]

> Mary is serving a long sentence in a low security prison (she was caught embezzling in an effort to pay off the student loans she accumulated while earning her on-line Ph.D. in the neural science of color vision). Mary is allowed unlimited phone use, but no books, television, or Internet. Also, the warden encourages Mary's interest in painting, since he considers it rehabilitating. Mary's miscreant friend Fred hatches a scheme. Recently, Jackson Pollock's painting Lucifer went missing. Fred knows unethical art collectors who would buy the painting if it turned up on the black market. Fred thinks he could sell these collectors a forgery. Knowing Mary paints, he calls her at the prison, pitches his scheme, and begins to describe the painting to her. Mary has never seen the painting, other Jackson Pollock works, or Pollock's imitators. In fact, because of a famously unusual childhood, she has seen no modern paintings. Not to worry, thinks Fred: they have years and years to talk. He'll just describe the painting at length to her. When she's done painting according to his verbal instructions, he'll come during visiting hours, she'll hand the painting over, and later they'll split the illicit gains.

The question to ask now is: could Mary make a decent forgery under these conditions?

DOI: 10.4324/9781003320685-1

This task is so impractical as to be nearly impossible. There are many reasons why. First, the telephone is a channel with a bandwidth that is just too low to convey all the right kinds of information. It is not that speech is in principle a medium incapable of conveying the required information. One could imagine devising a code that would begin to rise to the task. The canvas could be described in terms of small areas, each with a specific color. But then there are issues like the thickness of the paint, the sweep of the paint from one of these areas to another, and so on. Those are going to require more than just knowing which colors go in which small square area. Getting this over some conversations, no matter how long, is impractical.

Frank could offer Mary all kinds of advice on how to emulate Pollock's techniques, which might prove eventually sufficient for emulating that technique. But recall that she's not trying to emulate Pollock's techniques alone. She's attempting a forgery: the painting must look deceptively similar to the original Lucifer, of which there are many photographs. Learning to cast paint over the prone canvas is not enough. The paint must be cast to create the same patterns in the same colors.

Second, motor skills and perceptions both appear to be related to our reasoning skills in a way that would not facilitate this kind of transaction. Those who claim that consciousness is not physical make a great deal out of the fact that it is hard to say what a strawberry tastes like. But, oddly, they don't say much about the fact that it is hard to tell someone how to ride a bicycle (I'm not saying it's hard to give valuable feedback to someone riding a bike; rather the analogous case would be, imagine someone who's never ridden a bike, and your task is to talk to her, and only talk to her, so that when the conversation is done she can ride a bike). There are many things that we can do and recognize that are hard to learn through speech and reasoning. Part of the reason is that the skill is complex, and we're not built to convey that information through speech or reading; we get that information through learning by doing.

The task for Mary is practically impossible because there is just too much information in Pollack's painting to be conveyed over the narrow bandwidth of a telephone conversation, given human abilities to retain and integrate such information—not to mention that we suppose Mary is going to finish the task, if at all, during her lifetime. Note that this problem does not extend to all ways of conveying information about the painting. Seeing the painting or having pictures of the painting, for example, would be quite different. The information that one could glean from viewing Pollock's painting Lucifer is information that humans are able to recognize and even in some senses manipulate. An expert on Pollock's painting Lucifer would be able to recognize it by sight alone, would be able to distinguish it from other of Pollock's paintings and works by other painters, and would be the kind of person called to evaluate a Lucifer-like painting to ensure if it were original. An expert can imagine the painting (not in all its detail but in some detail), perhaps even imagine it upside-down. Thus, it is not the case that we cannot understand or recognize the painting, nor that we cannot manipulate some of this information.

None of us will claim that Pollock's painting is non-physical, or that it merely supervenes on but is not identical with the physical, or is an epiphenomenon of the physical, or is an ontologically simple or basic thing, or whatever other alternative to physicalism is on offer. If anything is physical, the painting Lucifer is. It's a brute physical object, made of other brute physical things like canvas and paint and wood. Mary cannot forge Lucifer under these conditions, not for any strange ontological feature of the painting, but because the features of the painting that matter to us, and would be required of a successful forgery, are descriptively complex.

The following situation would be similar. Suppose Mary were (for some reason) not to see color at the beginning of her life, but during this achromatic period, Fred frequently tries to explain what the experience of red is like through telephone conversations. Mary would not grasp the experience from the descriptions given by Fred—not because color experience is ontologically strange, but rather because, like the painting Lucifer, it is complex. No amount of practical theorizing and practical description of the kind we currently do will be sufficient for Mary to grasp (infer, simulate, etc.) the color experience. So, if one day Mary were to see color for the first time, she would learn something new. As the two cases are analogous, this suggests that the most parsimonious view about a color experience event is that it is no less physical than Pollock's Lucifer.

Consider another tale:

> Thomas wonders what it's like to be a bat. Thomas believes that some day, superfine resolution fMRI machines and other research techniques will allow us to record all the relevant information in a bat's brain while it performs an echolocation task; and Thomas wonders whether, if he can understand that information, he will then understand what it's like to be a bat. Meanwhile, to make a very small step toward discovering this, Thomas gets a research grant to use new higher-resolution fMRI machines to record bat brain activity while his lab bats are performing echolocation tasks. When the first recording is made, Thomas looks at it for hours. The file is many gigabytes of data. He looks at this data as changing color blotches on a computer screen, but at least on his first look he cannot see in the color blotches any patterns that help him better understand the experience of bat echolocation. Thomas starts to believe that it is impossible for science to ever reveal what it's like for there to be a pattern in this bat brain activity.

Should Thomas conclude that it is hopeless to know what it's like to understand the brain activation patterns of echolocation? It would be premature on Thomas's part to do so. He is only taking his first look at a huge set of data. A great deal of analysis might be required to identify the patterns. And, more importantly, it just may turn out that he is never able to see the patterns himself but is able to identify them using mathematical (e.g., software) tools that seek and discern very complex patterns. In such a case, the patterns there will not be the kind of thing that he can see in the form of data the fMRI machine produces.

But then should Thomas conclude that we, or at least he, can never know what these patterns are like? It depends on what he ultimately means by "know." But there is one sense in which he could be right about his fMRI hypothesis—that super-fine resolution fMRI will yield enough information about the bat brain activity to allow one to in principle understand what it is like to be a bat—and yet it could still be the case that he will never know. The reason is that the patterns involved may just be too complex for him to ever grasp with his theoretical abilities. This is no impediment to scientific study, however. Many phenomena that science studies are complex—the economy, an ecosystem, and the motions of millions of individual molecules in a gas. We do not call these phenomena non-physical because they are (in some cases) complex—not even if they are unpredictable because of their complexity. Furthermore, the fact that Thomas simply isn't built to be able to take in all that data and hold it all in his head does not mean that, if he *were* able to do that, he wouldn't know what it is like to be a bat. Perhaps if he could read off the fMRI data, remember it all, and "turn it around" in his head, he would experience echolocation for himself, as if remembering doing it.

The case is similar to Thomas's armchair musings about bat echolocation experience. Sitting in his armchair, trying to imagine what it is like to be a bat, Thomas concludes it is incomprehensibly strange. This might be true. Bat echolocation experience might be so complex that it is irreducibly strange. But this does not establish that it is not a physical event, nor that it is immune to scientific understanding.

Let's extend the story.

> After weeks of statistical analysis of the data, Thomas and his team use complex software to identify patterns in the data that reliably predict certain kinds of echolocation behaviors. These patterns are very complex, and are all of a kind we can call *E*-patterns. No human being staring at the fMRI data playing across a computer screen could see and distinguish patterns of kind *E* from most other patterns. It would be like distinguishing between two pictures of different television screens tuned to a dead channel. That is, the *E*-pattern is so complex that instances of it appear to us as random, as noise. And yet further research confirms that the patterns are there in the bats that he measured, and are reliable predictors of certain kinds of echolocation behavior. Now, Thomas's lab colleague David develops the following worry. What if there are—or even, what if there could be—bats flying around without this pattern of activity that this analyzing software has found in the bat brains they have so far studied? David calls these hypothetical bats "zombie bats," and he can't see any reason to suppose that they don't exist (or at least, could exist), because he can't see any contradiction between the claim that there is no *E*-pattern in these

zombie bats and the claim that they are echolocating. More specifically, what he *means* by "echolocation" and what he *means* by "*E*-pattern" are such that he can conceive of the former existing without the latter. Thus, he concludes, it can't be that the pattern the software found is what explains (or is necessary to explaining) echolocation capabilities. When some of his colleagues doubt his reasoning, he demands a proof that zombie bats are impossible; when they are unable to provide it, he concludes that belief in the possibility of zombie bats is warranted, and so he is warranted in believing the *E*-pattern is not a description or explanation of echolocation, nor a description of some process that might (in part, eventually) explain echolocation.

Should David (and you and I) now conclude that there are or there can (in some sense of "can") be zombie bats, and therefore that the appearance of an *E*-pattern is not essential to the echolocation experience?

No. David's apparent ability to conceive of the zombie bats could just mean that the *E*-pattern is so complex he cannot know its proper functional relations, and he cannot know when he is making claims that contradict the proper description of those functional relations. By supposition, the *E*-pattern is very complex. If his understanding of it is not equally complex, then his understanding must have thrown away some information,[2] and this lost information might be essential to properly explaining echolocation experience. Furthermore, his demand that his colleagues identify the contradiction (in the claim that there are zombie bats) is unfair, for it requires that his colleagues fully grasp the complex pattern and fully grasp what it describes, and then deduce a contradiction with the zombie bat claim, and then convey that to David in a way that he can understand. Because the *E*-pattern is *very* complex, reliably determining facts about it will require a complex theory or at least complex additional information like additional observations. Besides, David's colleagues have a fully adequate answer already: they can simply point to the empirical evidence that patterns of kind *E* are reliably correlated with echolocation in their random sample of subjects. Surely that is much better evidence than David's argument.[3] Thus, David's claims about conceivability do not tell us what is possible with respect to *E*; specifically because the pattern of kind *E* is complex and we don't fully understand it.

I hold that the same is true of the common claim that there could be phenomenal zombies: humans with a physical constitution like ours but without conscious (qualitative) experience. If the relevant phenomenal experiences were descriptively complex in the relevant ways, then we can *predict* that our simple theories will allow us to "conceive" of zombies and will also fail to help us identify the resulting contradiction, even if the phenomenal experience is a physical event. The anti-physicalist arguments mistake practical difficulties for metaphysical differences.

These three tales are analogous to the leading thought experiments given today to "show" that phenomenal experiences are not material or physical events. My contention is that there are two possible explanations for the judgments that these kinds of thought experiments encourage. That is, these kinds of thought experiments, and other arguments against physicalism with respect to consciousness, encourage us to conclude that phenomenal experiences are not the kind of thing that one could fully understand through a physicalist theory as offered by, say, reading books and attending lectures. Suppose this is true. There are at least two explanations for why this claim could be true. First, it could be because physicalism about consciousness is false. Second, it could be because the amount of information in a (paradigmatically mysterious) phenomenal experience is very great, much more than can be conveyed from one human to another in conversation or a readable text. The latter explanation, the one that I favor and will defend in this book, has many advantages over the anti-physicalist one, including its productivity and its parsimony.

A corollary of these claims is a novel form of denial of the common claim, taken by some to be obviously true, that (for at least some kinds of judgments) we cannot be wrong when we characterize our subjective qualitative states. On this view, when my subjective states are the thing about which I am making a judgment, then I cannot fail to be correct in my judgment. The reason for this epistemic certainty is that there can be no gulf between the appearance and the reality; when the reality I want to study is the appearance itself, then it would seem that they are the same thing, and so along with rejecting the appearance-reality distinction, one also rejects the possibility of error. There is no gulf out of which mistakes can arise. After all, "wrong" typically means that the appearance is not true of the reality; but if the appearance is identical with the reality, then the appearance must be true of the reality.

To consider an instance of such reasoning: a predictable response to the claim that paradigmatically mysterious phenomenal experiences are complex is something like, "No they are not. I can 'see' that my red experience is simple." But of course we humans can't see that at all. There is nothing in the experience that corroborates the claim that it is simple. All that such a claim corroborates is that if it is complex, we are unable to describe its complexity. This is not surprising. We are ignorant of almost everything the mind does, and we are demonstrably and highly fallible with regard to our understanding of the things that we are aware of that the mind does. Furthermore, we are well familiar with examples where experience seems to corroborate a judgment that we know to be false. For example, if you ask the layperson if she sees color in the periphery of her vision just as she does in the center of her field, she will say yes. But she does not, and so on. Our sense of how complex an experience is will be just as reliable as these judgments—which is to say, it is not reliable.[4]

There are many philosophers who attack infallibility or authority claims for experience, of course.[5] But using the concept of descriptive complexity explained in the following, we can offer a new and independent demonstration of why first-person beliefs regarding phenomenal experiences are fallible. One reason is that appearances are not the elements of our arguments. Our experiences are not constituents of our theories or our judgments—including judgments about appearances. Our *understanding* of our experiences is what constitutes the relevant content of our judgments regarding experience or our concepts of experience. Neither phenomenal concepts nor phenomenal judgments are identical with their target phenomenal experiences. Another reason why first-person beliefs regarding phenomenal experiences are fallible is that the events that constitute our experiences will not all be experienced. That is, there will be complex causes for our experiences that are not themselves experienced, but which must be described to properly explain the experience.

If our experiences are very complex, then our understandings of experiences are very likely to fail to capture all the relevant information of those experiences; indeed, if the information capacity of a judgment is less than (in a way to be explained later) the complexity of the experience being judged, then our judgment about the experience will *necessarily* leave out information; it will be an approximation not only which is fully capable of error but also which, in a sense, *must* be in error. In the same way that, in the first story mentioned earlier, Fred could not convey to Mary via speech all the information in the painting, our own conceptual understanding of a sight will not contain all (nor even much) of the information needed for an adequate explanation of that sight.

If we grant that paradigmatically mysterious phenomenal experiences are complex events and that the current arguments that the phenomenal experiences are non-physical fail, then it seems still the best bet that something not radically different from contemporary science can explain consciousness. That is, some form of physicalism appears to still be our best bet for the most promising research program. But we can say much more than this. The claim that paradigmatically mysterious phenomenal experiences are complex is in principle testable—testable in the near term. This stands in very strong contrast to the current crop of anti-physicalist claims, which either are not falsifiable or are falsifiable only at some unreachable limit (e.g., when we know all physical facts, or when we are ideally rational, etc.). Most importantly, this hypothesis points the way to productive research programs.

Before I can turn to these claims and corollaries, several clarifications are required. First, I must explain what I mean by "complex." If this notion is not made rigorous, then the claims that I aim to defend will be vacuous. I will explain descriptive complexity in what remains of this chapter. Second, I will need to outline the relation between our theories of experience, our understanding of our experiences, and our experiences themselves. I do this in the next chapter. Third, before I turn to evaluating the anti-physicalist arguments, I should offer a notion of what I will take "physicalism" to mean. I'm compelled to do this because it is difficult to have a discussion about physicalism without the debate becoming a muddle. We can avoid this with a clear notion of what we mean by "physicalism" in this context. I offer this in Chapter 3.

I have used the phrase "paradigmatically mysterious" several times now. By this, I mean the kinds of phenomenal experiences that appear mysterious to us and which we find it hard to describe and convey to others who lack the experience. These are the experiences that are held up as examples of non-physical or otherwise perplexing phenomena in anti-physicalist arguments. Most of the examples in the philosophy literature are color experiences, and the rest are mostly pain or other perceptions or sensations. I will have much more to say about this in Chapter 5, but, in brief, one of my contentions is that we have allowed an insidious sample bias to infect our discussion of consciousness. We focus always upon certain kinds of phenomenal experiences, like color experience, but we adopt eliminativism about, or aggressively ignore, others, such as the experience of believing that $2+2=4$. If you are not an eliminativist about the latter kind of experience, then it will be useful to have a way of distinguishing the ignored experiences from the widely discussed but biased sample of experiences. I do this by calling the biased sample the "paradigmatically mysterious phenomenal experiences." My suspicion is that the paradigmatically mysterious phenomenal experiences are mostly sensations or perceptions (e.g., sight, hearing, pain), autonomic awareness (e.g., the feelings accompanying terror), and combinations thereof. My central claim will be that the paradigmatically mysterious phenomenal experiences are precisely those that are descriptively complex.

1.3 Descriptive Complexity

The term "complex" is ambiguous. I refer here to a specific mathematical notion. But, even in the realms of mathematics and computer science, there are several different notions of complexity. A procedure is complex, for example, if it would take very many steps to perform (this is called "time complexity") or is complex if it would take very much memory to perform (this is called "space complexity"). Here, however, I intend to refer to a different notion of complexity: how much space it takes to *say something* or to *describe something*. This is called "descriptive complexity."

This idea is quite easy to grasp. Let us call any kind of ordered string of symbols we could write down, a "description." This is a very general notion. It is syntactic, but in a very liberal sense: not in the sense that a linguist uses "syntax" but rather in the very simple sense that we will measure complexity by looking at the quantity of the actual ordered symbols used to describe something. The insight of descriptive complexity is that some descriptions can be substantially compressed, but most cannot.

Consider the following two descriptions, which for ease of explanation are binary strings (here I adopt an example from Chaitin 1990):

(A) 1010101010101010101010101010101010101010101010101010101010101
0101010101010101010101010101010101010101010101010101010101010
1010101010101010101010101010101010101010101010101010101010101
0101010101010101010101010101010

(B) 0111110011110010001010101101101001110000101110100110011110101000000100111101001110101101110010011100101001011
1100000000111000110011100001111011101100100010011001110011110010001110001110111111111001

String *A* is quite easy to describe. We can say "string *A* is '01' repeated 100 times." Even a string *A** that was a million times longer than *A*, but with the same pattern, would be easy to describe. We would say "string *A** is '01' repeated 100 million times." String *B* is not easy to describe. Try to find a description of *B* such that, if you wrote that description down and gave it to another person, she would be able to reliably reproduce string *B*. You will find that your best strategy is just to write down *B* and give that to the other person. *B* is not simple. *B* is complex.

What is the difference between *A* and *B* that makes us want to say *A* is simple and *B* is complex? It is not their size. They are both 200 symbols long. It is not some traditional statistical property—if we were tossing an unbiased coin, counting heads as 1 and tails as 0, then each of these strings would have a 1 in 2^{200} chance of occurring. It is rather that we are able to *compress A*. We are able to describe it in a shorthand way that loses no information. We are unable, however, to compress *B*. There is no shortcut to describing it. If you must produce a description that will reliably reproduce *B*, you will have to write *B* down in its entirety. There is little information in *A*—after all, we could describe it quite briefly, but there is more information in *B*, so much that we cannot find a shorthand way to describe it unless we lose information (and thus lose the ability to reproduce *B*).

This intuitive notion can and has been made rigorously precise in a branch of mathematics independently developed by three mathematicians: Gregory Chaitin, Andrey Kolmogorov, and Ray Solomonoff.[6] The guiding idea of descriptive complexity is that the complexity of a description is the size of the shortest general recursive procedure that can reliably reproduce just that string. This can be made more familiar if we pick a machine that can produce general recursive procedures and with which we are all experienced: a computer or a universal Turing machine.[7] The descriptive complexity of a description is the size of the shortest computer program that can reliably print or recognize just that description. (I will use *recognize* and *print* as essentially equivalent demands. This is acceptable because determining either task will give, within a few bits, the same descriptive complexity value. Just as "print" means, reliably reproduce, to be able to recognize a string is to be able to accurately say *yes* or *no* regarding whether any arbitrary string has the property in question.) We typically assume this measure is expressed in number of bits (for example, if a program 100 bits long can print or recognize a string *S*, we say that *S* has a complexity of at most 100).

We noted earlier that *A* was rather simple. Descriptive complexity captures this nicely. A simple computer program that printed *A* could have a for-loop that printed "01" 100 times. If we can indulge in some pseudocode, we would have:

Program A:

```
FOR (I = 0; I < 100; I++) {
PRINT: "01"
}
```

Measured in bits, this program would be rather small, and if it were the smallest possible program that could print string A, then its size in bits would then express the descriptive complexity of A, measured in bits.

With about 13 extra bits, the same program could be modified to print $A*$— that is, it could print "01," 100,000,000 times.

Program $A*$:

```
FOR (I = 0; I < 100,000,000; I++) {
PRINT: "01"
}
```

This shows us that $A*$ is not much more complex than A, even though it is a million times longer.

The program that reliably prints B is not going to give us any shortcuts. It is going to require a line of code that looks something like:

Program B:

```
PRINT:"01111100111100100100010101011011010011100001011101001
10011110101000000100111101001110101101110010011100101001011
11100000000011100011001110000111101110110010001001100111001
111100100011100011101111111001"
```

And so this procedure, this program, cannot be shorter than B itself. Note then that if we had a $B*$ a million times longer than B but also incompressibly complex, our program would have to be a million times larger than this one—and thus very much larger than the program required to print $A*$, even though both strings $A*$ and $B*$ are 200,000,000 bits long when printed out. (Consider: this book has about 500,000 characters, so printing out $B*$ would require as much space as about 400 such books, whereas we have already given with *program-$A*$* earlier a description of the 200,000,000-bit-long string $A*$.)

In our time, most of us are now all very familiar with descriptive complexity, although we don't use that phrase to describe it. We understand that a high-quality digital recording of our favorite songs will be larger than a lower-quality recording; the reason, of course, is that the lower-quality recording threw away information. Similarly, we understand that a digital camera's quality in part depends on how many megapixels of information it can record; this is just a measure of how much information it is able to make into a binary description of the visual image that strikes the chip. And we are also now familiar with the constraints that descriptive complexity implies. My first computer had a 20-megabyte hard drive. It held some documents, but little more. It could not have held a movie, or a symphony, or even a lecture, by current recording standards. This is not because there is something radically new about current recordings, as if the ontological status of recordings has changed. It is because such recordings have a great deal more information in them than that storage would allow.

This easy-to-understand notion of descriptive complexity is enormously fruitful. A few important observations should be made.

First, I have said throughout that the procedure in question must *reliably* reproduce *just* the description in question or reliably be able to recognize it. This is an important point that often gets glossed over in explanations of descriptive complexity. It is important because a program that made use of some kind of random number generator and printed out various random strings would ultimately print the description in question, given enough time. Similarly, a simple program can be written that will print all strings of some alphabet. This is not what we mean here. The program must produce (or recognize) always and only the string in question. This is because you are trying to identify or reproduce that particular string. If you reproduce random strings or many strings, we are then confronted with the problem of identifying which is the particular string in question that we want to recognize or print.

Second, although for the sake of ease I contrasted a repeating with a non-repeating string, it is important to note that simplicity is not a matter of repetition. That is, it is not the case that a description is descriptively complex if and only if it is non-repeating. This would be an easy misconception to develop, and it is a common mistake to think that this is what is being measured by descriptive complexity. But π, for example, is non-repeating and has a low descriptive complexity—there are short programs that can print π. On the other hand, repeating descriptions of any descriptive complexity exist.

Third, we can see why it is useful to think of this as compression and as information. How much we can compress a description will indicate how its complexity differs from its actual size. The size of a fully compressed description is the complexity of the description. Similarly, it makes sense to say that there is little information in a string that compresses to a short program and, in fact, to identify the quantity of information with the descriptive complexity. This then captures the idea that a string with a great deal of information is a large string that is not (very) compressible. If it were, why not refer to the compressed form to assess how much information is in the description? I will follow this insight and identify the quantity of information in a description with its descriptive complexity. This measure is of a numerical magnitude. Given in bits, for example, it would be the number of bits in the shortest program that prints the string in question. Complexity can have a lower bound (0) but (for any language that will be of interest in this book) no upper bound.

Descriptive complexity also provides a very valuable notion of randomness. Look again at strings A and B: one of these strings I simply made up while typing at my keyboard and the other I created with a laborious and boring series of coin tosses. Which is which? Most people guess that A is the string that I made up (I've tested this many times with students, and not found an exception). But why? Normal statistical models will say that they are both equally likely to be produced by a coin toss—that is, both have a 1 in 2^{200} chance of being produced by coin tosses (assuming a fair coin, etc.). Why is it so obvious that A is the one I made up? The answer appears to be that we know that it is much easier for me to produce A than it would be for me to produce $\boldsymbol{B}$. Being told I produced one string via the easy way of just making it up and one string the hard way of performing and recording coin tosses, it seems most likely that A is the made-up string. And that's because the amount of information I had to have and use to make A is very small. This meant I could do it with little work (and probably also it means you assume philosophers are lazy).

A description that cannot be compressed we can call "Chaitin random." Note that the most compressed form of any description is by definition Chaitin random. An interesting fact about Chaitin randomness is that we tend to overlook how prevalent it is. We tend to ignore the complexities around us—probably because it's too much work to pay attention to them. Thus, the newspaper tells us the national debt is "twenty nine trillion dollars," or some nicely rounded simple number because that's a number that's easily compressed. If the newspaper reported that the national debt is $29,365,446,682,289.59, this would be hard to say, hard to remember, hard to read aloud, harder to reason about, and so on. We round to the simpler cases.

Interestingly, even in the crystal-clear rigors of arithmetic, many numbers are Chaitin random, and most are nearly Chaitin Random. The proof of this is rather simple (see Section 1.9.1), and a moment of reflection on this fact is a little shocking.[8] Many of us are inclined to think of the natural numbers as neat and orderly. In fact, almost all of them are nearly Chaitin random (that is, almost all of them can only be compressed a small amount); that means that much of what can be said about such numbers cannot be simplified, and often no patterns are to be found other than the brute numbers themselves. Number theory is a zoo of ever more, unboundedly complex, phenomena. These facts should warn us that in every domain of study, we are attending to the simple cases and often overlooking that many instances of proper descriptions of the relevant phenomena may be Chaitin random.

One other clarification is important. Not only descriptions of particular objects but also theories and descriptions of properties can have a complexity value. In fact, the idea of descriptive complexity is perhaps most clear when thought of as referring to theories: the smallest program that defines the descriptive complexity of a string can be thought of as including data and also a program to unpack that data; it is like a description and also a theory that one applies to the description to derive a prediction. It is important to note that a theory can be simple or complex, and also a description of a property of a phenomenon can be simple or complex.[9] It may be that a particular description has a property that we are interested in, and that this property is very complex. The property would be described as at least one posit of our theory. We could then also talk about descriptions of properties, which are captured in our theories, but a particular description, if it had that property, would also be exemplifying the property. Thus, we will sometimes need to clarify whether a particular description, or a property of the description, is of interest to us; and we will need to be clear about which we are identifying as complex. This matters because when we say a phenomenon is complex, we may mean that it has a complex property, so that it may sometimes be necessary to indicate the complexity of the theory that describes this property; or it may just mean that the particular description is itself very complex.

Descriptive complexity is a definition of a measure. The definition is clear and well defined, and we know that this measure has certain properties. There is a distinct question we can ask about descriptive complexity, however: how can we determine the descriptive complexity of a particular description? It turns out that this is undecidable—which means that there is no effective procedure to determine the descriptive complexity of any arbitrary description. This is not surprising; many interesting questions of mathematics that are very useful are undecidable. Even if we have challenges in determining the descriptive complexity of a particular description, this does not change that the description does have a descriptive complexity value; there is a fact of the matter about whether something is complex or not. Undecidability merely means we can't be certain of finding an arbitrary description's precise complexity. We may often, however, be able to say that something is complex, or that one description is more complex than another, in a reliable way. But, in any case, I will not be trying to determine actual descriptive complexity values in this book, so there will be no problem of running up against this limitation. It will impinge on none of my arguments.

More importantly, there is a family of statistical methods that captures the essential insight of descriptive complexity and allows us to always find an approximate measure of descriptive complexity to any required degree of accuracy. These methods are known as the *minimum description length* methods (often called "MDL") and have been developed by such scholars as Rissanen (1978, 1989). Thus, there are methods to find with sufficient accuracy the descriptive complexity of any description.

1.4 Quick Work With Some Common Objections

When first encountering descriptive complexity, philosophers tend to have a number of suspicions. In this section, I will address objections that I have encountered. If you are already familiar with descriptive complexity, or if you find descriptive complexity unobjectionable, you are invited to skip ahead to Section 1.5.

One suspicion that might arise is that this is a measure that will vary too widely. There are many computer languages and operating systems and hardwares. Won't the descriptive complexity of a description be wildly different, depending upon the computer we chose? We can generalize the question to the observation that there are infinitely many different possible universal Turing machines. We could of course agree upon a particular universal Turing machine, and then we would get the same measure (this is sometimes called "concrete" descriptive complexity). Also, we can predict that practical Turing machines, given our needs, will be quite similar (almost all of those infinitely many possible universal Turing machines will be impractically inefficient implementations). Finally, it seems reasonable as a measure to pick the smallest universal Turing machine we can find; if we later find an even smaller machine, its determination will be very close to those we developed using the first machine. But the real power of the concept of descriptive complexity arises from the fact that, regardless of which universal Turing machine we pick, the descriptive complexity of some description we aim to measure will not vary a great deal, when expressed by that universal Turing machine, from what we would have found using a different universal Turing machine. Thus, the answer to this question about variability is *no:* the descriptive complexity of a description will not be wildly different, depending upon the computer we chose. More significantly, it has been shown that the measure of descriptive complexity is independent of the particular universal Turing machine chosen, up to some constant. That means, your measure might differ from mine, but always within some particular finite bound. This result is not surprising when we remember that all computers are of equal power (in the sense of what they can compute, given unbounded time and memory), and so any universal Turing machine can simulate any other universal Turing machine given some finite program. And the smallest size of that finite program is the finite bound that may distinguish the descriptive complexity measures between these two machines. This is enormously important because it means that descriptive complexity is an objective measure.

A second suspicion the reader may have—one which I have found many philosophers raise when first learning about descriptive complexity—is that descriptions can be made more or less complex at will, simply by skipping whatever compression algorithm we are using, and instead adding ostensive terms to the elements of our language. This suspicion is related to an easy misunderstanding that can arise regarding arguments that I make later, so addressing it clearly now will be beneficial. The mistaken idea involved is something like this: I hereby christen the string *B* above "*b*." Now, I've compressed it down to a single element in my language.

This idea rests on an important insight: we do of course give complex things simple names so that we can quickly identify and discuss them. But this is not relevant to the arguments that I will make in this book, for three reasons. The first reason is that there just are not enough short names in any language to use as names for all the possible complex descriptions (see Section 1.9.1). This is why most descriptions of any language are very close to incompressible. That is, if this symbol "*b*" is meant to be a symbol that already exists in our language, then this strategy does not scale. You will quickly run out of names for complex strings.

But what, one might reply, if "*b*" is a new symbol, added to our language, and not one that already exists in our language? We in fact rule this move out in the definition of descriptive complexity because we assume that we start with some finite alphabet, and then must use that alphabet to describe each thing. It is hard to imagine how one would object to this assumption: it is meant only to capture the idea of how languages (broadly understood) work. We don't introduce new letters to the alphabet (that is, we don't introduce completely novel symbols) every time we name a new phenomenon. Still, to set aside this observation for a moment, suppose we did name *B* "*b*," and that "*b*" is a new symbol. Didn't we just make the descriptive complexity of *B* equal 1 (assuming now we've expanded the alphabet to include this new symbol "*b*")? This in fact turns out to be a strategy that cannot allow us to describe the world in any systematic way. To see this, consider again arithmetic. I mentioned earlier that there is a simple proof that there are many incompressible strings, which means in this case many incompressible numbers. Switching to base 10 numbers in order to make the example more familiar: imagine now someone said,

1,623,472,830,047,525,892,371,874,020,720,093,427 is not a complex number, because I'll just call it "α."

Where, we assume, α is added to our alphabet (it was not previously in our alphabet) and is not used to label any other object. Presumably, this can form a strategy for adding to our language as needed.

But this cannot be a global strategy. Consider, in our example earlier: what about the next Chaitin random number that we encounter? Shall we call it "β" (where β is a new symbol added to our alphabet of existing symbols)? The reader will quickly recognize the unmitigated disaster that arithmetic would be if, instead of using recursive numbering, with ten basic elements that we recombine, we instead introduced a new name for each complex number we encountered. The second reason this is not an exception is that it really depends on us keeping the complex description in mind. That is, if I ask you what α is, what can you say? A number smaller than β? Or must you point at a heap of 1,623,472,830,047,525,892,371,874,020,720,093,427 beans and say, "It's that many beans"? Or some other ostensive strategy? For us to know how to refer to α reliably, we will in fact have a compression algorithm or some kind of naming algorithm (e.g., for those familiar with programming: a hash table) that will allow us to derive that number from the symbol "α." But that means we did not gain anything in terms of compressing the information. Rather, we just gained something in terms of convenience in communication; we were forced to carry around a representation of the number in any case.

The end result of this strategy of introducing new atomic names as primitive additions to our alphabet is that we would need unboundedly many basic elements, along with our recursive language, and we would have no way to relate these elements to each other, and no way to identify them—except through some kind of ostensive reference. This strategy essentially denies what a language and a description are. And, regardless of that concern, it is the most *inefficient* strategy for description we could come up with, resulting in an explosion of naming elements. For example, since most natural numbers are nearly Chaitin random and so are descriptively complex, this would mean we would need an infinitely large alphabet of new symbols to name the complex numbers; we end up getting "short" descriptions by making the language have infinitely many elements. Obviously, that is off the table for human science and human mathematics. Thus, multiplying names is not going to spare a description from becoming complex if that description is of a complex phenomenon.

In this book, I'm going to make claims not about arithmetic but about brain events and mental events. Claims like *the physical correlates of a red experience are complex*. One can disagree with this claim as an empirical claim. But this claim cannot be shown false by saying something like "But that's not complex—I'll just call it 'red.'" A theory must ultimately take a finite set of symbols and build all its descriptions out of them. A theory about how brains perceive and interact with the world will by necessity have to develop specific and precise descriptions of the phenomena involved. The claims of a theory must have some relationship to the things being described in order to satisfy the demands of being a scientific theory. Merely naming things does not a theory make. When we develop a theory, we aim to describe phenomena in a way that allows us to do things like making very precise predictions. This requires a particular descriptive language. One cannot wave away the descriptive language of physics with some vague notions that languages are replaceable or arbitrary. There is nothing replaceable or arbitrary about the matter at all. The language is developed for a very specific task, and the accuracy and utility of the theories and descriptions concerned will require that their complexity reflects the complexity of the phenomenon as best we understand it.

There is, however, an important related point that we should separate out to avoid confusion. It is related to a concept called "relative complexity." The idea here is that sometimes, if one has a complex description D_1 available, then we might be able to identify some other complex description D_2 that is somehow related to D_1, and do so using less information than the complexity of D_2. This is rather obvious if we think of an example. Suppose that there is a very large Chaitin random number, which we will call D_1, and you and I have both memorized it. Suppose also that D_2, where $D_2 = D_1 + 1$, is a very complex Chaitin random number. Given that you and I have stored D_1, we can reference D_2 with only a little additional information. This is because much of the information in D_2 is stored in D_1.

Or, to make a different analogy, drawing on the arguments of this book: suppose that David and Fred (from Section 1.2) have seen and experienced all colors just as has any statistically normal human; also, assume that Mary has never seen colors (she sees only black and white). Suppose also (as I argue in Chapter 2) that a red experience is a very complex event. Then David and Fred can use a short description to identify information that they share—they can use a social custom that gives some of the precious linguistic real estate to naming this phenomenon; that is, they can just call it "red." But this will not help Mary. She lacks the shared information. (In Section 4.2, I claim that what underlies the knowledge argument is the fact that we intuitively understand that Fred and David can talk about red because they already share the information, but that they won't be able to explain to Mary what red is like because it requires too much information.)

The third misunderstanding about descriptive complexity is something like the inverse of the last objection. It goes like this:

> Can't any description be made very complex? You say 100 is not a very complex number. But I say, why not call this number something like {the number is not 1, the number is not 2, the number is not 3, the number is not 4, the number is not 5, . . . the number is not 99, the number is not 101, the number is not 102. . .}. Using strategies like this, might not anything have a description of any complexity?

This contradicts the very definition of descriptive complexity. The descriptive complexity of a string is the *shortest* description that will allow one to reliably recreate or recognize that string. The first description (stating "100") allows me to reliably recreate "100" (I repeat the description). The second description does also, but it is longer.[10] The descriptive complexity of the string is thus at most the size of the former and not the latter characterization.

Another misunderstanding that can arise concerns properties and generalizations about properties. As noted, properties can be complex also. If we want to explain some phenomenon, we may find that it has complex properties that will then require a complex description and in turn a complex explanation. But some philosophers assume that properties can always be described in simple generalizations. Frank Jackson commits this error with his account of physicalism. In his version of physicalism, a conjunction of all the physical facts, Φ, can *a priori* entail all the psychological facts. We might have worries about the descriptive complexity of this Φ, but Jackson claims we need not:

> when I say that Φ is a sentence, I mean that it is a sentence in some idealized language constructed from the materials that serve to give the full, complete account of the physical sciences—or of physics itself, if we have in mind a version of physicalism tied to physics rather than the physical sciences in general. We cannot actually construct Φ because we do not and never will know enough, and even if we did know enough, the task of writing or uttering Φ would be completely beyond our powers. It might be objected that this means that we do not really understand what physicalism is committed to. But consider the (true) sentence in English, "The average size of houses in 1990 is under 1,000 square metres." We know that this sentence is entailed by a very long conjunction made up of conjuncts of the form "—is a house in 1990 of such and such a size" together with a conjunct that says how many houses there are, in an idealized version of English with distinct names for every distinct house. Despite the fact that we will never get close to writing down this sentence, we understand perfectly well what has just been claimed—as is evidenced by the fact that we know it is true.

(1998: 26)

Jackson is erroneously assuming that there are no complex properties—or, at least, that there are none that matter to science and ontology. (This appears to be a common error: Richard Feynman reportedly once tried to explain a quantum principle in a manner suitable for Freshmen and said, "You know, I couldn't do it. I couldn't reduce it to the freshman level. That means we really don't understand it" (Goodstein 1989: 75). Feynman appears to have assumed that this property or phenomenon must ultimately be simple, and he did not understand it if he did not have a simple description of it.) The cosmos Jackson supposes is simple: we can always make sufficient and simple generalizations about anything in it. But this is strictly and provably false. The fact that we can make simple generalizations about phenomena of any descriptive complexity does nothing to show that there are not in turn properties of those phenomena that are complex. We might find that other phenomena we want to understand have properties that both must be properly described if we are to explain the phenomena, and also those properties are complex and so not properly captured by simple generalizations (the argument of this book is that the phenomenal characters of conscious events are just such phenomena). Thus, we do not know what physicalism, as he characterizes it, is committed to.

For an easy example, we can turn again to numbers. A very complex natural number is going to be either even or odd. This is a simple property. But that number might also have an extremely complex property that we cannot sufficiently describe (by which I mean, describe it well enough to answer some question we need to answer) in any other way than through using many bits of information. The Godel sentence *(This sentence is not provable)*, for example, is represented via Godel numbering by a natural number that is either even or odd, but the property of being a Godel sentence is much more complex (and requires significant additional information to be constructed) than the property of being even or odd. If we adopted Jackson's stricture here, we should fail to be able to describe the incompleteness of arithmetic, as Godel was able to do, because Godel's proof requires not just simple generalizations but also complex ones. We cannot assume on *a priori* grounds that there is any limit to the complexity of the generalizations that we might need to explain some phenomenon. That would beg the question in an egregious way but is also implausible for most natural phenomena, and it is provably false as a generalization about any recursive language.

1.5 A Clarification: Information Versus Representations

The theory proposed here requires some important clarifications about what, exactly, we claim is complex. And this begs another question: how does this notion of information relate to other uses of the term "information" in philosophy and cognitive science? I will turn to this second problem now and address the first problem in Section 1.6.

Philosophers and cognitive scientists will tend to think of information as something that is processed by minds and might assume then that a theory that makes claims about the mind based on a theory of information is committed to a theory of the mind as an information processor—including a representational theory of mind. However, this would not be accurate in the case of my arguments here. The complexity of consciousness claim is the claim that when we have an adequate theoretical description of a paradigmatically mysterious phenomenal experience, that theoretical description will be descriptively complex. But note then that this does not commit us to any view on the role that information processing plays in consciousness or the nature of the mind.

Consider an example of one distinction between notions of information. Anthony Chemero has offered a useful discussion of different theories of information (2003), in which he distinguishes between Gibsonian notions of information and those notions of information that characterize—for example—a view of the mind as an information processing system (this is typical of much of cognitive science). Gibson (1966, 1979) used "information" as a way to describe the "affordances" or opportunities for action and interaction that the environment supplies. On his view, and on related views often called "ecological," it seems that we will explain activity using this notion of opportunities supplied by the environment—and not, or at least much less so, as the result of some kind of information processing. For this reason, a view inspired by Gibson often aims to explain action with minimal reference to representations. In contrast, the view of the mind that arises in early cognitive science is of the mind as a thing that processes information (maybe by using algorithms somewhat like those that we use to program our computers; or maybe instead by using something like distributed parallel processing of a kind we now model with connectionist networks). On this view, an explanation of a mental faculty primarily relies on the view that the mind creates and manipulates representations of the environment; these representations may be very large (some propose, for example, that we create a whole model of the world, and then update it when stimuli contradict the expectations of the model).

This contrast is important because some who hear the term "information" may assume that we are referring to a theory of the latter kind: one committed to the mind being explained by information processing. But the theory proposed here is neutral with respect to the question of how much any theory of mind must make use of a theory of representation and information processing. Descriptive complexity is being applied to a theory; it is not being used to describe the contents of consciousness *as* information. (There is an important point related to this concern: we must distinguish information in an experience from information in a theory of the experience. I discuss this again in Section 2.4.)

Thus, someone with a Gibsonian theory—or another approach that stresses for example dynamical systems theory and non-representational accounts (see Clark 1997)—may deny the representational theory of consciousness (which is the view that we can explain phenomenal experience by describing it as representations). But presumably, they would allow that some sophisticated theory of vision will refer to the interaction of brain events, body events, and stimuli from the environment. If the Gibsonians are correct, and some adequate future theory of vision is like this, and if this theory is adequate to explain the quality of visual experience, the complexity of consciousness claim would (in this instance) entail that the relevant theory, and the descriptions required to make the appropriate explanations and predictions, will be complex. But there is no claim that the appropriate theory of vision will be one that describes vision as computations over visual representations.

For the record, I do believe that minds—such as human minds—create, store, manipulate, and guide action by using many and sometimes very complex representations. But I also believe that the Gibsonians and the enactivists (Noe 2004; O'Regan 2011) and those who argue for "embodied cognition" (Chemero 2009) are right in arguing that an explanation of perception and action must take account of the body and the environment—and they are right that the body and environment often need not be represented because the body and environment are reliably there to provide stimuli feedback. In fact, I defend the complexity of consciousness claim in part by drawing upon the work of enactivists and embodied cognition theory. Our experiences are normally dependent upon our interactions with our environment, and because of this, any proper account of those experiences will be very complex: it will require an account not just of some neural activity but also how this relates to motor systems, the body, and the environment.

1.6 Which Descriptions Are Complex?

The arguments that I will make in this book will turn on a claim that I will call *the complexity of consciousness claim*. Stated in a preliminary way, this is the claim that: a phenomenal experience is paradigmatically mysterious if and only if some of the properties necessary to that experience are very descriptively complex. By *properties necessary to that experience*, I mean some of the properties of the experience necessary to make it the phenomenal kind it is. In other words, an experience of red will have some properties that are necessary to make this experience an experience of red, and at least one of these essential properties is very complex.[11]

It is important (and illustrative) to distinguish the complexity claim from some weaker claims that would look quite similar but would be insufficient for the claims made and defended in this book. We might call the first the *weak complexity claim:* each paradigmatically mysterious phenomenal experience is a complex event. I believe the weak complexity claim is true. However, my theme in this book is that the essential properties or features of paradigmatically mysterious phenomenal experiences are themselves complex. This is a stronger claim and one that in turn sheds much more light on the challenges of explaining consciousness.

We can recycle the aforementioned analogy to illustrate this point. Suppose that N is a very large, Chaitin random natural number. Such a number is complex, by definition. But one can imagine a situation in which we are concerned not with being able to recognize or reproduce the particular number itself but rather just to determine if it is odd. This is a trivial, uncomplex property, and if we had the number in hand, one might just look at the final digit of the number to determine if it is odd. The analogy with consciousness might go something like this: the anti-physicalist could say,

> I agree that every paradigmatically mysterious phenomenal experience is a complex event. But my concern is with what makes red red, and what makes pain painful, and what makes fear feel the way it does. And in each of these cases, we are dealing with a primitive, simple property—let's call it a quale.

This is the position that I reject. The complexity claim is specifically meant to point out that (at least some of) the properties that we would need to refer to, recognize, and understand in order to *explain* the phenomenal character of the paradigmatically mysterious phenomenal experience are complex.

Another weaker claim, entailed by the complexity claim, is that a phenomenal experience is a paradigmatically mysterious phenomenal experience only if some of the properties necessary to that experience are very descriptively complex. This would also be too weak for some of the arguments that follow. I do not merely claim that a paradigmatically mysterious phenomenal experience has descriptively complex essential properties; I also claim that any phenomenal experience with descriptively complex essential properties is paradigmatically mysterious. In other words, the complexity claim is that *what makes a phenomenal experience mysterious is its complexity.*

A final point of clarification about the complexity claim is that some philosophers assume that a necessary condition of an experience having phenomenal character is that the subject is subjectively aware of the experience. This has a pleasing parsimony: we don't want to pile one mystery onto another and be confronted with the question, what makes a person subjectively aware of a phenomenal experience? But questions about subjective awareness are beyond the scope of this book. I will not contest the claim that a phenomenal experience is an experience of which the subject is aware. And I will gloss over the question of what makes an experience subjective by using a near-operationalization of subjectivity: for any of my arguments, it will be sufficient to take reportability as proof of subjective awareness. Here I use "reportability" very broadly. If a subject can report upon an experience or form a declarative memory of the experience, then the subject was subjectively aware of the experience. Furthermore, "report" need not mean voluntary verbal description. It can and must include things like forced choice responses. If someone can, for example, click a button in response to some stimulus in a laboratory condition, that could count as a report. I recognize that this notion of reportability need not be necessary for subjectivity. I only require that it is a reliable indicator. In the end, the border cases and strange cases (e.g., blindsight) are interesting but have no import to my central arguments. Thus, from here on, when I refer to a phenomenal experience, mysterious or not, the phenomenal experience must be subjectively conscious, and I assume this is indicated by the fact that the subject can report upon it. There are important details here that I am glossing over (like the question about richness or overflow), but I will discuss these as they arise and are relevant.

Since I will defend the claim that (so far) physicalism remains our best bet, I take it that the complexity claim entails: for any paradigmatically mysterious phenomenal experience, the physical correlates of some of the properties necessary to that experience are very complex events. At this point, it may still be unclear what such claims might mean. Aren't all physical things complex? For this kind of claim to be substantive, we must clarify what is being described.

Such claims are meant to refer to the description that our relevant scientific theory would provide us of those physical correlates. Thus, to say that the physical correlates of an instance of visual object recognition are complex would mean: given an adequate scientific theory of object recognition, the description of the phenomenon sufficient for that theory is complex.

The notion of being sufficient for the theory is meant to articulate a principle already in place in all scientific endeavors. This is the idea that a theory relates certain phenomena, and therefore describes those phenomena, but also in the interest of parsimony, only those phenomena. A theory in neural science, for example, will presumably not need to take into account the mass of the neurons it is describing, nor their gravitational attraction to each other or to the Earth, nor the exact quantity of neutrinos passing through each neuron, and so forth. It will matter, however, whether the neuron fires, what it is connected to, the kind of neuron it is, and so on. The things described in the theory, and required for the theory to make the kinds of predictions that it makes, are what will determine the descriptions used, and therefore these will help determine the complexity of the descriptions. All this may sound rather subtle, but really, it is exactly what happens in normal theory formation and normal theory use. It happens quite naturally in any scientific endeavor: the scientist only looks for and describes the relevant features of events and ignores the others. Every scientific theory already does what I am requiring here of our descriptions.

We might call this everyday scientific practice *minimal theory functionalism*. A scientific theory has an ontology, which determines the elements of the phenomena that it will describe; these are picked out and are related to the other elements of the ontology of that theory by predictions and explanations in the theory. This functionalism aims to be *minimal* in the sense that the formulation of it is weak: it simply says a theory describes kinds (such as kinds of objects or kinds of events) and functional relationships (in the weak, non-teleological sense of "functional") between these elements of the theory.[12] This is weak enough that it will not offend any physicalist who has worries about the stronger forms of functionalism. But this minimal view is required to make sense of any local scientific ontology. We know that there are very many more physical relations that exist for any physical phenomenon than some particular theory will treat as relevant. Again, my point here is simply that, say, a neural scientist may not need to reference neutrinos because they may not play a direct role in her theory; a computer scientist ignores implementation details to talk about steps in algorithms; an economist ignores many details about the goods moved by a market to describe other features of the market; and so on. In each case, a decision is made about what kinds of events and relations are to be measured and studied.

It is likely true that for most any physical phenomenon you could reference, that phenomenon is very complex if described from the perspective of the most fundamental of the available scientific theories of the constituents of matter. I call this the *information density claim,* and I defend it in Chapter 2. But it is not relevant to the formulation of the complexity of consciousness claim (though it is relevant to a certain kind of account of why the complexity of consciousness claim is true). Again, to say the physical correlates of, say, an instance of visual object recognition are complex will be to say that as described by a minimally adequate theory of visual object recognition, the event is complex. This means that the claim that the physical correlates of a phenomenal experience are complex is a substantive claim. It is not the claim that brain matter is complex or some such trivial observation. It is the claim that the phenomenon is complex, when described at the appropriate level of abstraction of the adequate theory (that is, described as simply as possible, while still allowing the theory of the phenomenon to be applicable and adequate[13]).

However, the claim that paradigmatically mysterious phenomenal experiences are complex does not require or entail that physicalism is true. If phenomenal experiences were non-physical events, then the claim that they were complex would mean that in the best theory of phenomenal experiences—which, then, by supposition would not be a physical theory—the adequate descriptions of these phenomenal experiences would have to be large. However, my primary interest will be to claim not only that paradigmatically mysterious phenomenal experiences are complex, but also that their physical correlates are complex. This also makes the argument much easier to follow—we are not stuck imagining an I-know-not-what-material of consciousness being complex. Furthermore, there is no cost to this—it does not beg the question—since my arguments in this book take the form that *if paradigmatically phenomenal experiences were descriptively complex physical events, then they would have the kinds of properties that we observe and often call mysterious.* From this conditional, I conclude that physicalism remains our best bet.

An important strength of the position I am developing should be noted at this point. I am not assuming anything like many of the subtle strategies that others have taken in response to the anti-physicalist arguments about consciousness. I will not adopt a phenomenal concepts strategy, for example, and argue that our phenomenal concepts are not concepts of physical or scientific properties. I will not make distinctions between facts of science and facts of experience, between *knowing that* versus *knowing how* (Lewis 1983b; Nemirow 1980), and so on. I am not adopting some kind of strategy that phenomenal terms are indexicals, or otherwise resistant to physicalism for purely semantic reasons.

I allow that scientific information, physical information, phenomenal information, whatever kind of information you might want to identify, can be treated generically the same (or, at least, can be treated generically in the relevant cases if physicalism is true of those cases). I hold that physicalism, if true, will in principle ultimately have a vocabulary for its descriptions of phenomenal experiences that can be translated conservatively over to descriptions of our phenomenal reports. This also means that my account of physicalism will not try to hide behind vague notions like "realization" or "constitution;" nor behind very weak relations that explain little if anything, such as (standard forms of) supervenience. I take the most stringent position with respect to scientific explanation: I will allow that a theory T explains a phenomenon of kind P if that theory is a successful scientific theory and given an event p_i of kind P, and some relevant historical information H about prior facts, it is the case that *(T & H)* entail that p_i.

I find all this a very pleasing feature of my arguments: they confront the anti-physicalist arguments about consciousness on their own grounds. The anti-physicalist is being given her strongest possible position from the start, and I am adopting a most demanding version of physicalism.

1.7   Complex Consciousness and Three Principles About Theory

We are nearly ready to outline one of the principal arguments of this book, which will show that because paradigmatically mysterious phenomenal experiences are complex, they will appear mysterious and otherwise resist explanation. In this section, I describe three ways in which we can expect the complexity of phenomenal experiences to potentially limit our understanding of these experiences. Fortunately, each of these limitations is independently sufficient for most of the arguments that follow in this book, so my position is strengthened by offering all three. I call these "principles," since I will evoke them repeatedly in the arguments that follow.

1.7.1   *The Modal Judgment Constraint Principle*

Almost all of the anti-physicalist arguments (that phenomenal experience will fail to be explained by a scientific theory) are arguments that require us to make judgments about possibility and consistency. We are asked to conclude that it is consistent that one could know a complete scientific theory of color vision, but not know what red is like; or that it is consistent that an organism could be physically identical to yourself but possibly have no experience; or that it is possible that we could have all the physical information about an organism and fail to derive the experiences that it is having; and so on. In all these arguments, there is a common core. We suppose some theory T and all its theorems $\{t_1, t_2, t_3, \ldots\}$ are consistent with the addition or subtraction of some claim Q about phenomenal experience q. We then conclude that Q is independent of T and therefore T cannot (alone) explain q.

But all these arguments overlook an important fact. Any determination of what is possible with respect to a theory and a proper description of some event is determined by the amount of information that we have about that event. To see this, consider a claim that is easy to understand because it will refer only to familiar properties and familiar facts about physical theories.

Suppose we consider our judgments about the possibility of an event (and such judgments are also judgments about "conceivability," in the formal sense that this term is used in recent metaphysics). The event will be the Quebec-to-Qatar trip of Smith. The theory that we will assume is some form of idealization of contemporary physics, which we will call T.

You slowly learn more and more about Smith's particular trip. First, I tell you claim Q_1, that Smith has been to Quebec and to Qatar. This is conceivable; we judge that this is possible, or physically possible, because we see that Q_1 and T are independent. Here a point made in Section 1.7.2 is relevant: of course, our scientific theory does not *alone* tell us that Smith exists, that Qatar and Quebec exist, and so on. These are particular facts that one must add to the theory in order to derive predictions or explanations. So, Q_1 is consistent with, and independent of, all the theorems of T—and it is consistent with the conjunction of the theorems of T and a host of physical facts independent of those concerning Smith's actual trip (e.g., facts like where Quebec and Qatar are).

But now let us add additional information. I tell you that Smith went to Quebec and Qatar on 1 January 2009; this is claim Q_2. This is conceivable, but it piques your interest. You know, for example, that transatlantic flights tend to stretch over the night from one day to the next. Then I tell you that Smith went from Quebec to Qatar on 1 January 2009, on the same afternoon—that is, between 12:01 p.m. and 5:59 p.m. (assume this is all Greenwich mean time); this is claim Q_3. You begin to suspect that I am exaggerating. You're not aware of any commercial plane that fast. Then I tell you claim Q_4: that Smith went to Quebec and Qatar, on 1 January 2009, between 1:00 p.m. and 2:00 p.m. You now think that this is very improbable. Finally, I tell you claim Q_5: that Smith went to both Quebec and Qatar, on 1 January 2009, in the nanosecond between 1:00 p.m. and 1:00 p.m. and 1 nanosecond.

Claim Q_5 is physically impossible. The conjunction of Q_5 and T, along with some facts like where Quebec and Qatar are, will render a contradiction. The reason is that Q_5 requires Smith to go faster than the speed of light. And, from this, a host of contradictions will spill out. We should conclude Q_5 (coupled with some basic physical facts like locations) is inconceivable. And so we end up realizing that the Quebec-to-Qatar trip of Smith is inconceivable, physically impossible, and so on.

Note that if Q_5 were true, then we could describe Smith's trip, *accurately,* with claim Q_4 or Q_3 or Q_2 or Q_1. That is, it could be that Q_5 and Q_4 and Q_3 and Q_2 and Q_1 are all descriptions of the same (impossible, inconceivable) event. So, what is relevant is that Q_5 provides more information than description Q_4, which provides more information than description Q_3, and so on. The descriptions with less information would be true if the inconceivable and impossible scenario were true but evaluated in isolation they make the inconceivable and impossible scenario appear conceivable or possible. The trip is ideally conceivable or ideally inconceivable—we will describe it as physically possible or physically impossible—depending upon how much information we know about it. This illustrates that the information we access in evaluating a conceivability claim or possibility claim will determine what seems conceivable or possible.

The moral for us is clear: if our descriptions of our phenomenal experiences (that is, the descriptions that we are able to generate in our philosophical debates, the descriptions that we offer when making these arguments, and so on) contain very much less information than a proper explanation of the experience itself would contain, then our judgments about what is possible with respect to that experience will be unreliable.

Call this then *the modal judgment constraint principle*: modal judgments (including conceivability judgments and possibility judgments) are unreliable when made about a phenomenon when we have less information than the full description of that phenomenon, and modal judgments (including conceivability judgments and possibility judgments) are unreliable when made about a property of a phenomenon when we have less information than a full description of that property.

1.7.2 The Contingent Information Principle

When we discuss theories in the abstract, it is easy to overlook that they require, in almost all applications, additional information, if they are to provide the kinds of explanations, predictions, and retrodictions that we want from them. Many arguments about phenomenal experience trade, I believe, off an ambiguity between theorem and prediction. For this reason, the principle I will describe here is important and useful.

It is helpful to start with a kind of simplified example. Suppose we have a theory of dynamics. Call this T_D. Scientific theories are very unlikely to be complete, in the sense that logicians use the word "complete" (meaning all the truths of the theory are provable by the theory); after all, all mature scientific theories require mathematics of a complexity known to be incomplete. However, the constraint I am concerned with here is a different one, so let us suppose that our theory were complete. Such a theory would still be, in and of itself, insufficient for the work we aim to use it for.

This is obvious when we consider an example. Our hypothetical complete dynamical theory will provide theorems that describe every possible kind of motion. But this complete theory will not tell us what bodies there are, what their mass and velocities are, and so on. Thus, in isolation, this dynamics theory T_D could not tell us that there is an Earth, that there is a moon, that the moon is in orbit of the Earth, and so on. These kinds of facts would simply not be theorems of any theory of dynamics. That there is an Earth and a moon, where they are, what their masses are, what their current instantaneous velocities are, and so on, would all be historical information. This must be *added to our theory* in order to allow predictions, retrodictions, and other kinds of explanations to be derived from the theory. Of course, these are related: the theory determines the kind of description that one needs to discover through measurement. But once that is determined, the actual particular facts to be described are independent of the theory itself.

The same will be the case for all other kinds of interesting scientific theories. Let us suppose that, against all reasonable expectations, a theory of color vision or some other or more general theory of neural science were complete; like other scientific theories, the theorems of this theory would be too general to capture particular facts. The theory will not tell us what brains are where, and it will not tell us what brains are instantiating various kinds of color vision events. These facts must be added to the theory so that the theorems can be applied to this information to derive predictions or other kinds of explanations.

Many philosophers describe physicalism as a claim about the completeness of scientific theory. I find this a very, very poor way to understand or characterize physicalism, but even if we adopted it, it is essential to ask what we mean here by "complete." It is absurd to demand of physicalism that it be complete in the sense that it predicts all events from physical theory alone. This is like demanding that the Peano axioms of arithmetic tell you how much money is in your wallet. Even if a physicalist theory were complete in the logician's sense, you would still need to add facts about particular events in order to predict other particular events. Another way of putting this point is that the kinds of things we aim to explain with our theories will not be the theorems of the theory; what we aim to explain will rather be captured through applications of those theorems to particular contingent historical facts to allow for inferences to other contingent historical facts. (Here "contingent" means not necessary for the theory—thus, not a theorem of the theory.)

This will matter when we look at claims that physical theory will not (be able to) explain phenomenal experience. Such claims miss the mark if they mean that some physical theory will not be able to produce, as a theorem, an account of some particular phenomenal experience. That is certainly going to be true of any theory of consciousness, but it is not inconsistent with physicalism.

Call this observation *the contingent information principle*: in most cases, scientific theories will not alone entail explanations of the particular instances of the phenomena we aim to explain. Rather, every scientific theory must be supplemented with historical, contingent information to offer up an explanation of (or prediction of, or retrodiction of) other historical, contingent information.

1.7.3 The Incompressibility Cost Principle

Descriptive complexity allows us to outline some important limits to theories. One of these is especially important to discussions of phenomenal experience. Because many readers may be only interested in the relevant principle, and not its proof, I offer an informal proof and technical details of this principle in an appendix to this chapter (Section 1.9). In this section, I will simply state the principle, explain it in an informal way, and then explain its relevance to a theory of phenomenal experience.

The incompressibility cost principle is the observation that, if we want to use a theory T to explain a very complex phenomenon P, where the descriptive complexity of P is very much greater than the complexity of T (which we write as $C(P) \gg C(T)$), then we shall need additional information of complexity at least of the quantity $C(P)—C(T)$.

Suppose we have a theory of visual perception that we believe is adequate. We want to use it to explain features of color experience. If that color experience is very complex, much more complex than our theory, then even if our theory is adequate, our explanation of the relevant experience will require the use of a great deal of additional information. This information might be descriptions of preceding physical states; that is the kind of information that we observed is required when we explained the contingent information principle. But the additional required information could also simply be the kind of information that we typically put forward in constructing a proof—that is, it can be information about how to derive the relevant facts from the given theory.

This latter claim might seem surprising, so I will use a very simplified example. Consider an example that only requires some familiarity with propositional logic. Suppose you need me to transmit to you a particular sentence, and you need me to do so as succinctly as possible (perhaps we are paying a per-bit transmission fee). Let T_p be a basic axiomatic theory for the propositional logic; this is usually a very succinct theory, with perhaps three axioms and a single rule (modus ponens). Let n be a huge, even, Chaitin random number, such that $C(n) \gg C(T_p)$. Let $\neg^n$ stand for n negations in a row. Then, where P_1 is some sentence of that propositional language, the following sentence:

$$\neg^n(P_1 \rightarrow P_1)$$

will be a theorem of T_p. Let us suppose that this is the very sentence I need to send to you. It will not be enough to send you T_p, along with the message that the sentence you need is a theorem of T_p. T_p is nice and succinct, and not costly to transmit, but it produces infinitely many theorems. How will you know which theorem is the one that you need? To help you find that sentence, I will have to include additional information. For example, if we have a way to enumerate the proofs of T_p, the proof of this sentence might be the mth proof of the enumeration. I could then send you T_p, and information on the enumeration scheme I used to enumerate the proofs of T_p, and also m.

But what the complexity cost principle tells us is that this information (in this example, T_p and the enumeration scheme and m) must be at least as complex as the sentence that I need to send to you.

Let us now apply this insight to the issue at hand. Suppose that phenomenal experiences of kind P are very complex events, with complex necessary properties. Our theories of phenomenal experience are not very complex. Thus, even if our current theories (or something not much more complex) were adequate and entailed theorems that would help us properly explain this experience, we must bring to such a theory a great deal of information in order to be able to identify and describe the relevant consequences of the theory. And this holds generally: a future scientific theory of consciousness either will need to be very complex or will require the addition of sufficient information, to properly describe **P**. This required additional information will typically be information about prior historical conditions (as noted and described in Section 1.7.2) but may be more. The quantity of information required will be at least the difference between the complexity of our theory **T** and the complexity of the property of **P** that we aim to explain.

Implications include those outlined in Section 1.7.1: if we lack all the relevant information about the experience, our judgments about what is possible with respect to the phenomenon, and whether our relevant theory is independent of the phenomenon, will be fallible. But the claim here is more general. If our description of a phenomenon and our theory of the phenomenon together are less complex than its essential properties, then we will not be able to properly identify and describe those properties. The kinds of descriptions of a color experience that we generate or imagine in our philosophical discussions, for example, are likely insufficient to distinguish the experience from another color experience. But then, such descriptions cannot be adequate to describe the phenomenon in a way that allows us to apply a successful theory of the phenomenon to derive the correct explanation or prediction, nor to conclude that such an explanation is in principle impossible.

1.7.4 Applying the Principles

To peek ahead, the moral should be clear. If paradigmatically mysterious phenomenal experiences are very complex phenomena, much more complex than our typical theoretical speculations and descriptions, then we cannot expect to explain those phenomena with our theories and a little bit more information—even if our theories were able (in the sense of being able to produce, in their endless list of theorems, a relevant theorem) to explain the phenomenon. And so from our perspectives, armed with our theories but without the addition of much more information, the phenomenon will appear to us as absurd and ineffable.

This nicely expresses the sentiment of all the worries that consciousness is beyond our ken. Pick at random any of a thousand earnest meditations from science or philosophy about the mystery of consciousness—here's one:

> Were our minds and sense so expanded, strengthened, and illuminated, as to enable us to see and feel the very molecules of the brain; were we capable of following all their motions, all their groupings, all their electric discharges, if such there be; and were we intimately acquainted with the corresponding states of thought and feeling, we should be as far as ever from the solution of the problem, "how are these physical processes

connected with the facts of consciousness?" The chasm between the two classes of phenomena would still remain intellectually impassable. Let the consciousness of love, for example, be associated with a right-handed spiral motion of the molecules of the brain, and the consciousness of hate with a left-handed spiral motion. We should then know, when we love, that the motion is in one direction, and when we hate, that the motion is in the other; but the "Why?" would remain as unanswerable as before.

(Tyndall 1871: 87)

(I pick Tyndall because his comments read as wholly interchangeable with hundreds of other such pronouncements, made over the span of the following 150 years.) Such claims describe a predictable problem that would arise if consciousness is ontologically strange, and if explaining consciousness will require fundamentally new ontological posits (that is, such claims would be a predictable consequence of the falsity of physicalism). But such claims would also describe a predictable problem if some conscious events are enormously complex. Both perspectives should lead us to expect that consciousness will appear absurd and irreducible and ineffable and as random-seeming as noise, and both perspectives should lead us to expect that our existing theoretical descriptions will seem as inadequate and irrelevant to the task as a description of left- or right-twisting molecules. But then phenomenal experiences might be mysterious not because they are best explained with new ontological posits, but rather because they are best explained with new information describing complex interrelations of the existing elements of our theories, or with additional complex historical information combined with our theories, or with the information required to derive complex results from our theories. This book argues that these possibilities are a more reasonable bet of what is happening.

1.8 Consciousness as Complex Event

I have clarified what I mean by complex: descriptively complex. I have tried to predict and ward off some confusions and then I introduced the three principles describing the limitations that confront us when we aim to explain complex phenomena. I am nearly prepared to lay out my argument. We need only clarify one additional point. Written in full, my fundamental claim is:

> **The Complexity of Consciousness Claim**: a phenomenal experience E is a paradigmatically mysterious phenomenal experience if and only if there is at least one property of that experience, R, such that it is necessary to explain R in order to explain the phenomenal character of E, and R is very descriptively complex.

The idea here is that there is some R that makes a red experience uniquely an experience of red, another R that makes a pain experience uniquely an experience of pain, another **R** that makes a terror experience uniquely an experience of terror, and so on.

The complexity of consciousness claim is of course not a complete theory of consciousness. It aims only to explain what makes some phenomenal experiences appear ineffable. However, establishing this can foster significant progress toward the development of a theory of consciousness.

At this point in my argument, the complexity of consciousness claim is vague: because descriptive complexity is a magnitude, the notion of "very" is unclear. In the next chapter, I make this precise by describing, and defending the plausibility of, two different comparisons for the complexity of consciousness.

1.9 Appendix: The Incompressibility Cost Principle

My purpose in this appendix is to more fully describe the incompressibility cost principle. I did not do this in Section 1.7.3 on the assumption that most readers would not care to see such details but for those who do I provide them here. The name for this principle is my own (it is not, to my knowledge, a principle that is made use of in the literature on descriptive complexity), but it is a straightforward corollary of a result that we can call "the incompressibility result." The incompressibility result most typically gets applied in a method known as the incompressibility method.

In this section, I will (1) clarify why most descriptions are Chaitin random or nearly Chaitin random; (2) review a standard proof of the incompressibility principle; and (3) prove the incompressibility cost principle and offer some illustration of what the principle means.

1.9.1 Most Descriptions Are Nearly Chaitin Random

Note that, for any language, the typical description has a complexity that does not deviate far from the length of the description. On the one hand, we do not need much more information than is in the length of a string to print or recognize that string. If we write $C(d)$ for the descriptive complexity of a description or string d, $L(d)$ for the length of the string, and c for some small constant value, then we observe that $C(d) \leq L(d) + c$. The idea here is that c is just a bit of overhead required to print or recognize d, if we already have the string in hand. That is, we should never need much more information than $L(d)$ to print or recognize d. That's an upper bound to the potential complexity of d, relative to its length.

On the other hand, there is the question of the lower bound of the information needed to print or recognize d. The floor is the more interesting issue.

In any descriptive language, many strings are Chaitin random, and most strings cannot be compressed more than a small amount. Pick some constant a for our target compression. For any finite set of descriptions of cardinality m, there will be at least *(m—$m2^{-a}$ +1)* elements of that set that have no compressed description of length less than *log m—a* (here I follow Li and Vitanyi 2008:

117). So, for example, if our set is of all the binary strings that are ten bits long, the cardinality of the set is 2^{10}; and if *a* is 1, meaning that we want then to find how many strings can be compressed 1 bit, we discover that about half of the descriptions in the set have descriptions that can be compressed to be about 9 bits long. About a quarter have descriptions that can be compressed to be 8 bits long, and so on. Note that this is just an observation about real estate: there just are not many shorter strings that can "stand in," under some compression scheme, for the string to be compressed. Once we pick our language, there are few strings much shorter than the string in question to be treated as a code for that string. Thus, most of those strings that we did compress by translating them to shorter strings in our code must be translated to strings that are only 1 or 2 bits shorter. Not only is at least one of our strings necessarily Chaitin random, but also the majority of the others are so nearly Chaitin random—within a few bits—that we might as well call them Chaitin random.

Note that this also means that for any theory and recursive language—and this includes any language that will matter to science or to a theory of consciousness—there will be no bound to the descriptive complexity of possible well-formed descriptions or of theorems. That is, there will be well-formed strings of any complexity in that language, and there will also be theorems of any complexity for that theory.

1.9.2 The Incompressibility Result

The incompressibility result is a very general result that tells us that any theory *T* cannot determine whether an arbitrary description much more complex than that theory is Chaitin random.

To show this, we need to remember that theories have a descriptive complexity. This is the smallest size of a description of the theory. Here I assume that a theory is finite, with finite rules, and that we can recognize when a formula is well formed in the theory. This is not very demanding; it is also what we usually mean by "theory" in logic.

The incompressibility result makes use of a version of the Berry Paradox, identified by Bertrand Russell and attributed by him to G. G. Berry. One version of the paradox is the sentence, "the least integer not nameable in fewer than nineteen syllables." This sentence names the integer but names it in 18 syllables. Descriptive complexity allows us to formulate a rigorous version of this paradox.

Suppose that we have a predicate *R* in our theory *T* that means *is Chaitin random*. Thus, *R(d)* would mean that description *d* is Chaitin random. Suppose that we can decide for any string *d* that it is Chaitin random. That is, for any description *d*, we can determine whether or not *R(d)*. This is our assumption for reductio.

Consider a number *n* very much larger than the complexity of *T*. Thus, $n \gg C(T)$. For our language (that is, for the set of all descriptions using our alphabet), we can lexigraphically order all the strings of the language. This means we can lexigraphically order the strings of length n. Now note, using T, we can (by supposition) go through these particular descriptions of length n and find the first such string in our lexigraphical ordering that is Chaitin random, by finding the first string d_f of length n such that $R(d_f)$.

This is a particular description that we have identified: the first Chaitin random string of length n in the lexigraphical ordering of descriptions of length n. But given this, we could now produce a description of d_f or we could recognize d_f using T and our lexigraphical ordering. This means that $C(d_f) \leq C(T) + c$, where c is the small overhead required for our lexigraphical ordering.

But now we have contradicted ourselves. Since the string d_f is Chaitin random, its complexity must be at least as great as its length. Thus, since $n \gg C(T)$, then we have that $C(d_f) \gg C(T)$, and so $C(d_f) > C(T) + c$.

We conclude that the source of the contradiction was our supposition that a theory T could identify whether an arbitrary description in the theory that was much more complex than the theory was Chaitin random. Thus, a theory cannot recognize whether an arbitrary description much more complex than the theory is Chaitin random.

Note that proving that a string d is Chaitin random will be equivalent to many other interesting properties. For example, what if some description d had a property R^* that turned out to be the equivalent of being random, because this is an irreducibly complex property? Then, T alone will not be able to prove that d had property R^* if d were much more complex than T.

1.9.3 The Incompressibility Cost Principle

In what follows, we are interested in a difficulty related to this incompressibility result: what might such a principle mean for a theory aiming to identify and describe and predict very complex properties—in particular, properties much more complex than the theory itself?

The incompressibility cost principle is that a description d that is very much more complex than a theory T cannot be identified as a consequence of T without the addition of information at least as great as the difference between the complexity of T and d. That is, suppose that $C(d) \gg C(T)$ but also that T, perhaps with some additional information, entails that d. Then we cannot identify the particular derivation of d from T without additional information of the size at least $C(d) - C(T)$.

The proof is simple, now that we are familiar with the proof of the incompressibility result. Suppose that theory T is of the relevant kind. Let H (for historical input) be any additional information that we may be using with the theory in any particular case. H is the kind of information discussed earlier in the description of the contingent information principle. So, if T were a scientific theory about dynamics, and we wanted to predict the future motion of an object, H would be information about this object: its mass, its velocity, forces acting on it, time, and so on. If H is empty (if there is no H), then any consequence of T alone is just a theorem of T.

We find that a theory T and information H cannot identify a description d if $C(d) \gg C(T) + C(H)$; that is, the theory and information will not be able to identify description d. The reason should now be rather obvious. Suppose using T and H we could identify d. Perhaps we do this by enumerating the proofs of T given H (this is the theorems of T and also the products of those theorems where we take H as a set of premises). We could write a small program that goes through this enumeration until it reaches the proof of d. How could we identify this proof, however? Suppose that we just take the overhead of our enumeration, our program, and some additional information, such as that this is the nth proof in our enumeration. Call the complexity of this overhead, c. We suppose for reductio that we can identify d using T, H, and c; and that $C(d) > C(T) + C(H) + c$. But if that were true, we would have a contradiction. For, using just information of complexity $C(T) + C(H) + c$, we could identify the string d. But then by definition of descriptive complexity, the description d would be of complexity $\mathbf{C(d)} \leq C(T) + C(H) + c$.

What the incompressibility cost principle reminds us is that, if some information describing a phenomenon is incompressible, then even if an adequate explanation of that phenomenon is a theorem of our theory, we will need to add to our theory at least as much information as is in the description, less the information in the theory itself, in order to identify or produce that description. And, given that any explanation will require that we at least be able to produce or identify the relevant description, this means that we cannot have an explanation of that phenomenon unless we add this additional information.

Another way to state the spirit of this principle is as follows. Note that it is not the case that a theory T is limited in the complexity of its theorems. Any typical theory T would be able to generate at least countably many theorems and theorems of any complexity. At first, it might seem that we contradict ourselves when we observe that a theory T can produce a theorem t_n where $C(t_n) \gg C(T)$; doesn't that mean we can reduce t_n to T, and thus it cannot be the case that $C(t_n) \gg C(T)$? But no: you still need to be able to identify that theorem if you are to make use of it. And this will require at least as much information as the difference between the complexity of the theorem and the complexity of the theory.

Here is where our ways of thinking about theories in philosophy can lead us astray. It is one thing for a sentence to be a theorem of our theory. It is quite another thing to find that theorem. What we care about in our actual use of our theories is whether we can find and use the explanations that we need; it is no help to be told that a theory can predict the phenomenon we want to predict, but that we cannot know how to get this prediction out of the theory. In the case of our theory T and a theorem t_n where $C(t_n) \gg C(T)$, it requires additional information to be able to get t_n out of T; and, on pain of contradiction, the quantity of this additional information must be greater than or equal to $C(t_n) - C(T)$.

A trivial example will help to make the incompressibility cost principle very easy to understand. Every language, including every set of theorems of any theory, can be coded in binary. It is trivial to write a program that outputs all binary strings, in lexigraphical order. Let *W* (for *Writer)* be such a program; then *C(W)* is very low. But *W* will output a string of each complexity (eventually). Given an interpretation of binary to Latin letters and punctuation, *W* will eventually output *Hamlet* and *The Origin of Species* and a proof that the continuum hypothesis is independent of ZFC. But obviously, *W* is useless. It is not a shortcut to great poetry or monumental science or long-sought theorems of logic. And we can see why: the information required to *find,* in this endless output of strings, *Hamlet,* or *The Origin of Species,* or the proof of the independence of the continuum hypothesis, is very great. We obviously get nothing for free from such an endless parade of symbols. The information that would be required to find *The Origin of Species* in the output would be about as much information as is in *The Origin of Species.*

Note that the incompressibility cost principle is so general that it will be relevant to many of the various distinctions that philosophers have used in recent years to cut finer forms of physicalism. For example, there has been an equation of physicalism with certain claims about possibility. Namely, if for a phenomenon *p* and for a theory *T*, it is possible that ¬*p*, while keeping the relevant features of *T* and the relevant historical facts constant, then we are to say *T* does not explain or reduce *p*. One difficult issue here is that the notion of *possible* is quite contentious. There are physical possibility, nomological possibility, metaphysical possibility, logical possibility, and epistemic possibility, to name five (not necessarily distinct) flavors. The incompressibility cost principle allows us (for the purposes of my arguments in this book) to cast aside this debate. If our theory cannot even identify the phenomenon in the proper way or cannot be used to practically produce a description of the relevant properties of the phenomenon, then we do not have to settle questions about the kinds of possibilities we think our metatheoretical account might require. Pick any flavor of possibility, and if *p* is much more complex than our theory *T*, then we will not be able from *T* alone to reliably explain *p*. Also, while the very notion of explanation is contentious, an explanation cannot both be adequate and also be unable to identify the phenomenon it aims to explain; so here again the incompressibility cost principle renders another fine-grained debate irrelevant: we do not have to settle what the proper account of "explanation" is.

Notes

1. I implore the reader to understand that the three tales that follow here are not meant to be arguments, nor even rigorous thought experiments, but rather illustrative hypothetical cases meant to motivate and make more clear the more technical claims that follow. And, of course, they are meant to also be spoofs. But nothing really turns on whether one agrees with my interpretations here of these tales.
2. There is an issue here concerning *a priori* versus *a posteriori,* or if one prefers rationalist versus empiricist, approaches to semantics. I hope to avoid semantics as much as possible in this book, since I do not believe that semantics can help answer metaphysical problems in any substantial way. Nonetheless, in Section 2.7, I devote some discussion to this matter. Briefly, here, we can note that: given that we can refer to complex things with a simple name, it cannot be that the meaning

of any such referential concept, as understood by us, needs to be equally complex as the referent. This holds for both the first and second intensions, for those who adopt a two-dimensional semantics; either the first or the second intension of a referential concept could be indicating a thing a proper theoretical description of which is more complex than our understanding has grasped and that the concept entails or embodies.

3. I am aware that David's reply will be that the empirical evidence corroborates that there is a physical or nomological possibility, and he is making claims about metaphysical possibility. But why would concrete evidence for physical necessity not also be taken as evidence for metaphysical necessity? It is surely a mistake to prioritize armchair reasoning over physical sciences in determining modal facts, in a case like this where we do not yet properly understand the phenomenon.

4. Interestingly, there is another kind of source of error that is overlooked in traditional epistemology. Error can arise not just from a gulf between appearance and reality. Error can arise if our description is less complex than the phenomenon described. And, if our abilities to describe the phenomenon are limited and can contain less information than the description in question, then we must err in a systematic way.

5. For example, an interesting recent critique is Schwitzgebel (2011). Furthermore, the mistake in question is likely a variation of a reoccurring error in philosophy, which Van Fraassen called the "bane of modern empiricism" (2002: 134): the conflation of awareness with judgments about that awareness. It turns out that this mistake is the bane of modern rationalism also.

6. See Chaitin (1966), Kolmogorov (1965), and Solomonoff (1964).

7. For those unfamiliar with the notion of a universal Turing machine: Alan Turing provided an astonishingly simple description of an abstract machine that is equivalent in power to any computer anywhere. We of course increase the speed and memory of our computers, but what the computers are able to do, given sufficient time and memory, is the same across all computers, and captured by Turing's machine. The machine is universal because it is programmable: its input includes a program telling it what to do with additional input. All of our everyday personal computers are universal Turing machines (assuming we are willing to give them more memory if they need it).

8. Gregory Chaitin's *Exploring Randomness* (2001) offers an exuberant overview of how much randomness there is in mathematics and explores some of the astonishing implications.

9. Furthermore, this means that we can have a simple theory applied to a complex description, to produce a complex outcome. In arithmetic, addition is not very complex. But one can add two very complex numbers and perhaps produce a third very complex number. In science, the equivalent could be that a simple dynamical theory applied to a very complex motion might make a very complex prediction. The inverse is also true: we could have a very complex theory applied to a very simple phenomenon. Some concepts of simplicity and parsimony make reference to particular kinds of things; some formulations of Ockham's razor, for example, define a description as simpler if it refers to fewer kinds of objects. Descriptive complexity is neutral with regard to questions like the count of the kinds of entities involved. We can have few complex kinds, many simple kinds, complex kinds in simple relations, simple kinds in complex relations, and so on. The descriptive complexity of each of these kinds of situations would not depend solely on the number of entities or their kind or their relations alone. Descriptive complexity is thus neutral with respect to questions of how to balance so-called "ideological" with "ontological" notions of parsimony.

10. The objection is actually doubly confused, since this funny description is in fact not very complex; it is easily constructed from the fact that the number is 100.

11. I have some concerns that this way of talking about the matter might lead some to opine that I am committed to a strong form of essentialism, in which essences were things, but that is not so. As complex phenomena, there need not be any well-delimited property shared by all and only the experiences we call "red experiences." Also, I believe it likely that what makes a red experience what it is is in part the relations of the relevant events to other events (or, said more correctly, this is what partly constitutes that information). We do not want to be misled by talk of necessary properties into thinking there is something simple and atomic and clearly delineated here—a traditional essence. For a parallel: there are senses in which we can speak of the necessary properties of hurricanes or of cats, and yet for both, there can be borderline cases where there simply is not a fact of the matter about whether something is a hurricane (e.g., a storm trembling on the edge of the definitional criteria) or a cat (e.g., an ancestor or descendent of a modern cat that lacks some common features of most modern cats). Because paradigmatically phenomenal experiences are very complex, we should not be surprised by this wariness about necessary conditions. Still, some things are cats or are hurricanes and have properties that are necessary to make them so, and the same is true of some kinds of phenomenal experiences.

12. I am only describing a property of theories relevant to the arguments here; I am not claiming that this functionalism characterizes all we need to know about theories or scientific method. Later I will discuss and reject a view called structuralism, which is not the view I outline here; see Section 4.5.

13. For this minimal functionalism about scientific theories, a theory can be called "adequate" if it can predict the relevant phenomena (given sufficient information about the prior events of the relevant kind it can predict the next events of the relevant kind) or retrodict the relevant phenomena (given sufficient information about the prior events of the relevant kind to an event that occurred, it would have been able to predict that event).

2   The Inadequacy Claims

2.1 Overview

My task in this chapter is to explain and defend two claims:

The Description Inadequacy Claim (DI): for any paradigmatically mysterious phenomenal experience E, our current descriptions of that experience and of its properties, even when combined with our best current theory of that experience and of its properties, is very much less complex than some property R of E that must be described if we are to explain the phenomenal character of E.

The Capabilities Inadequacy Claim (CI): for any paradigmatically mysterious phenomenal experience E, and for any human being, that human being's theoretical reasoning abilities have an information capacity that is very much less than the complexity of some property R of E that must be described if we are to explain the phenomenal character of E.

(In this discussion, I limit the domain of experiences to human experiences.) Each of these claims would be alone sufficient to explain the ineffability of consciousness and to render sound the refutations, offered in Chapter 4, of the leading anti-physicalist arguments. Therefore, I really only need the weaker of these, DI. However, I believe that CI has interesting corollaries; thus, it is worthwhile to try to motivate it also.

Why are these important? To briefly anticipate the argument, if the descriptive complexity of our phenomenal experiences exceeds the complexity of our current descriptions of those experiences, the complexity of our current theories of those experiences, or our capability to reason about those experiences, then the modal judgment constraint principle tells us that our judgments about what is possible with respect to these phenomena will be inaccurate; and the incompressibility cost principle tells us that we are not going to be able to reliably explain these phenomena until we bring much more information into our account. Thus, these phenomena would necessarily appear mysterious to us—they could even seem as inexplicable, as without apparent pattern or order, as noise.

DOI: 10.4324/9781003320685-2

As I noted in the last chapter, there is debate in philosophy about what an explanation is. I won't need to settle this here, because it is obvious that any explanation of a property *R* will require that we be able to identify and properly describe *R*. But since, the argument will go, we cannot reliably do that, then we surely cannot explain *R*. Debates about what an explanation is can thus, mercifully, be set aside.

We should reiterate two clarifications made in Chapter 1. First, we presume that the description in question of the paradigmatically mysterious phenomenal experience is the simplest possible to adequately allow the description of the experience in question, made in the correct theoretical language. If physicalism proves true, this will mean the simplest adequate scientific description of all and only the relevant features of the experience and the structures and events that enable the experience. If some anti-physicalist theory proves true, this will mean the simplest adequate description in the alternative anti-physicalist theory. Adequacy should at least include the ability to be able to describe the phenomenon so that it can be reliably identified and distinguished and also to be able to make new and surprising predictions about the conditions under which such experiences will occur. But, in the case of scientific theories, we can let the scientific method determine what are adequate theories. In this chapter, for the sake of formulating easy-to-understand arguments, I will sometimes assume physicalism about the relevant phenomena; again, this does not beg the question because my ultimate claim will be that if paradigmatically mysterious phenomenal experiences were complex physical phenomena, then they would appear mysterious to us in just the ways that they do.

Second, the reference in these hypotheses to a property *R* of *E* is intended to refer to some property that makes the experience the kind of experience it is. We hope that our best successful theory of consciousness will tell us what makes a red visual experience a visual experience and a red experience; we hope it tells us what makes an experience of terror an emotional experience and a fearful emotional experience; we hope it tells us what makes a pain "in the foot" be "in the foot" and a pain; and so on. This will require identifying and describing some distinguishing essential properties.

Finally, I should make an observation about the method. These claims (and the complexity of consciousness claim that is assumed in both claims) are empirical. My arguments here are meant to make these claims plausible and to help to clarify what the claims mean and what they entail. But, ultimately, it is a matter for a mature science of mind to prove that these claims are true. This means that in the end, my primary appeal is to productivity: I claim that the complexity of consciousness claim, the description inadequacy claim, and the capabilities inadequacy claim should be compelling to us at this time because of their ability to provide provocative and productive directions for research.

2.2 The Description Inadequacy Claim

I begin by defending the description inadequacy claim, DI. DI is sufficient for all the arguments that follow. This claim DI could be separated into two claims—one that our current descriptions are inadequate and one that our current theories are inadequate. However, as I will argue in the following, our theories of phenomenal experience are currently so preliminary that it is reasonable to observe simply that they add little to our descriptions. For this reason, although there are in principle two questions here (Are our descriptions sufficiently complex? Are our theories sufficiently complex?), there is no practical need to separate them out. Combining the points reduces the number of cases that the following arguments need to consider.

Let us start with an example. Consider the experience of fear. When a human being has a conscious fear experience—let us suppose, an intense experience of fear—a vast number of changes occur in the subject's body. The subject's

- Heart rate increases;
- Body temperature increases;
- Blood pressure increases;
- Skin begins to sweat;
- Muscles become tense;
- Eyes dilate;
- Body posture changes;
- Breathing becomes fast and shallow;
- Pituitary releases norepinephrine;
- Digestion is slowed or suspended;
- Memory formation becomes highly active;
- Memory recall becomes selective of fear-relevant facts;
- Perception becomes acutely primed to fast motion and other fear-relevant stimuli.

This is only a partial list, pitched at a very high level, of the features of fear (see for review Bradley and Lang 2000); this list leaves out a great deal of other autonomic and physiological changes and a great deal of other cognitive effects (such as emotional congruence in perception; see Niedenthal and Setterlund 1994). Also, every item on this incomplete list glosses over a very great deal of relevant detail (which would amount to a vast array of other effects). The effects on digestion, for example, are probably profound, very complex, and extensive and result in changes in the phenomenal experience (e.g., sometimes an acidic burning sensation in the stomach). The digestion system of a human being includes more neurons than the spinal cord; many of the neurons in this enteric nervous system are sensory neurons, and the enteric nervous system is highly autonomous (Goyal and Hirano 1996). Thus, this system alone is enormously complex and capable of conveying an enormous amount of information that shapes the quality of consciousness; the enteric nervous system responses alone are very much more complex than our descriptions of those features of our experience, and yet they are only a fraction of the felt effects of fear.

From these observations, we know that a proper description of the emotion would be very complex. I add to this one additional hypothesis: that explaining the distinct phenomenal character of the emotion will require a complex description—a description that uses some of this complex description of the emotion event or that identifies a complex property of some of this complex description of the emotion event.

And yet, in our own everyday descriptions, how do we describe our fear? Typically, we just identify it: *I'm scared.* If we strive for some literary detail, we might identify a few of the effects of the fear: *My skin crawls,* or *The hair on my neck stands up,* or *My heart hammers and I sweat.* The finest of novelists or poets would say little more, in describing fear. And yet, such briefs are merely labels for a collection of enormously rich and complex phenomena, and these phenomena are only a few of the phenomena that constitute a fear experience. Our descriptions serve to only point to the emotion or some of its effects; they are not attempts to, and are never adequate to, identifying and describing all (or even any!) of the phenomenal features of the fear, and in particular, they are never adequate to, nor identify and describe, the features of fear that make it fear. (For example, my skin might crawl because I'm cold; the hair on the back of my neck might stand in a shiver of aesthetic pleasure; I might sweat because I am running; and so on. These features of fear are not sufficient to constitute fear.) The case is no better for the scientist than for the poet. It is a great deal of detail, relative to what is usually said about a fear experience, to give a list and explanation like I have given earlier. But this list and paragraph are very little information indeed, paltry compared to even a single relevant feature of a fear experience.

In the case of an emotion, therefore, it is obvious that the phenomenon is enormously complex. My hypothesis is that explaining the phenomenal character of the experience would require a complex description, and yet our everyday descriptions are little more than pointers. If the hypothesis is true, then DI is true of such emotions.

The literature on consciousness largely ignores emotions—indeed, it ignores most phenomenal events. We can thus predict that the anti-physicalist will object: it is only an accident that our descriptions of fear are simpler than fear. Fear is not representative, because fear is special. Other kinds of experiences, the argument will go, are mysterious but not so complex. For example, visual experience does not include all these autonomic system changes, so is not going to be complex—or, at least, not for these reasons. But visual experiences are paradigmatically mysterious.

But is vision simpler than fear? Perhaps, but it is not simple. You know the cliché: a picture is worth a thousand words. This cliché, unlike most clichés, is, however, false—because it far understates the case. Consider a reasonable digital photograph. A contemporary digital camera of modest quality has the ability to take pictures with about 32 megapixels of information. Such a photograph in a reasonable compression algorithm, if taken of a complex phenomenon (e.g., a forest, not a white wall), will stand to be on the order of 4 megabytes. I have a copy of a translation of *War and Peace* that is 575,000 words, and uncompressed is 3 megabytes (and because this is uncompressed, the size of the file is only a rough upper bound on its complexity). A picture is thus worth at least three-quarters of a million words—or, if you prefer, one and a third of *War and Peace*. Given that a picture by a camera is not only inferior to our own visual experience but can also capture only a portion of our visual experience, then it is safe to say a visual experience can be worth *many* millions of words and thus dozens of *War and Peaces*. And, when we take into account the dynamic nature of vision, we no doubt will find that a visual experience is worth tens of millions of words.

Return to the example at the beginning of Chapter 1. A 4-megabyte picture of Pollack's Lucifer would not be of particularly high quality (which means, literally, that it would throw away a tremendous amount of information that we could otherwise potentially grasp with our visual systems). But we glance across such a picture and take in this information at that glance. We grasp the image in a few seconds and even recognize that it is crude and has lost infor-mation. (We are driven to make more powerful cameras and greater digital storage capacity *because* of our ability to recognize and act-appropriately-in-relation-to vast amounts of visual information.) Now, you look directly at the painting Lucifer by Jackson Pollock. Can you make some judgments about it that you can memorize and report to others, such that those judgments are sufficient to enable them to reconstruct Lucifer? You cannot (prove me wrong if you disagree: just make the judgment, call up a friend who's never seen Lucifer, report the judgment, ask her to sketch it, and see what she produces for you as a result). The reason is that there is more information in your visual experience of Lucifer than there is in any judgment you may make about it or any practical linguistic description you might offer. But that obvious fact is also very important, once we reflect upon it: it shows us that there is far more information in our visual experience than in any particular, and probably any sum of practically possible, judgments or statements about the experience. Reasoning and talking about vision are weak, whereas vision is mighty.

These practical experiences are consistent with what we know about the architecture of human vision. Our eyes contain about 130 million photorecep-tive cells, of two kinds: about 120 million of these are rods, and the rest are cones. Working over time, emended by the dynamic gathering of data through eye movements, they can produce a vast amount of information. The color processing system is complex also: we have three kinds of color receptors that work in opposition in pairs, determining color as a contrast between red-green and blue-yellow. What happens in our brains, to synthesize this dynamic data, is even more complex.

I do not know of any good current estimate of how much of the human neocortex is dedicated to visual processing, but at least one study has done this on macaques (Felleman and van Essen 1991). These relatives of ours have a visual system well comparable to our own. Felleman and van Essen found that much of the visual processing occurred outside the occipital lobe and that about 55% of the whole cortical surface was dedicated to or involved in visual processing. For the macaque, only about 3% of the cortex was dedicated to auditory processing and 11% to somatosensory processing. For humans, the percentage for auditory processing will be higher, but these numbers are perhaps close to representative. If we assume that the brain is relatively efficient (or, at least, equally efficient across functional areas), then this shows that much more information is gathered and manipulated by the visual system than by other sensory processing systems and by the other tasks that the neocortex enables (such as theoretical reasoning). In addition to having dedicated a huge portion of our neocortex to vision processing, there are many subcortical structures involved in visual processing, visuomotor control, and related functions like circadian rhythms. Given that typical estimates are that we have at least 10^{10} information-processing neurons in the brain, with at least 10^{13} connections, then we are talking about somewhere on the order of 10^{9} information-processing neurons dedicated to vision with at least 10^{12} connections. There is a tremendous amount of information in any visual experience. Of course, not all of these neurons are relevant and firing, and we are not subjectively aware of much of those that do. On the other hand, the firing of a single neuron can itself contain much information (for example, in firing rate).

But what about our descriptions of our visual experiences? These are paltry. Again, they typically are nothing but the sharing of labels, which have been learned through ostentation. We admire great writers for their ability to offer a striking visual image in words, but even the best such description will be tiny. This is, after all, what led James Joyce to have Stephen Dedalus so correctly observe in *Ulysses,* as he walks along the beach:

> Ineluctable modality of the visible: at least that if no more, thought through my eyes. Singatures of all things I am here to read, seaspawn and seawrack, the nearing tide, that rusty boot. Snotgreen, bluesilver, rust: coloured signs. Limits of the diaphane.
>
> (1986: 31)

Joyce is a genius: he does as well as anyone could do at describing the sights of the shore. But he begins with humility: all of these sights are ineluctable. They are beyond our control. And our everyday powers of description.

Thus, we corroborate again DI: nothing in our discourse about a visual experience is adequate to identifying and describing the elements of the visual experience that determine the kind of visual experience it is, sufficient for one to be able to recreate that experience. Yes, I can say, "I see the Duomo di Milano," but am I seeing it at night or during the day? Is the light bright or dark? How do the shadows play across it? Who is standing before it? How is the endless polishing of the Duomo going right now, as you look at it? Is it golden and clean, or dark from soot? From what angle are you viewing it? From how far away? Any normal human being would be able to discern extremely subtle differences between these and a thousand other dimensions that determine the character of her viewing experience. None of this is captured by a claim like, "I see the Duomo di Milano." And none of this information will be captured by even our finest poet setting out to describe what she sees when she gazes at the great cathedral of Milan.

My claims up to now have been uncontroversial, if not platitudinous. But, predicting my argument, and in an effort to save her own position, the anti-physicalist will no doubt want to contend that even these kinds of visual cases are not representative because they remain uniquely complex. Looking at a Pollack painting or a beach or a cathedral is different from a simple, mysterious visual experience. The preferred example here is a color experience, which many philosophers assume is representative in the relevant ways of all phenomenal experiences. The question we then ask is, *if I am having a particular red experience, could I describe it in such a way that I could enable another human being who has never had that kind of experience to know or have that particular color experience or to identify that particular color experience?*

I agree with the anti-physicalist that the answer to this question is no. The anti-physicalists argue that the answer is no because color experience cannot be properly described by physicalist language. It is worth noting that this is in fact a rather strange argument, given as it is without a positive account of experience, and for at least two reasons. Let me take a moment away from our argument to address these.

First, anti-physicalists with respect to semantic content, from the ancient philosophers to modern Husserlian phenomenologists, were traditionally concerned with explaining how we all grasped the same contents; they saw this as a very heavy burden put upon their anti-physicalist positions. After all, if our mental contents are not the same, it would seem we cannot understand each other, and many would see this as a *reductio ad absurdum* of the anti-physicalist semantics. But the contemporary anti-physicalists regarding experience invert this tradition, making phenomenal experience incomprehensibly isolated. In the eagerness to refute physicalism, they offer no account of how my red can be your red, and this allows for a range of absurd consequences. It allows for inverted spectra (my blue being your red); or for me having no experience while you have an experience, while we still both act similarly when we look at a red thing ("zombies"); and it allows for my phenomenal experiences to change like a kaleidoscope when I see a red thing but while I behave continuously as someone who has a stable experience. Again, such consequences would have traditionally been taken as a refutation of the position.

Second, the anti-physicalists have a position where the phenomenon is somehow essentially mysterious. That is, suppose that there are non-physical substances. This is surely possible, perhaps even reasonable. But now, why don't we have a theory of these? Why can't we describe these the same way we can describe rocks and trees and sunlight? Why are we unable to make any observations about it, other than to name our experience to others who are having the same experience? We should be suspicious of anti-physicalism for proposing a distinct kind of substance that they cannot describe in any way except to say it is the stuff of our experiences.

But, setting aside these concerns, the anti-physicalist explains the ineffability of the phenomenal experience as arising from ontological strangeness, which supposedly makes it theoretically inaccessible from our current physicalist theories. The point of DI is to argue that we could equally well explain the apparent ineffability of a color experience as arising from its complexity.

But how can we say that? Isn't a color experience a simple thing? The answer is no.

First, consider a real color experience. As I write this, I am sitting in my home office, facing a white wall. I perceive the wall as white. If you asked me its color, I would say "It is white." If you pressed me, I could say a bit more: I painted the wall myself, some years ago, using eggshell Behr paint, in a color called "White Lace." But now reconsider for a moment. The wall is not white. It is late in the morning on a January day. The sun is low shining through a south-facing window. The wall is on the south. The open door to the hall, obscuring part of the wall, casts subtle shadows, as do all the reflections of the sunlight off the polished wood floor and the other walls. The colors on the wall include gray, hints of yellow, hints of blue, and even, in the corner, a hint of green. It is brighter near the edge near the window and darker near the other corner and near the floor. I judge, in some sense, that the wall is uniformly white; for most purposes, I would be hard pressed to say much more about it (though my description earlier failed to even hint at the subtlety of the distinctions in its surface appearance). But my claim that it is merely white was a judgment; it is not a recapitulation of the information that directly enters my eyes nor even the information that I am able to attend to in my processed visual experience.

Our experiences of all colors are like this. We see colors on objects, in a variety of changing lighting, and we judge simplicity where there is great complexity. A patch of color in everyday experience is never uniform. And the colors that surround a patch will very significantly alter our perception of the color of that patch. Color is constructed out of a very complex interaction of objects with their environment and the observer.

Again, have I been unfair? What about a pure color experience? Part of my point here is that there is no (normal) pure color experience, but let us again attempt charity with the anti-physicalist position. Let us then imagine a patch of color that engulfs the entire visual field and is uniform. Perhaps such a thing is possible. In ideal laboratory conditions, we could perhaps recreate it. In this situation then, everywhere we look in our visual field, we see—let us suppose—a particular red.

Note the following. In this case, you will judge that you see red in your peripheral vision. Or rather, if you are a lay person, uncorrupted by the study of psychology or of the philosophy of mind, and I ask you, "Do you see red in the periphery of your vision?" You will answer, "Yes, of course." This hypothetical case is of great interest because it draws attention to the gross fallibility of our phenomenal judgments. It is something of a shock to learn we are practically colorblind in the periphery of our visual field. (To test this, get a box of different colored crayons or other small brightly colored objects with the same shape; set the box behind you; stare straight ahead; grab one of the objects at random; hold the object to the extreme right or left; decide what color it is; move it forward and try again; eventually, as the object nears the center of your visual field, you will see its true color, and you will find that your judgment when it was at the periphery was no better than chance—the exception being judgments with respect to, or influenced by, overall brightness.) And yet, all of us are fully convinced that we see color in our entire visual field. Even knowing that we are colorblind in our periphery does not change the perceptual judgment that we see color there.

Thus, our "experience" is convincingly that we see vivid color in our entire visual field. We do not. (This is similar to the blind spot, which exists but which we cannot get ourselves to "see," even when we know it exists.) What this establishes is that our phenomenal judgments are not only fallible, they are in many ways stubbornly and systematically wrong. By "stubborn," I mean that they resist cognitive correction. I *know* that I am colorblind in the periphery. I also undeniably make always and only the phenomenal judgment that I am not colorblind in the periphery. The phenomenal judgment that I see color there completely resists correction. So, any claim to authority for our phenomenal judgments, even with respect to the experience of a single color, are profoundly fallible. This includes any claims to "perceive" that color is a simple; such a claim is as reliable as the conviction that we see color in the periphery.

We can learn here from the enactivist theory of perception. The enactivists (Noe 2004; O'Regan 2011) explain this phenomenon with the posit that we have the experience of color in our periphery because we have the well-justified sensorimotor expectation that we *will* see color if we look in that direction. But this means that our judgments with respect to color experience are a very different thing indeed than just a simple input; they arise not from a direct and accurate sensation but from a kind of counterfactual expectation. Even in the case of a visual field engulfed in one color, our judgment will be dependent upon sensorimotor expectations. There is nothing simple about this case.

What about, in our condition of even "pure" color spread throughout the visual field, the instance when one attends to the center of the visual field? That, finally, is a simple thing, a quale, an atom of raw feel!

But no. First, note that we cannot even assume that our judgment about the center field is reliable. For example, if the anti-physicalist supposes that this is an atom of experience, we should expect as a consequence that she would notice if the atom changed. But in fact she might not. The well-documented, but surprising, phenomenon of change blindness occurs when a subject does not notice a change that would seem obvious once our attention is drawn to it. This phenomenon extends even to color experience. In a surprising experiment, O'Regan et al. (2000) had subjects fixate on digital pictures in which three different kinds of changes occurred: in some pictures, an object moved, in some pictures, an object appeared or disappeared, and in some pictures, an object changed color. In half of the cases, the change occurred in the area in the photograph of primary interest (as identified by other subjects). The interesting feature of the experiment was that the changes were made during eye blinks, which typically last about one-tenth or two-tenths of a second and occur about 30 times a minute. The results are surprising, if not shocking: about 40% of subjects failed to notice any change, even on repeated exposures, and even when the change was on a feature of central interest. Thus, a subject might look at a photograph of a scene with a car, and the color of the car might change dramatically during the blink, and the subject not know.

This reiterates the fallibility of our phenomenal judgments. They can be systematically unreliable. One's sense to be having a pure color experience, and the judgment that this is a simple, might in fact arise from two or more different colors in succession; or from a very, very slow change in color. But there is an additional consequence. The best interpretation of this phenomenon of change blindness is that *what we expect* and *what we are doing* determine what our experience is like. But that means our experience of color will hardly be a simple thing. It is essentially related to our attention, our expectations, our rich sensorimotor expectations and capabilities, and our conceptual state.

But finally can we not isolate some "pure" red experience? It is important to note that from the perspective of the physicalist, there is a fundamental confusion in this idea of "pure red" experience. It is not an idealization akin to frictionless surfaces or efficient markets; it is more like imagining motion without space or markets without the exchange of goods. This is because representations are fundamentally normative or teleological. Representations can be right or wrong. And, even if one has not adopted enactivism, ultimately we must explain this normative aspect of representations (and remember, we are talking here about actual, occurrent representations in human beings—not some abstraction like the semantic content of "red") in terms of their relation to action. A representation *must* be related to action, in some way. So the idea of a representation that is "pure" in the sense of being divorced from all possible connections to other representations and possibilities of action is meaningless. Such a thing can at best be a causal correlation. It cannot be a representation. Thus, if one considers the representational theory of consciousness a contender, or even if one grants that red can represent, then this demand for a "pure red" experience is question begging. It is like asking for a non-representational version of red experience.

Let us try to be neutral, and instead of a "pure" red experience, consider something like a true judgment made about the center of the visual field when exposed to an unchanging field of red light. Can we not consider this, if not a "pure" red experience, at least some kind of simple?

The enactivist view is that the phenomenal character of red is determined by how red will change and react in relation to action, to sensorimotor control. This puts the lie to the infamous inverted spectrum thought experiment (which is at least as old as Locke 1975 [1689]) and the metastasizing variations on it (such as twin-Earth colors, Block 1990). Red is a color that behaves in certain ways in relation to motion, light, and reflectivity. This is why my red cannot be your blue. My red must act in relation to these factors as does what you call "red." This information about the changes in light, reflectance, and other features, as a function of motion, *constitutes* what a red experience is. This information is the phenomenal character of red. Thus, red experience is not a simple atom of information. It is a complex web of information relating to expectations and capabilities of motor control with reliable forms of interaction with the environment.[1]

A red experience is complex, but what of our descriptions of red? Our descriptions of any color are very impoverished in comparison to the richness of the color. Other than names, we have a few adjectives that we typically rely upon, like "bright" or "pure." These descriptions will fail to amount to even a fraction of the complexity of the experience itself—and, more importantly, will not begin to approach the complexity of the brain events that are required for one to have a red experience. Because it is sufficient to label red phenomena, given the inter-human reliability of our perceptions, we have not striven to develop an accurate description of the information in a red experience, nor are we well equipped to do so.

Color, like fear, is representative: each paradigmatically mysterious phenomenal experience is very complex. Each of these experiences is constituted by complex events that determine why it is the kind of experience it is. But our language for describing experience, and for describing its properties, is very impoverished. Each of these descriptions is so impoverished that one cannot properly identify the essential features of the phenomenal experience from the description.

It will be helpful here to consider a potential objection to this position, well articulated by William Robinson. Robinson offers the following summary of an argument for dualism or anti-physicalism (2018: 60; I slightly edit the argument):

RS1. The physical properties with which qualia are correlated are complex.
RS2. Qualia are relatively simple properties.
RS3. No property can be both complex and relatively simple.
RS4. Qualia are not identical with their physical correlated properties.
RS5. Qualia are not identical with physical properties with which they are not at least correlated.
RS6. Qualia are not identical with any physical properties.

My reply is to reject RS2. But here is the rub. The dualist claims that they observe this simplicity of experience directly. Suppose I reply that water looks simple, even though it is really a complex arrangement of H_2O molecules. The anti-physicalist reply is:

> the pattern in the water case is that when a thing does not appear as what it is, a distinct property is involved in the way it does appear. Applying this pattern to qualia should lead physicalists to say that qualia are complex

properties that have a distinct property involved in the way that they appear. But this result concedes the need for properties that are distinct from the complex properties with which they are correlated.

(Robinson 2018: 61)

I refute the intuition that guides such arguments in Section 4.3. Here it may be useful, however, to make a few observations. First, I deny that we actually perceive these qualia as simple. We are not reliably able to discern the structural requirements of our experiences, just as we cannot observe the structure of water. I have already given examples of how we can be systematically inaccurate in judgments about perception. Second, in Section 2.6, I show that this claim is not an observation but rather a theoretical posit, revealed by the fact that lay people reliable agree with me, and not with anti-physicalists, on this matter. Third, there could be an issue of relative versus absolute complexity which underlies the theory-laden claim that, for example, a red experience is simple. Recall that we discussed in Section 1.4 that sometimes a very complex description can be simply explained if we already have some other additional information. A person who sees red has already poised within her brain and mind the many capabilities that constitute the perception of red: the ability to distinguish frequencies, the understanding of how red behaves under different lighting, how it relates to action, how red appears relative to other colors, how it changes under lighter or darker shades, and so on. With all this information already poised for use, only a slight additional amount of information may be needed to actually identify an instance of the color red; it may be that we are inclined to mistake this additional necessary information as the sum of sufficient information.

Having argued that our paradigmatically mysterious phenomenal experiences are complex, what then about our theories? We can be quick with the defense of DI with respect to our theories because our current theories of consciousness are really meta-theories—they are hypotheses about what the right kind of theory might look like. As such, they are enormously simplistic. This is not a criticism, but rather just a recognition that we are in the early days of the science of consciousness. For example, the fine previous work on the representational theory of consciousness (e.g., Lycan 1996; Tye 1995) is aimed at making the approach plausible and at answering very general objections. It does not begin to make progress in describing the particulars of any kind of experience. The situation is the same for the other physicalist philosophical theories: they aim at approaches and do not provide descriptions that are sufficient for prediction or reconstruction.[2]

In the sciences, the situation is similar. Although more detailed than philosophical theories, nonetheless, the current scientific theories of consciousness are highly preliminary. Also, most are aimed primarily at explaining subjectivity rather than phenomenal quality. Thus, for example, Bernard Baars has developed an influential theory of consciousness as a global workspace (1988). The theory and variations of it (Dehaene and Naccache 2001) are our best current theories of subjectivity, but they are pitched at the level of gross structural and functional relationships. They do nothing to describe individual experiences. Work in perception probably comes closest to what we need— for example, there is a sophisticated vocabulary and there are sophisticated theories available to those who study color vision. But even these are highly preliminary with respect to phenomenal quality since they are not developed to explain the phenomenal quality of experience but rather to determine some of the limits of color capabilities.

An interesting exception here is the Integrated Information Theory (IIT) proposed by Tononi and his collaborators (e.g., Oizumi et al. 2014). This theory is preliminary in the ways that I identified for the theories discussed earlier (that is, IIT is not yet, to my knowledge, able to distinguish particular kinds of phenomenal experiences), but it does offer a sophisticated and provocative model. IIT is a physicalist theory of consciousness; it identifies consciousness with complex brain events. These events are maximally complex integrated information states, called "Φ^{MAX}," which constitute the kind and quality of an experience. What is of interest here is that, for this theory, phenomenal experiences are locally maximally complex states of integrated information. Given that information integration in the brain is presumably normally complex, then these maximal states must be highly complex. Thus, these Φ^{MAX} events will themselves be very descriptively complex, to a degree that satisfies the complexity of consciousness claim. If this is so, then IIT entails the complexity of consciousness claim, and all the arguments of this book are consequences of IIT and thus are available to the defender of IIT as additional means to bolster the theory.

Our current theories are thus (as of now) inadequate to the task of sufficiently describing our experiences and their essential properties. This corroborates the description inadequacy claim, DI.

These arguments for DI are preliminary, I recognize. But my claims have two benefits, in addition to the explanatory power explored in the rest of this book: they are falsifiable, and they are productive.

2.3 Capabilities Inadequacy Claim

DI is alone sufficient for the arguments that follow. However, I want to defend a more radical possibility, the capabilities inadequacy claim, CI. This claim is that our ability to reason about paradigmatically mysterious phenomenal experiences does not have the information capacity to allow us to properly entertain (think about, speak aloud, etc.) the descriptive content of a paradigmatically mysterious phenomenal experience. I believe that CI is true, but the argument that follows is preliminary and tentative, and so I am compelled to reiterate that the key arguments of this book do not depend upon CI.

I made some passing defense of CI during my defense of DI. But, in this section, I will make two arguments for CI. The first is based on observations concerning disassociations between our capabilities for phenomenal judgments.

The second is a kind of efficiency argument. Both arguments are made from a physicalist perspective and require a minimal modularity assumption: I assume that some portion of our brains is dedicated to theoretical reasoning, and not all portions of our brain can be used for this kind of theoretical reasoning. Thus, we cannot take the portions of the neocortex dedicated to color processing or motor control or hearing and use them for doing a math problem (at least, not in the way that we normally do the math problem). This is, I should note, trivial for anyone familiar with basic brain anatomy. The controversies about modularity with respect to reasoning arise over how general, and perhaps how distributed, our reasoning abilities are. For our purposes here, reasoning abilities include the ability to learn and follow an algorithm in a self-aware way, or to do mathematics, or to reason about logical implications and consistency. (This last ability is the one that will matter most in response to the anti-physicalist arguments, in Chapter 4, since the anti-physicalist arguments require judgments about possibility and implication.)

Concerning dissociations between capabilities, consider a phenomenon like prosopagnosia. The prosopagnosic, as a consequence of damage to the fusiform gyrus, is unable to recognize faces but is otherwise not visually impaired. What is of interest here is that the prosopagnosic cannot learn some algorithm to recognize faces. Imagine a denial of CI: one asserts that in fact our reasoning abilities are no less capacious than our perceptual abilities, such as our visual abilities. We are able to reason about theories, and this requires a certain amount of information, and we are able to recognize faces, and (the denier of CI might claim) this requires about the same amount of information. The two may be significantly different tasks, but if we deny CI, then we believe that the capacity of reasoning is not bounded such that it cannot do both.

But if that were the case, then one should be able to "cure" prosopagnosia through therapy. We should be able to develop a face recognition theory and train prosopagnosics to use it. In this therapy, the subject will learn and then apply face recognition rules to the visual information that is otherwise unimpaired for the prosopagnosic. These would be the kind of rules that our face recognition algorithms use in our computers. As a result, the prosopagnosia will disappear: the subject will learn to recognize faces using reasoning alone. And, after all, such redundancies are possible, and some forms of redundancies in our mental capabilities are relatively familiar. A person with poor balance uses visual information, for example, to better judge her orientation to the ground. Thus, if the capacity of our theoretical reasoning abilities were not bounded in a relevant way, and it had complete transparent access to all visual information, then the prosopagnosic should be able to develop and use a theory to judge whose face is before her. The agnosia should be curable with a little extra reasoning effort.

But we cannot cure prosopagnosia through such a therapy. Since the visual information for the prosopagnosic is unimpaired—she can describe the color of the hair, the color of the eyes, and all the other features of the face before her—we need some explanation of why she cannot recognize the face by simply learning such an algorithm. Presumably, after all, such an algorithm is embodied in the normal functioning of the fusiform gyrus.

The explanation is that there is more information required to distinguish two similar faces than we are capable of manipulating in our theoretical reasoning abilities. That is, the reason we cannot cure or work around prosopagnosia through therapy is that CI is true with respect to the information distinguishing one face from another.

The claim of CI is that the ability to understand and act appropriately in relation to paradigmatically mysterious phenomenal experiences is not unlike the ability to recognize faces. We cannot teach the person with achromatopsia how to see color based on some inferential algorithm applied to changes in light as affected by motion with respect to colored objects, for example. The anti-physicalist claims that this is because color experience is not something that a physicalist ontology can explain, and anyway this phenomenon experience has no structure or parts to describe. One either has it or does not. But we would also not be able to teach the person with achromatopsia the trick of distinguishing some colors if the task were just too complex for the kind of reasoning abilities that the person with achromatopsia (and you and I) have.

The efficiency argument for CI requires a strong assumption. We assume that the brain is relatively efficient. As a result, the volume of structure dedicated to a certain task is a rough measure of how computationally demanding that task is. This is obviously a significant claim and one that will no doubt be controversial to some philosophers. However, a moment's reflection should suggest that something roughly like this efficiency claim must be true. The brain is a very demanding organ. It consumes a significant number of our calories, for example. An organism that struck upon a more efficient way to perform mental tasks would have a potential fitness advantage. We do not need that evolution is perfectly optimizing to expect that as a rough rule brain volume should map onto computational demands.

But if we grant this assumption, we immediately recognize that most of the real estate of the neocortex is dedicated to sensation and perception, and another significant fraction is dedicated to motor control. A relatively smaller portion is dedicated to theoretical reasoning and other general cognitive skills. If the efficiency assumption is true, then this indicates that much more information is generated and manipulated by sensory and perceptual processing portions of the neocortex than is by theoretical reasoning.

One fact that corroborates the efficiency assumption, and also helps to corroborate CI, is that we lose the ability to imagine or dream a sense when we lose the relevant neocortical area. Thus, for example, Sacks and Wasserman (1987) report on a painter who suffered head trauma that resulted in brain damage rendering him unable to see colors. He also lost the ability to imagine colors or dream colors. Such efficiencies make good evolutionary sense: why would imagination or dreaming make use of a redundant structure, and rather not just use the very structure that enables color processing in vision? But, like the case with prosopagnosia, we should ask ourselves, why can't the person with achromatopsia just use her theoretical abilities to imagine or dream in color? The answer, of course, is that color is more complex, it contains more information, than her theoretical reasoning capabilities can manage.

Of course, the anti-physicalists claim the person with achromatopsia cannot think red because red is not a physical kind, and for some reason, this means that our logical capabilities alone cannot recreate the experience. Since even the anti-physicalists grant that my brain obviously causes phenomenal experiences, it is in fact a little odd that I cannot just reason my way to a red experience. If my visual cortex causes the non-physical event, why can't some little bit of my frontal lobe do it through reasoning? Yes, the idea is that if I reason with my physical theory I can't reason my way to a red experience because the experience isn't physical, so my theory doesn't get it right. But why can't my frontal lobe just do whatever my visual cortex does which causes the non-physical event? The anti-physicalist has no answer to this question. Her best answer, in fact, would be to say that the color experience is complex and those brain regions dedicated to reason aren't up to the task, but then that would make her anti-physicalism such that it does no work (since, as I will repeatedly show, the only thing that her anti-physicalism explains—the mysteriousness of phenomenal quality—is already explained by the complexity claim).

We do not have a good understanding yet of what enables theoretical reasoning of the kind relevant to the anti-physicalist arguments, which typically require that someone make judgments about logical consistency between metaphysical claims and phenomenal claims (e.g., all physical facts could be the same but no color experience exists). However, some preliminary work in this area is fully consistent with the claim that only a small portion of the cortex is dedicated to such reasoning. Monti et al. (2007) studied logical reasoning using problem tasks on subjects being measured by fMRI. They identified a network involved in this reasoning that was independent of reading and language abilities. The network was highly distributed but notably very much smaller than the amount of neocortex dedicated to visual processing. If we assume that there are efficiencies here and that the occipital lobe is not wasting all that real estate, then it is impossible to take the information in a visual experience, in its entirety, into our theoretical reason. There simply is not the capacity there.

This is consistent with our everyday experience of logical reasoning. We typically are only able to reason with a small amount of information. Our short-term memory has a capacity of less than ten items, where the items are themselves rather simple (like a single-digit number or a single short word). We do not have the experience of being able to remember and add together two very large numbers, for example. And yet such a thing would be simple relative to the amount of information that constitutes a visual experience. If we cannot remember, turn around in our reasoning, and add together two numbers that are a few hundred thousand digits long, why should we expect to be able to turn around in our reasoning both all the information in color experience, along with our prejudices about what physicalism amounts to? (Both would be required to accurately judge if they were independent of each other.)

The kind of reasoning that many of the classical anti-physicalist arguments indulge in—and this reasoning is typical of many arguments concerning consciousness—is that if we have an experience, then it is wholly available to reason. This is to assume the Cartesian mind, a transparent and structureless whole where nothing is hidden, where all the information is freely available to all kinds of cognition. But this is simply false. To have an experience of some kind, like a red experience, is a completely different thing than to reason about red experience.

Finally, I will observe that many philosophers accept a massive modularity thesis about the mind. On this view, our mental capabilities are constituted by the operation of mental organs, which are brain structures (these can be distributed) dedicated to that task. There is debate about how widespread modularity is in the brain (ranging from massive modularity theses like Cosmides and Tooby 1992 and Carruthers 2006, to limited modularity such as proposed by Fodor 1983), about whether modules are dedicated neural structures (see Samuels 1998), and about whether modularity extends to various cognitive capabilities (see Sperber 1994). But even those critical of most modularity claims (Churchland 1988) will presumably grant that there are dedicated structures performing complex information processing that are distinct from and more capacious than some other dedicated structures. A massive modularity thesis would seem likely to entail CI (we would need to know the details of the particular form of the theory to confirm this) since we should expect that dedicated reasoning organs are unlikely to have the immense capacity required to allow them to manipulate sensory information in those modules. But one need not accept the massive modularity thesis to accept CI; one need only accept that our reasoning capabilities are not as capacious as the information in our paradigmatically mysterious phenomenal experiences. Either a massive modularity thesis or the various much weaker views about capacities and modularity are consistent with CI. That is, CI does not require a modularity thesis, but most modularity theses, emended with some minimal observations about brain structure, likely entail CI.

I have assumed a physicalist view throughout my arguments. As I have already noted, this will not beg the question in any of my arguments. But, of course, the anti-physicalist will resist such physicalist accounts. Note, however, two things. First, the anti-physicalist should recognize on phenomenological grounds that CI is true. We cannot teach the prosopagnosic to recognize faces. We cannot just bounce around in our short-term memory or our theoretical capabilities all the information that we know is in a visual color experience. Second, the anti-physicalist is in a very difficult position. She cannot explain why paradigmatically mysterious phenomenal experiences are correlated with complex brain events. If they are ontologically different things, why would they need to be so correlated? I discuss this more in Section 4.5 of this book.

What these considerations make clear is that the complexity of paradigmatically mysterious phenomenal experiences exceeds the capacity of our reasoning capabilities. We simply are not capable of articulating all the information in a sight or sound or taste and then considering that information the way we can consider something like a math problem. The taste of a strawberry contains not only more information than we can reason about, but also at least one of the essential properties of the taste of strawberry is more complex than our reasoning capacity can manage.

It is perhaps necessary to ward off two possible confusions here. First, we can of course reason *about* our experiences, and in turn, our experiences can of course inform our reason. In these cases, the capabilities constituting, say, a color sensation are available to reason. We can reason about this information and in various ways access it. But we cannot shift that information *into* our reasoning capability. Second, CI is not the claim that we cannot have a theory of consciousness nor the claim that we cannot (in some sense) understand a theory of consciousness. It is rather the claim that some of the theoretical kinds of the theory of consciousness will be too complex for us to hold them in our theoretical reasoning capabilities. We can imagine someone objecting, "You've overstated your case. Why should we believe that any natural phenomenon can be captured by our simple scientific theories? You've stated that most phenomena, even most numbers, are complex; why shouldn't all our theories find these phenomena mysterious?"

Here a few reminders are required. First, we must note that what we are looking for when we develop our theories is patterns; that is, we are looking to compress the data. So we look for, find, and largely have a bias to notice such patterns. The success of science does not mean the world is simple (see DeLancey 2011). Second, neither the DI claim nor the CI claim entails that we cannot use other methods to store and manipulate information, thereby bypassing our own limitations. Computers allow whole new realms to be explored because they can manage ever more information. We can still in principle develop a scientific theory of consciousness. The complex descriptions required could be stored and manipulated on computers. Such modeling is now common in many disciplines that deal with complex phenomena, such as the weather. Third, it may be that often we simplify by idealization and that this allows us to step up toward highly useful theories that admittedly throw away some information (see Weisberg 2007; Potochnik 2015; Winsberg 2006). Finally, remember the discussion of the incompressibility cost principle from Section 1.7.3 and the related discussion of the contingent information principle in Section 1.7.2; there we stressed that even very simple theories can have consequences of any complexity. Thus, there may be some revealing and relatively simple patterns in some very complex phenomena, but that does not reduce its complexity.

2.4 The Overflow Claim and the Inference to High Complexity

My claims about consciousness have interesting parallels in one of the important debates in recent work on consciousness, sometimes called the "richness debate" or the "overflow argument." I will call it the "overflow claim." This debate depends on a distinction that Ned Block made famous, between "access consciousness" and "phenomenal consciousness" (Block 1995). Access consciousness refers to information—representations, on Block's account—that is available for cognitive processing. These are the kinds of things that constitute reports. "Phenomenal consciousness" is instead what it is like for the subject to have the experience. I will let Block describe the overflow claim, as it concerns visual perception:

> The overflow argument appeals to visual iconic memory . . . to argue that a conscious perceptual system that has "rich" contents "overflows"—that is, has a higher capacity than—the sparse system that cognitively accesses perception.
>
> (Block 2011: 567)

It is curious that scholars active in this debate are comfortable with phrases like "has higher capacity than" but do not take the additional step to recognize that this only makes sense if they are talking about information. My own rephrasing of this would be to say that there is more information in the phenomenal experience than there is in the capacity of whatever brain event that constitutes access consciousness. This is similar to the CI claim.

Defenders of the overflow argument believe its best evidence comes from experiments by Sperling (1960) that show subjects can remember information when properly cued to do so, in such a way that makes clear that the information was present in some way in the mind before being accessed. Sperling did this by showing subjects a grid of letters for a very brief time. Subjects are unable to report what all the letters are, although they report the experience of having seen all the letters. However, if cued to recall a row of the letters, they can do so with an accuracy better than chance, showing that the information was present in some sense. Those who see this as evidence for the overflow claim interpret the experiment as showing that a visual representation with more information than is available to report was present, for a short period, allowing for some information retrieval. There have been challenges to this interpretation, but it remains plausible and at least as good as the alternatives on offer.

Additional important evidence for the overflow argument comes from phenomenology: subjects report that they see more than they can recall and accurately describe. Look out at the rolling hills across the lake—are you not having a visual experience that is full of information? The primary alternative theory to the overflow argument, and to these kinds of reports, is that we form unconscious memories of the stimuli, that these are accessed in the Sperling experiments, and also that our access to these unconscious memories results in the illusion that we have a rich phenomenal experience. This illusion is sometimes called the "refrigerator light illusion" (O'Regan 2011). On this view, we believe we have a rich phenomenal experience because we know that we can access a lot of information if we need to do so. Supposedly, this is like believing the light is on in the refrigerator when you close the door.

I am critical of arguments that are common in the philosophy of consciousness, which go something like: you are saying consciousness is like this, but I am saying consciousness is like that, and because it is my notion of consciousness that I am trying to explain, your account is useless to me because you are trying to describe or explain something other than what I mean. The problem with such replies is that they can allow one to define consciousness in a way that fits it to your preferred theory. Nonetheless, in the case of the supposed refrigerator light illusion, I find myself compelled to make just such an argument. The claim is simply not credible. Those who propose it are saying that while listening to a symphony, or eating a pizza, or staring out across the lake at rolling green hills, you have a few bits of information that you are conscious of in working memory (or some such proposed "access consciousness" buffer), and the belief that you have a rich and varied experience is an illusion. The only response one can give to this kind of claim is that it denies that the phenomenon exists. Or, to follow the spirit of the otherwise problematic argument form, in this case, then I should say to the defenders of the "refrigerator light illusion" that I want to explain the richness of the illusion.

However, even if we should have no patience for the refrigerator light illusion claim, one can grant that there is a difficulty in the formulation of the overflow argument. The distinction between access and phenomenal consciousness, like the difference between subjectivity and experience, is clear enough as a conceptual distinction, but as an empirical matter, it can be puzzling. This is because we must rely upon reports to study consciousness, we must recognize that those reports can be in error, but we are also distinguishing between the ability to report on consciousness and the conscious experience itself. It is always tempting to conflate those two and call it a victory for parsimony. But even if we do not conflate them, one may well be perplexed by the idea that I know I experience more than I can report I experience. Unfortunately, by contrasting access and phenomenal consciousness, this appears quite puzzling. I could claim—indeed, I believe—that a report is an attempt to describe, and our experience is not our theoretical description, and a range of experiences shows us that our theoretical or verbal description is inadequate. However, the overflow claim rests on not a contrast of description and experience, but rather on access and phenomenal consciousness. As a result, it seems to set up a contrast between our access to our experience and our experience, which is more difficult to understand.

The view I defend here has obvious echoes with the overflow claim. I can add that I believe that something like the overflow claim is true, if we contrast the kinds of descriptions we can generate of our experience, with that experience (this is just to assert DI and is a consequence of CI). But the arguments in this book need not rely upon the overflow claim.

The overflow claim does draw our attention to another important issue that I only briefly discussed before. The overflow claim relies upon the claim that the information *in* the conscious experience, as an experience, exceeds the information capacity of access consciousness. To clarify with an analogy: imagine that my conscious experience of vision is, in this instance, like a picture on a television screen (it is nothing so static, but the analogy is here just to make a point). Then the picture is full of information. We might store the image in a computer file, and we could measure the descriptive complexity of that file; the information in this image and that we measured would thus be information that directly constitutes the information that is in the experience as experience. We can contrast with this another kind of information: the information in the sufficient theoretical description of the brain events (if we assume physicalism, for the sake of argument) that constitute the visual experience. To return to our analogy, this would be a description of the television itself and also of all the events occurring in the television that enable it to project the image on the screen.

We might call the former, "information in the experience," and the latter, "information required to explain the experience." Within certain constraints, there is some correlation between these; we should expect that it will take a theory and descriptions with a great deal of information to properly describe the brain events necessary to generate and constitute an experience that has a great deal of information. But, in any case, the complexity of consciousness claim is concerned with the information required to explain the experience. It claims that there is at least one property of the experience, as described by an adequate theory, that both are necessary to explain the phenomenal character and that also is very complex. That is, in saying that a paradigmatically mysterious phenomenal experience has at least one property R that is essential to its phenomenal character and is very complex, one is not committed to the idea that all the information in a description of R is information in the experience. It causes the experience, it is essential to the experience, but it may not be that all the relevant information can be perceived directly—or, perhaps, it could be that some, but not all, can be perceived directly.[3]

This does not change that I believe that the information in the experience of a paradigmatically mysterious conscious event is itself complex. Furthermore, I believe that the complexity of the information in the experience is related to, in some essential way, the complexity of the information required to explain the experience. Thus, I agree with the spirit, though I am uncertain of the details, of the overflow claim. But the point here is to recognize that the causes and essential properties of an experience need not themselves be experiences, and my claims are not equivalent to the overflow claim nor do they entail the overflow claim. My opinion is that we are able to access much of the information required to explain a complex experience, but that there is no clear sense in which it need be available for report or theoretical reflection all at once. How such reports or reflections, or our capabilities used for theoretical reflection, relate to "access consciousness," as Block understands it, I do not know.

2.5 Why Are Some of Our Mental Representations Complex?

One might wonder why some of our mental representations are complex. Here I want to offer some arguments meant to explain why something like our visual representations would have a great deal of information in them. The arguments are somewhat speculative, and my other arguments do not depend upon their soundness. There are two claims that need to be defended: first, that many phenomena in the environment are very complex, and second, that in some cases there could be a fitness benefit to better representing such phenomena.

There is no practical upper bound to the possible complexity of physical phenomena. Given that our physical universe is very large and has many objects in it, there are no practical bounds to how we can recombine matter into new combinations and interactions. To deny this is to claim that there is a largest computer program and most complex computer program, a most complex expressable number, a most complex expressable theory, and so on. But for any computer program, one could add another line, for any represented complex number one could add to it another large complex number, for any theory one could add another claim, and so on. (The only practical consideration here is that the universe may have finite mass and finite size. Then there could in principle be some upper limit—albeit incomprehensibly large—for complexity. This is why I added the caveat "practical." But such an upper bound would be so high that it cannot be relevant to any question we will consider here.)

Given that there is no upper bound, does it follow that the phenomena that matter to a mind are very complex? Here we need to consider two issues. First, are the phenomena around us simple, or are some of them simple? Second, would the complex phenomena around us (if there are any) have any relevance to our survival because of their complexity?

To answer that first question, I want to introduce the concept of *information density*. We will say that a phenomenon is maximally information dense if and only if a full description of the phenomenon will require at least as much matter and energy as constitute this phenomenon. This could be expressed as a ratio: the information density of P = the matter and energy required to fully describe P divided by the matter and energy that constitute P.

We know from the idea of the Bekenstein boundary that the amount of information that can be contained in a given finite region of space with a finite amount of energy must be finite (Bekenstein 1981). But the question being asked here is different. What is the cost of representing that information? The claim that it requires less space and energy than the region being described seems unlikely. In any case, even if some compression is possible, the representation of that information must have a cost. My proposal is that most of the physical world has a high information density. Take a table, a chair, a hurricane, and a frog, and if you wanted to describe that thing in full, missing not a single feature, not a single atomic particle or its position and momentum (we are setting aside issues of measurement here), then it would take at least as must energy and matter as the thing being fully described. Of course, we never make such descriptions, and we don't need to—the question here is, how "deep" can an analysis of some natural phenomenon go? I would argue it can go very deep, such that there are few if any natural phenomena that can be fully represented without paying a great cost.

But if most phenomena are information dense, it does not follow that we need to represent them with a great deal of information. Why not represent just a few things, with a low-information representation? The problem is that representation is how we distinguish things, and the more information in a representation, the more it will be able to distinguish.

To see this, consider predation. All animals evolved in an environment where they had to play the role of stalking predator or evasive prey—many animals have to play both roles. Predation and evasion, along with other kinds of competition, create an arms race for representational capacity. An octopus, for example, is hunting organisms, including fish, that try to evade it. It must learn to recognize those fish and be able to track them in order to hunt them. But many of the fish are constantly evolving new strategies of evasion and camouflage. Better representation of the environment is going to be the only tool for the octopus to distinguish hiding prey from things like rocks or weeds. This means that it becomes worthwhile to spend the cost of developing more discerning perceptual organs and the enormous cost of neural tissue needed to use these organs to distinguish phenomena. But the fish are in this arms race too. They will get a benefit from having better camouflage. Also, they need to recognize the octopus, which itself has a very effective camouflage. They will get a fitness benefit if they can see and distinguish the hiding octopus. Predator and prey are in a perceptual and information-representation arms race—in this example, one where improved camouflage can drive improved perceptual sampling which drives the need for improved camouflage. Such a race should drive organisms toward the maximal benefit for the consumption and use of more information.

Other challenges to an organism will require information to make distinctions—motor control, of course, but also identifying foods, identifying potable water, and avoiding many kinds of threats other than predators. Sexual competition will benefit from the ability to distinguish better mates—many potential mates often cheat by trying to appear better pickings than they are. Indeed, once we recognize that most animal behaviors require representations to function, we can see that there will be innumerable benefits to increased information in our representations, bounded by high caloric costs of neural tissue and sensory organs. Thus, a natural organism competes with predators, prey, and peers in a very complex environment, and one of its most important advantages is the amount of information in its representations of its environment. It is thus predictable that we would find things like the human visual neocortex capable of creating enormously complex visual representations.

2.6 Theory and Observation of Complexity

I have argued that the very complex events that constitute a perception or emotion, to take two examples, have complex properties that distinguish them from other kinds of phenomenal experiences. As I noted earlier, this is an empirical claim, and so my task as a philosopher will be to show the implications of the assumption, and I hope that the entire theory that I develop offers some evidence for the assumption because of the explanatory power of the theory. However, I do suspect that people understand, albeit in a limited and intuitive way, that their conscious experiences are very complex, and have complex distinguishing properties. I make use of this claim in my argument in Section 4.2, but it is otherwise independent of my other claims.

We are aware of the complexity of the character of our experiences for a range of reasons: we distinguish many kinds; we find them very distinct; we find they come in very fine gradations along broad continua; we learn and have constantly reiterated to us our inability to verbally describe these experiences; and, above all, we compare our experiences with our descriptions and our (typically folk) theories.

Reflect upon our everyday experience. We learn, without reflection, that we cannot describe most experiences in a way that conveys those experiences. Rather, we learn shared names and use those to refer to the experiences. Confronted with a new experience, we know that we cannot describe it in a way that would allow someone to reconstruct or have that experience. We compare it to the best analogs we expect our listeners to have ("It tastes like chicken. But not really.") and then encourage them to have the experience. Over a childhood in which we learn to coordinate action with others, we quickly learn that experience far outstrips our ability to describe. We intuitively understand that there is far more information in our paradigmatically mysterious phenomenal experiences than we can explain to others. Thus, we have an unreflective but accurate understanding of DI.

Again: I am not claiming that we observe that our experiences are complex. Rather, our experience provides reasons for the general understanding that our experiences are complex. Such a claim is not an observation, nor is it *a priori* true.

I can say with confidence that a claim that paradigmatically phenomenal experiences are simples is neither an observation nor *a priori* true because it is possible to demonstrate the contrary. If the claim that phenomenal experiences were simple were an observation, or otherwise *a priori* true, or if it followed *a priori* from what we mean by, for example, "red (experience)," then the lay conception of phenomenal experiences would be that they were simples. And this is not so. I have demonstrated this through a simple survey.

In a philosophy experiment undertaken for another and independent purpose (to determine if interpretations of thought experiments were easily influenced by the framing of the experiment), I surveyed 330 undergraduate students regarding a version of Jackson's knowledge argument. The version went like this:

> Anne can see but she is born with a disease that makes her unable to see colors. Anne speaks English and as a child she learns many facts about colors from other people who see colors, such as "grass is green" and "the sky is blue," but Anne sees the world in black and white. When she grows up, Anne goes to college to study neural science and she earns a Ph.D. in neural science. She becomes an expert in the science of color vision, and learns all that science can tell us about color vision. All this time, Anne cannot herself see colors. After Anne has been a practicing neural scientist for many years, some doctors discover a cure for Anne's disease. Anne takes the cure and her vision is repaired so that she can see color.

Readers familiar with Jackson's thought experiment will note that his version had Mary locked in a colorless room. I changed the thought experiment because experience had taught me that students frequently had objections which were not immediately relevant. These include "Doesn't Mary see her hands?" "What if Mary presses on her eyelids?" "What if Mary cuts herself?" and so on.

The non-control subjects of this survey were given a dummy question that suggested interpretations of the thought experiment; the control subjects instead were not given suggestions for the interpretation of the thought experiment. The surveys were collected over several years. Effort was taken to ensure that the subjects were likely to be naïve to the thought experiment. Only 9% of the control sample were majors in philosophy and related degrees; surveyed individuals were not drawn from metaphysics classes such as the philosophy of mind but were mostly drawn from introductory logic or introductory ethics classes; students were asked if they were familiar with the thought experiment and removed from the sample if so. About half were my students, but those who were my students had not taken the philosophy of mind or any other metaphysics or philosophy of psychology class with me. I had never discussed or mentioned consciousness with them.

Only a few of the control subjects said that Anne would not learn something new when she saw red for the first time. The control condition of this survey had 100 subjects who agreed that Anne learned something new. These 100 control subjects were asked this follow-up question (the order of the answers varied randomly among their surveys—except that "none of the above" always came last—to ensure that there were no choice-order effects):

> Why do you think that Anne learned something new when she sees red for the first time, even though she had a Ph.D. in neural science and knew all the science about color vision? Please choose only one of the following options which best explains why.
>
> a.   A red experience is not a thing that interacts with the physical world, and sciences only explain interactions between physical things.

    b.   A red experience is something we use to get around in the world, like being able to walk or ride a bike, and scientific knowledge gives us facts not skills.

    c.   A red experience is too complex for someone to learn what it is like from just reading neural science textbooks, lectures, and the other kinds of things scientists typically learn from.

    d.   None of the above (there is another reason not listed above).

Interestingly, of these options, Jackson's own was the least popular; only 8% of the control subjects chose that a red experience is not something that interacts with the physical world. The next most popular was "none of the above," with 12% of the vote. The view that consciousness is a skill, and not a fact, earned 18% of the vote. And, 62% of the subjects answered that a red experience is just too complex for someone to learn what red is like from reading a textbook.

I am not citing this as evidence that color experience is complex. I do not believe that semantics, or lay conceptions, are guides to metaphysical truths. Rather, I mean only to indicate that this result shows that it is not "obvious" or "intuitive" or any other kind of "common sense" that color experiences are simples. Nor is it (part of) the meaning of "red experience" that it is a simple. The only evidence I am aware of—the evidence I gathered and cite here— shows conclusively that the view that a color experience is complex is com- pelling to far more lay people than is the alternative that Jackson first offered. Thus, the view that a color experience is some kind of phenomenal simple is a theoretical claim, or at most a philosophical prejudice, not a lay conception and not an observation and not an expression of the meaning of "red."

The fact that most people don't hold to the belief that a red experience is simple shows us that the philosopher inclined to claim a red experience is a simple is in fact defending a theory—namely, anti-physicalism with respect to consciousness—and not engaging in phenomenology nor in the conceptual analysis of the concept of "red (experience)."

2.7 The Dread Question of Semantics

It is my contention that semantics cannot provide substantive insight into meta- physical issues. For example, I do not believe that claims about what we mean by our concepts reliably shed light on the properties of the referent, nor that we can quickly rule out a kind of explanation by claiming that our seman- tics has somehow not been satisfied by that explanation. Furthermore, claims about what other people mean by our concepts, or claims about what our concepts normally mean, are highly dubious (as should be obvious from the prior section). Even claims to have analyzed from the armchair what a concept means for one's self are dubious—none of us is likely able to articulate what we mean by any concept we freely use. Furthermore, most of our referential concepts need only guide everyday actions, and thus really are indeterminate when a philosopher demands that they apply in novel ways to unusual cases or phenomena.

In my arguments, I have sidestepped the issues about reduction and semantics that have characterized much contemporary debate about consciousness. Because an appropriate description of a phenomenon must be present in any explanation of the phenomenon, if I have shown that we currently lack the proper description then I need not address other questions about semantics.[4]

But it is necessary to head off a potential objection to the two inadequacy claims. The objection would go like this: a red experience cannot be more complex than my description, my theory, or my reasoning capacities, since (1) what I mean by "red experience" is not something very complex and (2) my meaning must be adequate because it succeeds in referring.

The first claim can be quickly refuted. If someone wants to claim that what she means by "Jupiter" is a god glowing in the sky, it won't be of much use to argue with her. She is claiming that by definition she is working with an incommensurable conception, and that's her prerogative. We cannot make her pledge allegiance to a different definition. Similarly, if someone says what they mean by "red experience" includes that it is a simple phenomenon, I can only respond that that's not what I mean by "red experience," and furthermore I don't believe it is what anyone else (without a theory to defend) would mean by "red experience." And, in any case, we are not interested in what the anti-physicalists mean by "red experience." We are interested in red experience.

The second claim, however, is more problematic. Some philosophers adopt a rationalist or *a priori* approach to (some) meanings and hold that in some senses they cannot be wrong about (some aspect of) the meanings of their terms. The idea would be that, since they can use their concept of red experience reliably, the concept must be accurate in some relevant ways. This too I find implausible.

We might reject such a claim because we adopt an *a posteriori* or empiricist approach to our semantics. On such a view, it is experience and the world, and not our own armchair reasoning, that ultimately must determine the referents of our referential concepts. Thus, our hypothetical person who meant "bright god in the sky" by "Jupiter" would be able to use this concept to track Jupiter and refer to it and say things about it in many kinds of situations. Though her expressed conception is mostly bunk, we would find we could talk to her and disagree with her, because we could point at Jupiter, we could get her to agree that she also meant *that thing,* we could get her to state the kinds of properties Jupiter must have if she is right, and then we could show her the view through a telescope and reveal that Jupiter lacks those properties, and so on. We could get her to eventually say, "Jupiter is not a god," and this would not be a contradictory sentence, even for her.

But some scholars resist such appeals. Fortunately, we do not need to settle the question of empirical versus *a priori* semantics. We need only a weaker claim: the complexity of a referential concept need not correlate with the complexity of the referent.

Consider: does someone's successful use of a simple referential concept provide any evidence that the referent is simple? *Red experience* is a simple referential concept, let us grant. Does this lend evidence to the idea that red experience is simple? The answer is no. We can see this by way of a *reductio* argument. Suppose then that a referential concept being simple demonstrates that its referent is simple. Then, it would follow that we could never refer to complex things with a simple referential concept (such as a proper name). For, if we could, then we would contradict the claim that a simple referential concept ensures a simple referent. But surely, we do refer to complex things with simple referential concepts. We can, for example, have a referential concept like *the smallest ninety-billion-numeral incompressible number*. On pain of contradiction, it cannot be that the smallest ninety-billion-numeral incompressible number is simple, just because the referential concept used is simple. (And we would learn nothing about the number from someone who claims it's simple because they feel that their concept of it reveals it is so.) Thus, it cannot be that the complexity of our referential concepts sheds any light on the complexity of the referent.

This should be obvious, after a moment's reflection. If we are to move around in a world full of complex things and are not going to be constrained in our reference to these complex things, then of course we should adopt the semantic strategy of sometimes (often) using simple referential concepts to refer to these complex things. This can be successful if there is some way to recognize the referent sufficient for whatever need is at hand. Reference will be constrained by our needs to coordinate certain kinds of actions and accomplish certain kinds of ends. If I sometimes only need to "point" at an object, rather than fully describe it, to accomplish my ends, then for the sake of saving time and energy, I should do so. I want to be able to say, "A hurricane is coming," without having to fully describe the hurricane. This is sufficient to motivate action like moving away from the coast, and that might be the only thing we need our concept to do, and so there may be no need for the concept to be more representative of the complexity of its referent. Reflections on examples like this make clear that any language actually *requires* that our referential concepts be such that they cannot be any kind of *a priori* guide to the complexity of the referent.

All that any semantics needs from its referential concepts is that they succeed in reliably referring to the right kind of thing in the kinds of situations where this has proved useful in the past. Even a strict descriptivist would grant that the descriptions that constitute the referential concept need only be sufficient to reliably be true of all and only that kind of thing *in the relevant (normal) contexts*. This is a very different thing from providing an adequate theoretical description.

Thus, no *a priori* knowledge about the nature of our referential concepts can determine the complexity of the referent of those concepts.

2.8 The Ineffability of Consciousness

We now have in place the tools to make the argument that explains what makes paradigmatically mysterious phenomenal experiences mysterious. DI tells us that our descriptions and theories of our experiences are not as complex as the essential properties of these experiences; CI tells us that our theoretical reasoning capabilities have a capacity that is less than the information in these experiences.

From DI, we get the consequence that our descriptions of our phenomenal experiences will contain less information than is in those experiences or is in an adequate theoretical description of those experiences, and consequently, from the modal judgment constraint principle, we can conclude that our judgments about what is possible with respect to those experiences will not be reliable. For example, our descriptions of red experience will significantly underdetermine red experience, but then we cannot reliably determine what is possible with respect to red experience.

DI also reminds us that both our descriptions and our theories of phenomenal experience are currently less complex than those experiences. The incompressibility cost principle tells us then that we will not be able to generate an adequate explanation from any such theory without adding to it a great deal more information, be that additional theory or additional descriptions.

From CI, we get the consequence that our individual reasoning about our phenomenal experiences will contain less information than is in those experiences or is in an adequate theoretical description of those experiences, and consequently from the modal judgment constraint principle, we can conclude that our individual reasoning about what is possible with respect to those experiences will not be reliable. Other tools—most notably, computer models—may allow us to generate more complex descriptions of red experience, but the philosopher in the armchair is not going to manage it.

CI also reminds us that both our theoretical reasoning and our conceptual descriptions of phenomenal experience are currently less complex than those experiences. The incompressibility cost principle tells us then that we will not be able to generate an adequate explanation from any such individual reasoning alone.

Each of these is sufficient to explain the ineffability of consciousness.

These findings are consistent with physicalism; that is, they are consistent with the expectation that consciousness will prove to be constituted of physical events. Considerations of productivity and explanatory power suggest then that a physicalist theory of phenomenal experience is still our best bet, and we should first and foremost pursue such a theory in our efforts to explain consciousness. If we pursue a physicalist theory, we know how to continue with productive research programs that have clear goals and outcomes.

If we deny that paradigmatically mysterious phenomenal experiences are complex, however, we need some other reason to explain why they are mysterious. The suggestion of the anti-physicalists is that phenomenal experiences are a different ontological kind. This claim has an enormous cost: no anti-physicalist has offered a productive research program for the study of phenomenal experience. No anti-physicalist has made testable predictions. Instead, they have only been able to hold out the hope that new methods might be invented in the future to study these phenomena.

On the other hand, DI and CI make testable predictions. We predict that as our scientific understanding of the physical correlates of phenomenal experiences grows, then we will discover that these are complex. DI predicts that they will be more complex always than our current theories. CI predicts that they will prove more complex than the capacity of our short-term memory or our theoretical reasoning capacities.

This points to productive research programs, also. It tells us that we should continue to study the physical correlates of phenomenal experience and aim to develop models that can capture and describe enormously complex properties. Again, all the anti-physicalists have to offer is a hope that meditation or maybe some new form of phenomenology might evolve into a satisfactory tool for the study of consciousness. That is a very unproductive starting place.

Finally, note that the anti-physicalist is burdened with a very significant problem. If they grant that phenomenal experiences are complex, then their claims that these phenomena are not physical do not work (since the complexity of the phenomenon is now sufficient to explain their mysteriousness). On the other hand, if they deny that phenomenal experiences are complex, they have an equally useless fifth theoretic wheel. There is no reason, on the anti-physicalists view, that the physical correlates of a paradigmatically mysterious phenomenal experience should be complex. So why are they complex? If the phenomenal experience of fear is not constituted by the vastly complex events occurring in the body when afraid, then why can't we also feel fear when a single neuron is firing in the brain? Why can't the person with achromatopsia dream in color, using whatever part of her brain is generating the narrative of the dream? And so on. If paradigmatically mysterious phenomenal experiences are simple, then the complexity of the physical correlates of such phenomenal experiences is absurd. After all, there are many physical phenomena for which some forms of complexity don't matter. For example, we can treat two masses that attract each other as points masses, sitting at their centers of gravity. The complexity of the shape of the mass is irrelevant for calculating their mutual gravitational attraction. But the anti-physicalist is in the absurd position that the complexity of the causal correlates of phenomenal experience *should* be irrelevant; they should have no correlation to the kind of experience. So why are they reliably complex?

Two questions now loom before us. First, what does it mean to be a physicalist? Philosophers have not formed a consensus on this. I address this in Chapter 3. And second, what about the influential arguments against physicalism with respect to phenomenal experience? Don't those independently show that physicalism is not our best explanation of paradigmatically mysterious phenomenal experiences? I refute these anti-physicalist arguments in Chapter 4.

Notes

1. Other kinds of associations may matter to the phenomenal character of the experience. For example, there is some evidence that color can affect cognitive activity, such as creativity. In a widely cited experiment, Mehta and Zhu (2009) demonstrated that subjects were more critical when exposed to red and more open and creative in problem solving when exposed instead to blue. Subjects need not be

aware of these associations in a way that makes them ready for report. But they are there, and they influence perception and other cognitive capabilities, and—this is the important point—it is plausible that they constitute what a particular red experience or blue experience is like, by way of these kinds of associations and effects.

2. This theoretical poverty is even more true for the anti-physicalists, who offer no theory but rather only critiques. Indeed, the indescribability of conscious experience is typically a central assumption of the anti-physicalist position, so that a result similar to DI follows *a priori* for the anti-physicalist, since their claim is that our theories fail to properly describe our phenomenal experiences and this is because new ontological kinds (of which we currently lack a proper description) are required.

3. There are some subtleties here that prevent us from assuming that a lot of information in an experience entails that there is a lot of information required to explain the cause of the experience. For example, one could imagine a simpler system that—perhaps using the environment as a seed for information—creates some random experiences, which then have higher information than the normal cause. On the other hand, it is obvious that one could have a complex system produce a simpler output. I'm not saying that either is true of phenomenal experience, but rather I'm just pointing out that we cannot just assume that there is, in all situations, a clean linear correlation between these two quantities of information.

4. The kind of debate that I aim to avoid is, for example, the one about whether scientific explanations require "a priori and transparent" reductions. A primary source here is Chalmers and Jackson (2001). I am satisfied with the kind of refutation made of this position we see in Block and Stalnaker (1999) or Polger (2008). But, as I said, I believe mixing semantics and intuition and metaphysics creates a hopeless muddle, and I have sidestepped these issues in my argument.

3 Strong Physicalism

3.1 The Problem of Physicalism

I have claimed that physicalism about phenomenal experiences remains our best bet on what a successful explanation of consciousness will be like. But what do I mean here by "physicalism"? Many philosophers are simply willing to take this as a primitive, but I am not. I think too much depends on how we flesh out the details, and so I owe those details to the reader. In this chapter, I propose a theory of physicalism. This theory escapes the problems that I believe render other formulations of physicalism so vague that they are nearly useless. But the real benefit is that the theory is very strong—by which I mean, it is very demanding, and as a result, it is falsifiable. It is the most falsifiable form of physicalism that I am aware of in the literature on physicalism.

Perhaps the most common characterization of physicalism is the view that everything is physical. We might call this *global physicalism*. Then, we can think of physicalism about a kind of phenomenon P as the more modest claim that the kind of phenomenon P is a physical kind. We would like a robust notion of the physical, and of physicalism, sufficient to evaluate such claims. There are two separate problems here. The first is to find a satisfactory concept of the physical sufficient for making sense of a claim like phenomena of kind P are physical. The second is to define the relationship to the physical sufficiently to understand what it means to be a physicalist about phenomena of kind P. This includes clarifying what kinds of reductions or relations to the physical are to be sought (e.g., entailment, supervenience, analysis, constitution, realization), the kinds of modal claims involved, and so on. Arguably, the first of these two problems is the more basic, since reduction to other kinds of things is also possible; this will be my focus here.

3.2 What Is the Physical?

Many of us share the conviction that our best source of understanding of what the physical is—and therefore of what kinds of things should count as physical, and also of what kinds of explanations and reductions are physicalist—should come from our best sciences. We can call this (following Poland 1994) the

DOI: 10.4324/9781003320685-3

a posteriori strategy. Such an approach to understanding physicalism seems properly grounded in the empirical. Furthermore, it makes clear the link between physicalism and partly epistemic conceptions of naturalism, by framing physicalism as a commitment to certain kinds of methods being sufficient to explain the relevant phenomena. I am going to adopt and defend an *a posteriori* strategy in this chapter. However, it would be useful to first review, however briefly, the alternatives, and our reasons for abandoning them.

3.2.1 Alternatives to the A Posteriori Strategies

The simplest approach to identifying the physical would be an *a priori* one: if we were able to describe the necessary and sufficient properties of the physical before we are familiar with all kinds of physical facts (that is, if we were able to describe these conditions now), then we could identify the physical and as a consequence narrow our definitions of physicalism. But such *a priori* approaches to define the physical have failed. The most familiar such attempt is Descartes's claim that things extended in space are material. The problem with this specification is that it seems plausible that physical sciences could treat of unextended entities, and we would still want to call these entities physical. For example, on some accounts, a black hole is a point mass. It has no extension in space. But it would seem perverse to argue that matter, shrunken to a point, becomes immaterial—especially when, first, it retains many other features of matter, such as gravity, and, second, it is already recognized as a physical phenomenon by contemporary astrophysics. Conversely, it seems that we might discover something which was extended in space but which we did not consider physical. Ghosts are a traditional kind of fictitious but relevant example.

A priori specifications of the physical are making something of a comeback in recent years. Some philosophers have argued—often for the purposes of denying physicalism—that the physical has certain *a priori* features. For example, David Chalmers argues that sciences only explain "structure and dynamics" (2007). The problem here, however, is that these criteria are simply too vague. It is unclear what a structural property is, it is unclear what a dynamic property is, and—most importantly—it seems that the very kinds of posited non-physical entities that are raised in these discussions themselves have structural and dynamic properties. For example, Chalmers argues that science only explains dynamic and structural properties and that consciousness is not explicable by physical science, but obviously many phenomenal experiences have structural and dynamical properties. A visual experience of a red square is structural (it has shape, and red exists in relation to other color experiences through relations like the spectrum, etc.) and may be dynamic (the experience could start dim and grow more bright, etc.). Ultimately, these criteria seem neither necessary, sufficient, nor even remarkably typical, of the kinds of things we consider obviously physical. (I discuss this at greater length in Section 4.5.)

If we cannot determine the nature of the physical before looking at the physical, it seems we have five strategies left.

The first is to generalize from an ostensive definition. This is the strategy taken by Frank Jackson when he writes that,

> physicalists can give an ostensive definition of what they mean by physical properties and relations by pointing to some exemplars of non-sentient objects—table, chairs, mountains, and the like—and then say that by physical properties and relations, they mean the kinds of properties and relations needed to give a complete account of things like them. Their clearly non-trivial claim is then that the kinds of properties and relations needed to account for the exemplars of the non-sentient are enough to account for everything, or at least everything contingent.
>
> (1998: 7)

There are two strategies implicit here: the ostensive definition and the negative strategy (the physical is the non-sentient). I will address the ostensive definition strategy first. Let us pick one of these objects: that chair. It has been often recognized that such a definition can turn out to be too broad. The reference could prove too broad because something could go into determining the reference that we ultimately agreed was not physical. The classic argument here is that suppose we discover panpsychism is true, and the chair is sentient or otherwise has phenomenal experiences. Then if physicalists want to say panpsychism is inconsistent with physicalism, the ostensive definition would steer them wrong (Montero 1999). Less fanciful possibilities are also problematic. Suppose that we discover mental events are not physical events. It is also plausible that "chair" is a functional kind, definable only in reference to artifactual uses of agents with mental events. Then, we would not be able to explain all the features of the chair—in particular, we would not be able to explain why it was a chair—without reference to events (like intentions) that we might want to exclude.

But the more important problem with the ostensive definition is that it may prove too narrow. We now have an active search to identify dark matter. Suppose that there is dark matter in the spaces between galaxies and that it generates a new force, dark energy. It could well be that neither dark matter nor dark energy is required to explain the nature of the chair. Perhaps dark matter and dark energy only exist in deep space, in cold places, and so on. But then if we used the reference to fix our definition of the physical, dark matter and dark energy would not be physical. That seems an undesired outcome. New forms of matter and energy, which are measurable and have influence on other kinds of matter and energy, and which are actively being sought by physicists and already posited by physicists, would seem exemplary of the physical.

The problem with ostensive definitions is fundamental: we cannot know beforehand whether a sample is sufficiently representative of the physical. And, if we stipulate that the sample defines the physical, then we may end up with artificial boundaries to the physical.

Another common strategy, implicit as a secondary strategy in Jackson's claims mentioned earlier, is the *via negativa* strategy: to define the physical in negative terms, or otherwise in contrast to something else. An intuitive way to do this is to define the physical as what is not mental (Schiffer 1990; Spurrett and Papineau 1999; Montero and Papineau 2005; Howell 2009; Gocke 2009; Brown and Ladyman 2009), or to at least stipulate that a necessary feature of the physical is that it is not mental (Wilson 2005). However, this strategy is ultimately unhelpful because it requires us to know what the mental is. Without a test for the mental, we cannot determine whether something is physical. Furthermore, it is unclear how this strategy is to work if we discover that mental events are explicable by something like contemporary physical sciences. Does that then mean that there are no mental events? Or does it mean that we have instead just defined the whole world as mental and therefore non-physical? That is, a simplistic *via negativa* strategy seems to require eliminativism or idealism. The way out is to have a sophisticated *via negativa* strategy that draws a distinction between basic and non-basic properties (or a similar distinction) and defines physicalism as a view that mental events are non-basic (e.g., Levine 2001: 25ff). But now we are back on a similar treadmill: we need to know what the basic properties are. This is at least as hard as defining the physical.

The fourth option is to define the physical using a notion of causal closure: the physical is what is related to the physical by way of causation. We take causation as a relation generating an equivalence class, and this class is the physical. Although some consider this strategy an elegant solution, it is hard to take it seriously. The quintessential examples of dualist (that is, not physicalist) theories that we have—e.g., Descartes and all his followers—argued for causal interaction between the physical and the non-physical. It is unhelpful to argue that Cartesian souls are physical because they causally interact with the physical. The move eliminates most dualist theories by re-definition.

The fifth and final alternative considered here is to think of physicalism as a stance. This is the view that physicalism is merely a commitment to the methods of natural science. I have some sympathy for the view of physicalism as a stance. The motivation, as I understand it, is that there is no coherent form of physicalism that is not question begging in pernicious and self-refuting ways. For those who defend the stance, it seems that the articulation of physicalism with some kind of fundamental principles is doomed to rest on non-physicalist principles; or its reliance on science makes it doomed to be revised into something indistinguishable. This leads to a dilemma. On the one hand, the advantage of treating physicalism as a stance is that it escapes what Van Fraassen (2002) called the "false consciousness" that can result from treating physicalism as a factual but universal claim (e.g., all is physical). On the other hand, however, if we adopt physicalism as a stance, we cannot address the anti-physicalist arguments. We treat them as uncouth, rather than as substantive and false. We say, we're not going to entertain the kind of claims you make, we refuse to talk with you in that way.

It would be preferable if we had an alternative to the view of physicalism as a stance that allowed our disagreements to be substantive and our claims to be falsifiable. Otherwise, "stance" views quickly descend into claims about special perspectives. Those who disagree with your stance are derided as failing to understand its normative nature, as unfairly trivializing the stance, as being simplistic, and so on. This is unproductive.[1] Put more gently, it would be an improvement to be able to allow, and answer, specific criticisms. It would be an improvement if one's view was actually falsifiable; or, at least, if one's view seems to contradict another view, it would be an improvement to be able to say whether it did so contradict the view, and if it did, it would be an improvement to have some hope of determining which of the contradicting views was more justified.

In this chapter, my claim is that we can escape this dilemma. We do this by recognizing the incoherence of the universalist ambitions of claims that "all is physical." In analogy with logic and mathematics, I call the resulting position "constructive physicalism." Constructive physicalism has something of the stance to it, since it amounts to a series of bets—or, if one prefers, many particular stances, taken one after another about one particular phenomenon after another. But my approach generates a form of physicalism robust enough for falsification, and it allows us to address the anti-physicalists on their own terms.

These remarks are brief, but they do establish that there are good reasons to believe that the *a posteriori* strategy to identify the physical is an important one, since the alternatives are, if not refuted, then very contentious. If we have no satisfactory *a priori* account of the physical, if we cannot identify it reliably via ostensive definition, and if we cannot define it negatively in relation to other categories, then it does seem that our best remaining strategy is to identify the physical as the stuff that is studied and described by the sciences. We might also prefer this strategy simply because it is the strategy most suitable for a scientific approach to the physical; that is, a scientific world view suggests that we should expect it to be an empirical question of what kinds of (physical) things there are.

3.2.2 The Dilemma for the A Posteriori Strategy

In the *a posteriori* approach, we turn to science to tell us what the physical is. The challenge with the *a posteriori* approach, however, is that there is widespread agreement that future scientific progress will likely change the scientific ontology. This seems to entail that if we aim to *fix* the nature of the physical now, any reference to actual sciences as arbiters of the physical will require some kind of projection to a limit or unrevisable form of science. And any such projection confronts two dilemmas—Hempel's dilemma and Stoljar's dilemma—which present insurmountable problems.

Stoljar identifies theory-based physical properties in the following way:

> F is a physical property if and only if F is expressed by a predicate of a physical theory.

> (2010: 75)

This in turn allows us to determine the truth conditions for a relevant kind of global physicalism:

> Physicalism is true if and only if every instantiated property is necessitated by some instantiated theory-based physical property.

(2010: 71)

This captures nicely the relevant goal: we will rely upon scientific theories to discover what the physical is. Stoljar, however, identifies a significant problem. A complete interpretation of this claim requires that we settle whether the notion of scientific theory is to be identified by actual or by possible theories. That is, we must decide between:

> *F* is a physical property if and only if *F* is expressed by a predicate of a physical theory that is true at the actual world.

Or:

> *F* is a physical property if and only if *F* is expressed by a predicate of a physical theory that is true at some possible world or other.

(2010: 75)

We now have a dilemma: either option appears inconsistent with what we want out of our notion of physicalism. For, if we mean true in the actual world, then there are possible worlds that we would like to call wholly physical, but they will not count as such. Stoljar gives the example of a world with laws like our own but with some different fundamental properties; a "twin-physics" world akin to Putnam's Twin Earth thought experiment, but with twin-mass, twin-charge, and so on. A world that had different fundamental particles, for example, but in which beings managed to explain everything in terms of these fundamental kinds using recognizable scientific methods, would seem to be a world in which we seem to want to say physicalism is true. The actualist reading is too restrictive.

On the other hand, take a world like our own except that something like (what we would here call) immaterial minds causally interact with material brains. It seems the "science" of this world might include new fundamental entities, which are the kind of thing that many want to rule out of the notion of the physical. The possibilist reading would be too permissive.[2]

If, like me, you experience nausea during travel to other possible worlds, there is a way to stay home and rephrase Stoljar's point. What we want from physicalism, Stoljar is revealing, are two quite different things. On the one hand, we know we want it to capture the kind of stuff that is revealed by our sciences. And not just our sciences right now, but rather all the kinds of truths about our world that our sciences will capture. That's the actualist case: we want physicalism to capture what's true here. On the other hand, we want physicalism to be a general metaphysical thesis. Part of our motivation for this is that we know we do not yet know many physical facts, but we hope to be able to generalize in a way that will cover those undiscovered facts. We want to say, regardless of how those facts turn out, they will share certain features. But that is to say that there are different possible scientific theories that we could call physicalist. That's the broad possibilist reading of "physical."

These desires pull in different directions. Satisfying one of those pulls will contradict some of the basic intuitions we aim to satisfy in defining physicalism. The solution would seem to be to find criteria to narrow down the possible cases until we got just those possible cases we wanted to have. Then we could use not the actualist but a narrower possibilist reading. But to find another notion of the modality of physicalism would require some additional criteria for physicalism, which we lack and which is why we set out on this exercise in the first place. That is, the narrower reading of the possible would be precisely what we mean when we say, *physical possibility* (or, what some call nomological possibility). But of course we need to know what is physical in order to be able to specify the physically possible. If we seek a fixed definition of the physical, suitable for projections into all future scientific discoveries, then the solution to Stoljar's dilemma requires that we already know what we aim to discover.

The second problem for the *a posteriori* strategy is Hempel's Dilemma. This dilemma is widely familiar, but a brief review might be useful. What we will mean here by "Hempel's Dilemma" (and what is usually meant by this) is a metaphysical version of a linguistic or logical criticism that Hempel made of some suggestions by Goodman:

> the physicalist claim that the language of physics can serve as a unitary language of science is inherently obscure: the language of what physics is meant? Surely not that of, say, eighteenth-century physics; for it contains terms like "caloric fluid," whose use is governed by theoretical assumptions now thought false. Nor can the language of contemporary physics claim the role of unitary language, since it will no doubt undergo further changes too. The thesis of physicalism would seem to require a language in which a *true* theory of all physical phenomena can be formulated. But it is quite unclear what is to be understood here by a physical phenomenon, especially in the context of a doctrine that has taken a decidedly linguistic turn.
>
> (1980: 194–195)

Hempel recognizes that if we say, "the physical is what is revealed by our scientific theories," then we face a dilemma in determining which theory. By the pessimistic induction and also by the simple expectation that scientific progress will occur, we know that our current physical theory is very likely to be revised. But then, that could render a current global physicalist claim false in the future. The alternative that Hempel suggests here is a kind of ideal theory: the results of physical sciences when they are at some satisfactory state of advancement, at which our scientific theories are true or unrevisable. Then, from this unrevisable body of science, we would glean an unrevisable conception of the physical. The problem with this, however, is that it is without sufficient content. We simply do not know what an unrevisable physics will posit as the fundamental kinds of entities, so we do not know what the physical is for the unrevisable theory.

Some scholars have described this dilemma in a slightly different way. One horn is that we use current physics as our guide to the physical, but as noted that physics is likely to be substantially revised. The alternative is to refer to an unrevisable and *complete* physical science, which must by definition have expanded to include all kinds of entities in its ontology. Therefore, looking to the future unrevisable physical science is objectionable not just because it is unknown but also because, at least on some understandings, it will by definition include all the kinds, thus rendering physicalism trivially true (Crane and Mellor 1990; Ney 2008).

Stoljar argues that these kinds of arguments, reconstructed from Hempel's remarks, are unsound (2010: 96ff). The notion of "theory" used in both current and ideal theories, he holds, is actual theory, and therefore is impaled on the first horn of Stoljar's dilemma. This appears correct, but it also threatens to obscure the important point of Hempel's dilemma, which is that relying upon a better theory to tell us now what is physical is like buying clothes now for a future friend: you can't tell what fits.

We can save Hempel's insight from the actualist horn of Stoljar's dilemma if we read Hempel's dilemma as showing that even the too-strong condition for physicalism expressed in the actualist case fails to clearly identify a well-defined subset of the physical. That is, even if we set aside concerns about other possible scientific theories or other physical histories, and grant that the actualist criterion is too strong because it will identify properties that not all scientific theories need to have, it still is the case that the actualist reading identifies one notion of the physical that should satisfy physicalism. In other words, we might not want to limit our notion of physicalism to our particular scientific theories, but our best scientific theory will be physicalist. Our actual theory is then sufficient but not necessary to identify (at least some subset of) the physical. Hempel's dilemma shows that even this narrower sense of "physicalism" and consequently of the "physical" either fails to be true or fails to be contentful; the dilemma shows that even the strong actualist sense of "physical" either is too constrained or is vacuous.

3.2.3 Solving the Problem of Projection

The *a posteriori* strategy seemed the best strategy to identify the physical, but it stumbles over two profound dilemmas. The problem for three of the four horns of the dilemma was a problem of projection. We project in two ways. First, we want to turn to empirical results to guide our understanding of the physical, but we want also to project beyond current empirical results in a way that goes beyond the generalizations of the theories in question and speculates about an unrevisable or true theory. Second, we want to project beyond any particular phenomenon described in physical theory, to a global characterization—all phenomena, all facts, all of the world.

At first glance, it would seem that we cannot do without these projections. Most of our claims in metaphysics that a physicalist explanation is possible are made when we do not have the explanation. We are speculating and so projecting, offering arguments that an explanation will ultimately be found. And, physicalists seem committed to developing general claims about all phenomena, and not just particular phenomena.

However, we need neither the projection to ultimate theories nor the projection to all phenomena. We can project not to a science that has achieved an unrevisable maturity and describes everything but rather to current science and its next steps *with respect to a particular kind of phenomenon*. On this view, we claim that a particular property, object, or kind is physical if it is a fundamental posit of, or otherwise explained by, contemporary science or a minimal extension thereof.

We can illuminate this proposal by looking at scientific progress as a kind of strategic game (here I follow insights of Solomonoff 1964, and reconstructions of Solomonoff of the kind found in, say, Li and Vitanyi 2008: 348ff). The scientist plays the game with nature. She begins with a theory and set of observations, some of which the theory explains. The theorist can keep the existing theory or she can propose a revision of the theory that does at least as good a job as the existing theory of explaining (retrodicting) past observations. In either case, she then makes some novel predictions. Nature's move is to offer observations, in the context of experiments, which either confirm or contradict the predictions. In response, the scientist compares her extended theory with the old theory and keeps only whichever does best. Then she starts again. The game continues until revisions are not possible. We add the idealization (nothing will turn on this in my primary argument) that this theory is the conjunction of all scientific theories, and our observations are ranging across diverse phenomena.

On this view, actualist physicalism is the claim that physicalism will be fully described by the theory proposed by the theorist when, in our world, the game is done. The physical will be whatever is referred to or otherwise explained in that theory alone. Possibilist physicalism is the view that physicalism is described by whatever is shared by all possible terminal games.[3] The second horn of Hempel's dilemma is that we simply don't know what the final (or much later) moves of the game will look like; if Stoljar is right, Hempel is referring to the final (or much later) moves of the game as played in our world.

But we do not need to project to the end of the game. We should think instead of physicalism about a kind of phenomenon *P* as a bet. The bet is that this phenomenon *P* will be explained by something very like contemporary science. When we argue for physicalism, without actually discovering the relevant explanation, we are arguing that an explanation using something like contemporary science is possible. More formally, we should redefine a basic particular physicalist claim thus:

> *P is physical* if *P* is, or will be, explained by successful contemporary scientific theories *T*, or a minimal extension of those scientific theories.

We who do not have the explanation of *P* in hand, but think we see how it might go, are therefore betting on this proposition that *P* is physical.[4]

Three parts of this definition obviously require clarification. First, we should be willing to be ecumenical about the kinds of sciences that are stipulated in the definition. I used the phrase "successful" instead of "physical." This will help avoid circularity that would result from defining the relevant sciences as physical sciences. A reasonable criterion for success would be that the science is able to reliably make testable, surprising (not predicted by alternative, otherwise equally productive, and simpler theories), and confirmed predictions. Such a criterion would allow most of physics, chemistry, and biology; much of psychology; and very little of economics. But I also believe that we can follow Ladyman et al. (2007) and observe that even if this definition is not fully satisfactory, we can allow that the *practice* of science can offer us a reliable indicator of successful science.

Second, the notion of "minimal extension" can be made sufficiently rigorous. I propose two accounts—one rigorous and the other of which allows for a little bit of liberality. The rigorous account is that a minimal extension of a theory *T* is any extension that adheres to the methods of science and that *adds only mathematical theory* to *T*. That is, the extension would not posit new entities. Such extensions are not uncommon in the sciences, and many are celebrated as classic examples of reduction. A bit of additional mathematics is used to show how some phenomena can be explained using the existing ontology. This is the gold standard of a minimal extension; indeed, most philosophers would not even consider such a thing an extension. I will also call a minimal extension one that adds an axiom (law) that describes complex interaction between already recognized entities. Laws are often seen as revolutionary, but a law that posits no new entities should typically not be seen as extending our ontology.

Some scholars may want to allow some weakening of this notion of minimal extension—metaphysicians might want to defend stronger or weaker forms of physicalism, based on their other commitments. For example, we might want to take the practice of science as a good indicator of what is, and is not, a minimal extension, even when scientists posit new entities. Results that are recognized as revolutionary, and require very careful and rigorous re-testing before being accepted, are just those results that are considered non-minimal. Results that posit new entities but are not considered revolutionary would be recognized as minimal extensions. I won't need such a weaker characterization in the arguments that follow, however, so nothing in this book turns upon this openness to liberality in defining "minimal." (In the rest of this book, I will assume the definition of "physical" given earlier, and I will mean cases where we add at most more mathematical descriptions or laws to our theory.) I will add, finally, that a necessary condition for a minimal extension should probably also be that it does not contradict the prior form of the theory (this is usually assumed in the definition of "extension" in logic).

Finally, it is useful here to use the vague general notion of "explain." The reason is that the notion of physicalism I am developing should be available to those who are committed to distinct views on the reduction or explanation relation, such as supervenience, realization, and so on. (As already noted earlier, my critical arguments in this book can allow us to remain liberal about the notion of explanation, as long as we recognize that any explanation must require adequate description.) My own view is to adopt the strongest standard of explanation: it requires the ability to make robust predictions about the phenomenon, and the ability to make such predictions can be taken as indicative of (although not synonymous with) successful explanation.

I'm well aware that the devils are in the details. However, in this case, my main claims in this chapter and in this book will stand regardless of how we flesh out these details regarding what will count as T and how explanation should be described. That is, there are many accounts of these details that we might want to try out and compare—and, in general, if we are explicit about those assumptions, then the rest of us can take or leave the relevant bets as we like. None of these variations would reduce the position to the kind of global and limit physicalism that I am opposing, and all of these would be consistent with the constructive version of physicalism I develop later. And so, it is not essential to my argument here to settle these issues in some definitive way. Rather, our bets just need to be transparent.

One might object that there could be a lack of consensus on T. It might be an embarrassment if we have competing successful theories that for some reason we do not merge, but if they are both successful scientific theories, then we have competing physicalist outcomes. If there are two successful competing scientific theories T_1 or T_2, and T_1 succeeds in explaining P while T_2 fails, we will have vindicated physicalism with respect to P (my remarks in the following, on the first horn of Hempel's dilemma, apply here with respect to T_1 versus T_2). But what, one might add, if there were another group of contemporary scientists who begin with a theory T but add to it a posit of a thing most of us would consider quite like a Cartesian soul? Call this T_3. The researchers using T_3 make a bet that both relies on these Cartesian souls and is inconsistent with the bet made by the researchers using T. Suppose that the T_3 researchers are proved right. The objection goes, we now added souls to our physicalist ontology, and this is unacceptable.

But such a worry would miss that, if the souls that are posited in T_3 are like Descartes's souls, then this would mean that T_3 is not a minimal extension of existing theory but rather is a revolutionary extension. It posits new kinds and presumably contradicts some other existing successful scientific theories or principles (e.g., conservation of energy). Also, P is now explained by a theory that by definition includes kinds that cannot be studied by a science (that is, presumably our access to these souls is via subjective introspections not amenable to third-person confirmation), and so T_3 is no longer (only) a scientific theory. Of course, that's the very kind of case in which we want to say that physicalism about P has failed. Thus, the existence of competing scientific theories would not undermine this notion of the physical.

We can use this formulation of a particular physicalist claim, with its focus on a kind of phenomenon, to then formulate a general theory of physicalism. I will call the general form "constructive physicalism":

> Constructive physicalism: for phenomena kinds $P_1 \ldots P_n$ of which we are developing theories in successful sciences, it is the case that
>
> $\{P_1$ is physical or P_1 will be eliminated;
> P_2 is physical or P_2 will be eliminated;
> . . .
> P_n is physical or P_n will be eliminated$\}$.

The criterion that we are developing theories about $P_1 \ldots P_n$ ensures that we do not allow into our scope of generalizations references to all kinds of things. Here, following the spirit of the constructivists in mathematics, we are not going to allow ourselves to refer to the phenomenon-I-know-not-what. Rather, we must construct the "all" of any claim that "all is physical." The motive should be familiar: I suspect that the notion of *all phenomena* is as incoherent as the notion of *the set of all sets*. To avoid this kind of reference, we should be able to specify in principle which particular kinds of phenomena we are claiming are physical. (I discuss later other and independent reasons why I find global physicalism objectionable.)

The disjunction between explanation and elimination is in the specification of constructive physicalism because it would be absurd to demand that physicalism explain non-existent phenomena. No physicalism should be defined such that eliminating a supposed phenomenon proves physicalism false. Only the positing of a more successful explanation that added to the current ontology would prove a constructive physicalist claim false.

Finally, the constructive physicalist is not forced to assume all unexplained phenomena are not physical. For some phenomenon for which we do not have a successful scientific explanation, the constructive physicalist can either strive to describe how we might expect future extensions of our sciences to explain the phenomenon (an activity that already constitutes much of contemporary metaphysics) and thus place the physicalist bet on the phenomenon; or the constructive physicalist can remain agnostic about the phenomenon. In other words, the constructive physicalist is not committed to the mysterious (that is, the unexplained) being by default non-physical.

I will call "strong physicalism" the version of constructive physicalism that defines "minimal extension" as an extension that adds only mathematical description or theory but no references to new kinds of entities. To many people, this version of physicalism may seem too easy to falsify. I will make two observations. First, that most formulations of physicalism are so vague as to be unfalsifiable is not a virtue. Second, we should remember that I am limiting my application of physicalism in this discussion to physicalism about the phenomenal experience. It is very likely that future sciences will discover new kinds of entities. But constructive physicalism is not a global claim that all phenomena are physical. It is a local claim, which can be made only about specific phenomena. Thus, if cosmology or some other endeavor adds to our ontology, that may not matter to the question of physicalism with respect to consciousness. Strong physicalism about phenomenal experience is the claim and expectation that we will not need to add to our ontology any new entities and will be adding only theory and mathematics, in order to explain the phenomena of consciousness. If we discover that we need to add some new kind of entity to our ontology—primitive qualia, for example—then I would gladly recognize that as overthrowing physicalism (as we meant to use the term "physicalism" prior to that addition to our ontology).

Constructive physicalism (and therefore strong physicalism) can now be shown to be a form of *a posteriori* physicalism that escapes the four horns of the dilemma.

For Stoljar's dilemma, and the second horn of Hempel's dilemma, the problem lies in the move to the limit of the sciences. For Stoljar's actualist or possibilist account, or Hempel's limit case, we should understand physicalism, and the physical, as everything consistent with the claims in the final move of the game of scientific discovery. But my proposal is that we limit ourselves to speculating solely about the *next* moves in the game and limit ourselves to claims about particular kinds of phenomena. We are not gored on the actualist horn of the dilemma because we have offered no commitment to the actual final or true science. We are not gored on the possibilist horn of the dilemma because we are not making any claim about all possible kinds of physical theory. And, neither of these horns gores because we have made no global commitment—we have not said, "all phenomena are described by this actual or this possible science." We have said only, "*this* and *this* and *this* phenomenon is or will be explained by these sciences."

And, we are not gored on the second horn of Hempel's dilemma on either interpretation of that dilemma: we are not proposing a notion of science that is without content because so far beyond us, nor are we referring to a notion of science that is trivially assumed to explain everything. We are referring to our current science and its immediate progress.

What about the last horn of the dilemma, Hempel's dilemma for current theory? This is the worry that our current sciences will be revised, and so they cannot be relied upon to tell us what the physical is. The first thing to note is that this has no impact upon any particular claim that P is physical, as I have proposed we understand such claims. Such a claim is made with respect to one current theory or a minimal extension thereof. It is not the claim that the theory

T is true or otherwise unrevisable, but rather it is a claim that *T* or a minimal extension thereof will explain *P*.

However, I recognize that this doesn't really touch on the spirit of Hempel's concern, which is more clear when we ask, what about constructive physicalism? Hempel's worry is that our theory *T* will be significantly revised. I have argued that physicalism should be constructive physicalism, the sum of the explanation cases (the sum of the particular claims of the form, P_i is physical). Hempel's worry applied to constructive physicalism is that we will eventually revise our theory *T* into something significantly different.

We need to consider the possible cases that could arise then for transition from a theory *T* to its extension *T** with respect to a kind of phenomenon *P*. We note for each theory there are three possible cases: *T* explains *P*, *T* does not explain but does not eliminate *P*, and *T* eliminates *P*. We can ignore the case where our initial theory *T* eliminates *P* because we are then placing no bets about explaining it later. That leaves six logically possible cases of transition.

(1) *T* explains *P* and *T** explains *P*.
(2) *T* explains *P* and *T** does not explain *P*.
(3) *T* explains *P* and *T** eliminates *P*.
(4) *T* does not explain *P* and *T** explains *P*.
(5) *T* does not explain *P* and *T** does not explain *P*.
(6) *T* does not explain *P* and *T** eliminates *P*.

If we had placed the physicalist bet with respect to phenomenon *P*, then cases (1) and (4) would render our bet a winner, assuming the extension is minimal. It would not matter whether the theoretical explanation changed in case (1); our scientific theory still explains *P*.

Case (6) arises if our new revised theory has an ontology that makes our posit of *P* superfluous, and we decide that we were wrong that *P* even exists. By the definition of constructive physicalism, neither case (6) nor case (3) is inconsistent with physicalism. I am unaware of any instance of theory progress like case (3). It is difficult to see what reasons a skeptic could offer us to believe that case (3) would arise with respect to phenomenon *P*. We would hope that our descriptions of kinds of phenomena are not so theory laden that we end up eliminating phenomena that we once explained and that once played significant roles in our theories. However, even if there is an example or two of an important kind of phenomenon being eliminated, there will not be enough such cases to mount a pessimistic induction of the form: we eliminated phenomena in the past, and we will therefore eliminate *P*.

It appears to me that cases (1), (4), and (5) are the historical norm. We do not find our new theories abandoning phenomena. This in part follows from the fact that one of our standards for evaluating new theories is their conservatism with respect to the phenomena. Elimination seems to be something we should have avoided in our choice of descriptions of observations since hopefully the phenomena we aim to explain are not so theory laden that we find we were mistaken to even claim to observe them. Caloric or the ether or vital spirits were posits of theories, not phenomena. But, in either case, if elimination is possible, it is not an exception to constructive physicalism. I included the criterion that we will explain or eliminate *P*, because of course it would be perverse to expect a theory to explain something we agree does not exist.

The situation is similar for cases (2) and (5). These are the cases where we begin with a theory *T* (and we claim that *T* or a minimal extension thereof does or will explain *P*), and our new theory *T** does not offer an explanation of *P*. Consider first case (2), where *T* did explain *P*. I am unaware of any scientific revolution in which we abandoned an explanation for a kind of phenomenon. And, even if someone can dig up a few cases, they are not going to be sufficiently frequent to offer evidence for a new and narrow kind of pessimism—that is, they are not going to be sufficient for a reapplication of Hempel's dilemma, whittled down to attack constructive physicalism. Such an attack would be based upon a new pessimistic induction: in the past, we dropped explanations of phenomena, so we predict that we will do so for this phenomenon *P*. Since we have no cases or few cases, we are well justified then in dismissing this worry. Consider instead then case (5) where *T* did not explain *P*, though we were betting that it would. Then, we find ourselves in the same position we were in before. Presumably, we should want to make the same bet on *T** with respect to *P*. Of course, if we asserted that *P* is physical, and we did not manage to explain *P* in our extension, then if we have reason to believe that our failure indicates something suspect about *P*, we should re-evaluate our expectation that *P* is physical. However, if nothing has changed our conviction, and our reasons have not changed for expecting some extension of our scientific theories will explain *P*, then we may be well advised to double down: we should assert again that *P* is physical, on the expectation that some extension of *T** will explain *P*. In either case, it is the role of the metaphysician to make that decision, and the decision is not significantly different from what it was before we extended theory *T*.

The primary difference between constructive physicalism and physicalism-as-a-stance is that constructive physicalism remains falsifiable. The cases listed earlier presumed transitions between scientific theories. Another possible case is the following: *T** does not offer an explanation of *P*, but we introduce a theory *M* that posits additional ontological posits (perhaps that must be studied through new methods), and together *(T* & M)* explain *P*. For example, we posit a Cartesian dualist theory and a method of introspection to accompany it, and only by adding this to our theory *T** are we able to explain *P*. This is the kind of case that would render our bet on a scientific theory a loser. The distinguishing feature is that we added to our ontology. Such a case *should* refute constructive physicalism.

Thus, the first horn of Hempel's dilemma cannot gore constructive physicalism. The underlying reason is unsurprising: scientific change has rarely if ever resulted in preserved (that is, not-eliminated) *phenomena* being lost to the domain of science, and so no pessimistic induction can shed doubt on each of the individual explanation claims that constitute constructive physicalism. Even though we certainly expect our scientific theories to undergo significant revisions, we do not expect the phenomena we aim to explain to be evicted by those revisions.

Note that we escaped the first horn of Hempel's dilemma because constructive physicalism does not include some claim like *all phenomena are physical*. For such a claim, it might then be reasonable to expect Hempel's first horn to gore. For example, let A be the set of physical phenomena, as determined with reference to some kind of projection of current theory—something like all possible phenomena that could be explained by T. Let A^* be the set of physical phenomena as some kind of projection of a revised theory T^*. Presumably, $A \neq A^*$. This would arise even if T itself were in some sense final, or true, or unrevisable with respect to the phenomena it aims to explain, and the extension T^* just added theory to T because we discovered independent new phenomena. Thus, we can get into merely logical difficulties because of the global imperialism of classical formulations of physicalism. But not only do I think the global projection is incoherent, we simply do not need it. On the constructive physicalist view, we have no claim that "everything is physical." We instead have a constructed set of identifiable kinds of phenomena.

Recall that strong physicalism is the combination of constructive physicalism and the claim that a minimal extension of a theory T is any extension that adheres to the methods of science and that *adds only mathematical theory* to T. In the arguments of the following chapters, I am only concerned with strong physicalism.

My next task is to show that constructive physicalism is not only sufficient for our needs but also offers new ways to understand explanation.

3.2.4 Constructive Physicalism Is Adequate for Ontology

Would constructive physicalism, and the particular explanation claims that constitute it, be able to do the work that we want it to do? Not only is the answer yes, but also a stronger response can be mounted. All the interesting arguments in metaphysics about physicalism are in fact much better considered as particular explanation claims or as constructive physicalist claims, rather than as part of any global physicalist claims.

It is obviously beyond the scope of this chapter to consider all or even many cases, but a few can illustrate that constructive physicalism preserves, in a systematic way, the essentials of our debates. Consider then some arguments concerning free will, purpose, and consciousness.

One version of the free will debate, as it exists after the scientific revolution, asks us whether a view in which each event is causally determined by prior events is consistent with a robust claim that human beings have free will. The challenge for those who adopt some version of either libertarianism or compatibilism is to explain how we might make sense of free will in a universe that our sciences describe as requiring each event to be either necessary or random. Note that this problem does not require that we refer to a completed physics. Even obviously incomplete, it seems that contemporary physics is enough for this problem to become acute since our best understanding offers us only necessitated or random events; our best science of brain and physiology is consistent with this, and we have no examples of phenomena that suggest a prospect for some robust kind of agent causation.

In this context, our best theories to answer the problem are framed in relation to, and are consistent with, contemporary science. For example, a widely discussed recent compatibilism is Frankfurt's Humean view that a desire is free if we desire to have that desire (1971). Since we lack a successful science of human desire, we cannot be sure that desires are physical events. However, this is a problem we have independent of the free will problem, and the expectation that desires are physical events is not inconsistent with any current scientific knowledge. Thus, Frankfurt's theory can be formulated as a kind of compatibilism plausibly consistent with constructive physicalism; it is not necessary to refer to ultimate physics for the free will problem to be pressing and for his compatibilist solution to be compelling and suggestive of productive future research opportunities.

The debates about teleofunctions begin with the observation that not only in the arts and in ethics does talk about purpose seem necessary but even in the biological sciences, it seems (at least practically) necessary to rely upon reference to purposes. We describe the organs of organisms, for example, in terms of their purposes. Medical notions like health and well-being appear irreducibly teleological. How then can we make sense in *contemporary* scientific terms of a claim like "the purpose of the heart is to pump blood"? Here again, the problem does not require that we refer to some ultimate physics in order to be formulated. It is a problem for contemporary sciences that, if we want to restrict our discourse to causes (as much as possible), then we need a causal account of these purpose attributions. Constructive physicalism, with respect to current sciences, is sufficient to formulate the problem.

The program of the etiological theory of purpose, championed by Millikan (1984) and others (e.g., Neander 1991), identifies teleofunctions with the selected roles of the structure in question. Hearts cause many things: they cause noise, they cause the production of carbon dioxide, they generate heat, and so on. But it is only the act of pumping blood that ensures that the trait of having a heart contributes to the ability of that organism to reproduce. Therefore, pumping blood is (at least one) purpose or teleofunction of the heart. This compelling theory is consistent with contemporary sciences. It refers to current theories and currently recognized relations and entities. It is thus fully consistent with, and can be formulated with respect to, constructive physicalism.

These two metaphysical problems and the two approaches discussed could be formulated without change using constructive instead of global physicalism. Some debates in metaphysics would require some alteration. However, the alteration would be an improvement. To see this, consider again the knowledge argument, which asks us to imagine that a woman Mary has never seen color and yet knows all that science can tell us about color vision (Jackson 1982);

later revisions of the argument make Mary into a god, who knows all physical information (Jackson 1986). The question is, does she gain new knowledge when she first experiences a color? Most (but not all) philosophers are inclined to claim that she does learn something new. But if Mary learned something new, even though she knew all the (relevant) physical facts, it seems then that color experience is not a (relevant) physical fact. Proponents conclude that global physicalism is false.

The argument is intended to refer to ideal, unrevisable physical theory to make sense of all relevant scientific knowledge, or to all ideal, unrevisable physical factual claims to make sense of the notion that Mary is a god who knows all physical facts. We should expect only worthless intuitions to arise from the contemplation of either claim, requiring as it does wild speculations about future possible knowledge and the insights of omniscience (and, as I have already noted, I believe that references to "all phenomena" or even to "all physical phenomena" are incoherent). However, we can easily rephrase the argument to suppose that Mary knows all the relevant scientific facts of *contemporary* science and that the physical information that she has is the information that plays a role in contemporary science or in a minimal extension of contemporary science. The argument still goes through; and now, for those of us who accept the conception of constructive physicalism, the argument is actually more revealing: what is at stake is whether we're on the right track *now*, or whether we should try out some more radical alternatives to understanding consciousness. We should explain why Mary's personal scientific knowledge is insufficient. This would have the benefit of also explaining why philosophers are inclined to believe that Mary learns something new (since, after all, they *must* be judging the thought experiment on their own limited knowledge and limited theoretical abilities). And, if we should go looking for new kinds of knowledge, then we should place some more diverse research bets, perhaps even bets on non-scientific approaches, since we have come to believe that minimal extensions of contemporary knowledge are not going to be sufficient.

The most developed contemporary physicalist theories about consciousness in philosophy are formulated in terms that are consistent with constructive physicalism. Consider for example the representational view of consciousness (Lycan 1996; Tye 1995). On this view, phenomenal experiences like color experience are representations. We have theories that attempt to make sense of representation in terms consistent with contemporary science. The representational theories of consciousness in particular are compelling *because* they are plausible extensions of current scientific theory.

These three cases are representative of the role that physicalism plays in contemporary debates in philosophy. As such, they show that we lose nothing by treating physicalism as constructive physicalism: in most cases, the problems and our best solutions will remain unaltered. In the other cases, the problems will benefit from the discipline that constructive physicalism would force on the debate.

3.2.5 The Benefits of Constructive Physicalism

With constructive physicalism, we escape the two dilemmas for global *a posteriori* physicalism, and we lose nothing in our metaphysical debates. But do we gain anything that we otherwise did not have?

We gain something very substantial: a clear and important role for physicalism to play in philosophy and in science. To see why, consider a thought experiment contrasting two fanciful situations. In both situations, we discover a reliable oracle. Let us say, in both cases, an enormously intelligent and scientifically advanced extraterrestrial organism pays us a visit, assures us that it has a rigorous understanding of constructive physicalism and that its sciences are vastly beyond our own, and then it provides us with a single insight on consciousness. In situation (1), the oracle reliably tells us that physicalism about consciousness is true. In situation (2), the oracle reliably tells us that physicalism about consciousness is false. Our oracular visitor falls silent after this.

What would be the practical differences between these two situations? In neither situation did the oracle tell us any additional information, such as what the true or best theory of consciousness is. So, we've not learned something that has obvious direct applications. But we can predict that there would be important differences between these situations—or, more importantly, we can say that there should be. In situation (1), our decisions about resource allocations for the study of consciousness should be invested wholly in current physical sciences and philosophical theories of the kind we now know are consistent with physicalism. In situation (2), we should continue with those scientific endeavors concerning consciousness that shed light on other phenomena (like self-awareness) or related phenomena, but we should also invest resources in other radically new approaches—first-person phenomenology, the development of new information theories, explorations of meditation, and so on. Most of these programs are risky and will fail to answer our questions, but if we know that physicalism will fail, we have to start looking in these other places.

We can draw a useful analogy with finance. Call the *unpredictability of progress* claim the (hopefully obvious) claim that we are not able to predict the specific results of future scientific progress (where progress is defined as requiring theory revision or the adoption of a new additional theory). This is why we do research, particularly experiments. If we could reliably predict all future scientific results, we could save the cost of laboratory equipment. This principle of the unpredictability of progress—that we cannot predict where our sciences will end up, other than through the brute work of actually doing science—should sound familiar. In the sciences, we strive to share all the relevant information freely, and what we want to know then is what is not yet known; the way to learn it is to do research; and so the outcome is unpredictable. This is quite similar to the situation of an efficient market. In an idealized free market, every entrant knows as much as every other entrant, and the outcome of the market would be random (Fama 1965; Samuelson 1965), because the known information would already be priced into the market. What remains is by definition the unknown, which is by definition unpredictable. This is also the situation of research. Ideally, all scientists come to their science knowing what has been established. What remains for them to discover is what is unknown.

But then what role is there for physicalist ontology, and why ask the questions we have about physicalism? To follow the analogy, ontology should play the same role with respect to theory development that portfolio managers or other investment analysts play with respect to future states of the market. If efficient market theory is true, then portfolio managers cannot predict where the market will go. But that doesn't mean there is not an important role to be performed by these managers. The resources available for investment are limited, and as a result, decisions must be made about how to best invest those resources. Portfolio management theory offers a way to systematically manage scarce resources: ultimately, one balances expected risks of various kinds with expected or possible returns and volatility, with the risk preferences of the investor, and factors like the time horizons of the investor. Each particular decision requires some assessment of likelihoods about what is admittedly unpredictable.

The traditional conception of the role of physicalism is to strive to determine how various phenomena might ultimately be explained by the sciences. But this outcome is unpredictable: we don't know what the sciences will ultimately allow as physical. But what we can do is make assessments of likelihoods and, as a result, recommend what we think are the best bets. We should understand physicalism in this way: as advice regarding the best bets on theoretical progress. For example, instead of claiming or denying that a conscious experience is a physical event, we should be claiming or denying that contemporary science, or a minimal extension of contemporary science, is likely or unlikely to explain consciousness.

Since we lack the oracle of the thought experiment, the philosopher engaging in a defense or critique of physicalism regarding some phenomenon is the next best thing. She can be seen as advising upon the best bet in the relevant research directions. She is striving to show us that it is likely, or unlikely, that something like contemporary science will explain consciousness or some other phenomenon. Why would this be a worthwhile thing for a philosopher to do? Resources for research are limited. The allocation of those resources requires us to bet wisely upon different directions of research and also to manage our portfolio of research programs—placing more on the conservative bets, perhaps, and less but still some on the risky bets. In this way, such a bet or bets, if educated, can ultimately help us better allocate resources for research. The philosopher investigating physicalism should be thought of as offering advice for those who must decide upon the allocation of research resources, with the aspiration of favorably influencing resource allocation decisions. Note that the traditional global physicalist, with her idea of final physics, can offer no such guidance. When she says that *P* is physical, she tells other scholars nothing of practical utility. That is what Stoljar's dilemma and Hempel's dilemma show: the global physicalist refers to a limit phenomenon that is vacuous and indeterminate.

I of course have no illusions that grant boards will read philosophy journals to decide between, say, giving research funds to meditators or psychologists, nor that physicists will ever read philosophy journals to determine what equipment they should buy next year. Any influence on such resource allocation decisions would be profoundly indirect and weak. But our lack of influence doesn't mean that this is not the best understanding of the endeavor. Besides, getting clear about what the endeavor is, and thereby improving how we undertake the endeavor, could ultimately increase its influence.

Three other benefits should be noted for constructive physicalism.

First, the formulation of constructive physicalism as strong physicalism is falsifiable. If we discover some new phenomenon that cannot be explained by some extension of our sciences, then physicalism about that phenomenon was false. This means that constructive physicalism is unlike the view that physicalism is a stance or is an ideal theory of everything. As a stance, physicalism is a commitment and cannot be false, just as it cannot be a robust ontological claim. As an ideal theory of everything, physicalism is trivially true of everything described in successful theories some day in the future. But, as some interpretations of Hempel's dilemma already demonstrated, physicalism construed as the position of an ultimate science is also unfalsifiable, as a consequence of being without any content that we can refute.

Constructive physicalism might be too easily falsifiable for some. We should expect that some non-conservative extensions of science may occur; by definition of constructive physicalism, these would identify the relevant phenomena as non-physical; and yet, future philosophers may very well call those phenomena "physical." But such an objection would miss the point of my initial arguments. There simply is no *a priori* characterization of the physical. We should then expect it to change over time. But when we now, at this moment, say that "*P* is physical," this claim need not be vacuous.

A second benefit of constructive physicalism is that it does not require that there is a fundamental level. Often, physicalism is portrayed as a commitment to the view that everything will be ultimately described in microscopic terms (e.g., all facts will be entailed by microphysical facts if physicalism is true; Pettit 1994) or in terms of some other special class of "base" facts.[5] I share with Schaffer (2003) the suspicion that this is not a fruitful way of conceiving of physicalism. I share with Ladyman et al. (2007) embarrassment that the "facts" that philosophers tend to pick as potential base facts are generally baldly inconsistent with our best science. Constructive physicalism entails no commitment to an ultimate base.

Third, this formulation rules out the claim that "everything is physical" or similar kinds of claims. Other philosophers have argued that there is something problematic with this claim (e.g., Stroud 1986). I share these doubts and think they apply even if one were to develop a strong version of physicalism other than the version offered here. The claim that "everything is physical" seems certain to end up being perniciously circular. So many kinds of things are called "things" that surely not every thing is a physical thing. Fictional things, for example, are not physical; on some rather conservative views that many would consider physicalist, mathematical entities are not physical. To avoid such "things," we will find ourselves in the situation of having to say, "by thing, when I say 'everything,' I mean . . ." And then we will need to fill in the blank with some properties which are no doubt going to be an alternative way of saying, physical. The result is again that we will have to know what makes a thing physical in order to give a global specification of the physical. Furthermore, I think that there is something contradictory in the very idea of "all phenomena" and "all physical phenomena." Thus, I think it is a benefit that, for constructive physicalism, we cannot in any robust way mount a claim like "everything is physical." By definition, constructive physicalism describes an expectation about the phenomena that are in the scope of our sciences. We can set aside questions about whether science is about "everything" as unproductive.

In conclusion, note that one could make a case that physicalist claims never were anything more than something like the kinds of bets described here and that, in practice, physicalism never amounted to more than constructive physicalism. Since we do not know what future science is going to be like, we never really were arguing over anything other than physicalism as we understand it here and now. The best examples of progress in physicalism—by which I mean things like the three examples earlier: the representational theory of consciousness, Frankfurt's compatibilism, and Millikan's teleofunctional theory—are all attempts to make coherent the claim that something quite like contemporary science will be able to explain the relevant phenomena. Indeed, it is hard to imagine how one could undertake a serious effort in ontology that referred to yet-undiscovered entities or tried to explain all phenomena. Physicalism always has been the placing of bets on contemporary science with respect to particular phenomena. And so it should be.

Many will find constructive physicalism too demanding. It does mean, for example, that the shift from atomism to Newtonian physics, for example, would count as a failure of physicalism with respect to, say, gravity. But I think that this is a virtue. What the old atomists meant by "physical" (or rather, "material") was indeed proved inadequate when we added fields to our theories. And there is another virtue to my approach in the context of this book: I want to always take the most demanding position with respect to physicalism in arguing that physicalism remains a reasonable bet with respect to our efforts to explain consciousness. Strong physicalism is a very demanding, and clearly falsifiable, metatheory.

3.3 What Is the Relation Between the Physical and Other Phenomena?

I have used constructive physicalism to argue that we have an account of what the physical is. The other aspect of physicalism is to determine what kind of relationship must exist between an object and the physical in order for that object to count as physical. Examples include constitution, realization, supervenience, and entailment. For example, we won't expect our basic physical sciences to be concerned with chairs. But, we want to say that chairs are physical. What then is the proper relation between chairs and the stuff posited in the basic sciences? The constitution view is that each chair is physical if each chair is constituted out of things posited in our basic theories.

I find either a constitution or realization account the most compelling. I find the supervenience accounts least compelling. But in this book, I will not need to take a stand on these. Whatever the relation, my primary arguments should remain the same. Again, this follows because if we cannot even properly describe the phenomenon without additional information, then we can expect that we will not be able to offer an account of constitution, realization, entailment, or supervenience.

3.4 Reduction and Emergence

Although nothing in my arguments that follow will turn on this observation, it is valuable to recognize that this account of physicalism, combined with an appreciation of descriptive complexity, allows us to recognize a specific sense in which many phenomena can fail to be reducible. Philosophers tend to equate failures of reduction with dualism. There is literature on non-reductive physicalism, but it largely amounts to a hopeful assertion that there can be such a thing. However, there is a sense in which we can rigorously describe a kind of non-reductive physicalism (consistent with strong physicalism) using descriptive complexity. The point here was already made, implicitly, earlier when we introduced the notion of "minimal extension" of an existing theory: we defined it as adding additional description and mathematical theory, but not entities, to the relevant physical theory.

If we have a collection of entities and relations that we grant are physical, and if these can be arranged in new ways with sufficient generality, then we will have as a consequence that there can be arrangements of physical materials that are highly complex. They will not be reducible only in this precise sense: there will be no shorter way to describe them—any theoretical account of this complex arrangement cannot be replaced with a simpler description. Most philosophers would consider that consistent with physicalism. But it is important to note then that we should not equate "physicalism" with some kind of claim that it is the same as "reduction," if the latter means an explanation that is relatively simple.

At least two consequences of this are of interest to ontology. First, the proper description of such phenomena cannot be reduced to a description of the constituent parts and our physical theories; it sometimes must include descriptions of the arrangement itself (this is what I refer to as the contingent informa-tion principle in Section 1.7.2) or otherwise information about how to derive the description from the existing theory (as per the complexity cost principle described in Section 1.7.3). We must remember that explanation (whatever your theory of explanation) will require a description of the phenomenon. Sec-ond, this could mean that some of these complex systems can act in ways that are complex. Such systems, if in principle predictable, may require a great deal of additional contingent information in order to be predictable. Complex physical facts are thus all around us. Most of the physical facts that would interest us are presumably complex. Physicalism, contrary to the view of many of its defenders, should never be confused with the view that nature is simple (see DeLancey 2011). This is also plausibly why sciences must fork: as they encounter more and more complex phenomena, the practical strategy is to spin off new disciplines that can assume certain complex information in their local theory so that the study of the relevant phenomena can be eased (recall the notion of relative complexity, discussed in Section 1.4).

There has been significant literature on "emergence" in philosophy. The general idea is that there may be some kinds of entities or events that "emerge" out of simpler entities or events. I do not think there is enough consensus on what "emergence" is for one to be able to say if this kind of complexity would count as emergence. My own sense is that it does not. It seems that the notion of an emergent entity or event is meant to be more robust. Furthermore, the most cited discussions tend to be deeply concerned with questions of causation (see Bedau 1997; Wilson 2013, 2016). I have offered no account, nor do I have one, of how one should understand complex entities in terms of causation. Thus, it seems safest to conclude that this notion of complex phenomena is not what most scholars mean by "emergent" phenomena.

3.5 Conclusion: Consciousness as Physical Event

I will argue in what follows that strong physicalism about consciousness is our best bet (and, as noted, from this point on in this book, "physicalism" is taken to refer to strong physicalism about the phenomenal experience). What then is the best relation to propose between the physical and other phenomena, if we are to be physicalists? The relation I have proposed is very demanding; I am claiming that if one is a physicalist about irony or beauty, then one claims that a minimal extension of current theories will explain in a direct scientific way (e.g., by making falsifiable predictions) irony or beauty. But the trick here is that I put no constraint upon the complexity of the theory. In practice, I suspect it is a fool's errand to seek a physical theory of irony or beauty. The resultant theory would have to refer to social events, language, expectations and beliefs, and so many other phenomena and complex relationships that it would be pro-hibitively complex. The physicalist need not, I have argued, be committed to their position being practical. Rather, they bet it is true. For the arguments of this book, we are in a slightly better position. Although I think that phenomenal experiences are complex, I don't think that they are as complex as strange things like irony or beauty.

But first: there are specific arguments against physicalism with respect to consciousness. Any defense of physicalism should address these. This is the task for the next chapter.[6]

Notes

1. Criticisms of Davidson's views on mind were typically defended in this way: it is a misunderstanding to argue against his ontology, he is making normative claims about the essentially normative nature of our understanding of each other. Never mind that he was also making explicit ontological claims that contradict claims made by others. Or, Van Fraassen offers the religious stance, in which we treat god as a person, and a person is not reducible to objectified kinds (2002). Thus, the atheist who says there is no god is unfairly objectifying. But, after all, what about the atheist's claim? If we simply dismiss it by saying she is being too simplistic about the theist's stance, we allow for an ontological claim to both contradict a rival claim and be impervious to the appropriate criticism.
2. As will be clear from my remarks later, I'm not sure that we should have this concern. I believe that part of the motivation of the *a posteriori* strategy should be the epistemic commitments it carries: the domain of science is not determined alone by what *exists*, as Stoljar seems to suggest with this rejection of the possibilist reading of global physicalism but also by what can be studied by the scientific methods. The Cartesian soul objected to here by Stoljar would not be physical, on such a view, if the methods required to study it were not scientific methods. However, my answer to Stoljar's dilemma is independent of this point, so I set this point aside.
3. It is an interesting question what the possibilist physicalist really should be proposing here. She could propose the union of the ontologies of all terminal games, the intersection of the ontologies of all the terminal games, or, perhaps, some metatheory describing the common features of all the terminal games. Nothing in my argument turns on settling this issue.
4. As I noted, I think that there is something valuable to the view of physicalism as a stance. Here it is captured in the idea of reductive physicalism about **P** as akin to a bet on explaining **P**. Namely, the physicalist is guided by an optimistic metainduction. She expects the success of the sciences to continue. This expectation is similar to physicalism as stance, but it is now based on a substantive and defensible, and ultimately falsifiable, reason.
5. We can include here those who defend in metaphysics an "*a priori* entailment thesis" that all physical facts are deducible from some special or base facts (Jackson 1998). The various versions of this view appear to assume that there is some fundamental kind of physical fact, from which other less fundamental facts can in principle be derived.
6. Considerations of space require me to pass over certain issues regarding physicalism, such as the *a priori* entailment thesis (Joseph Levine 1983, 1993; Terrence Horgan 1984; David Chalmers 1996; Frank Jackson 1998; Chalmers and Jackson 2001; Jaegwon Kim 1999, 2009; it also has a venerable history including Samuel Alexander 1920; C. Lloyd Morgan 1923; C. D. Broad 1925; and Laplace 1902) and the physicalist entailment thesis (Lewis 1983a; Jackson 1993; Balog 2012). All of these theories require an account of what the physical is, so we have addressed them with the defense of strong physicalism. But I believe I can also show that these theories of global physicalism are inadequate because they ignore the complexity cost principle. But this would be a different book—one about physicalism, and not consciousness—if I took the space to address all such theories.

4 Refuting the Anti-Physicalist Arguments

4.1 Overview

My task in this chapter is to demonstrate that the most influential arguments against physicalism with respect to phenomenal experience are all either trivial (and thus question-begging) or unsound. I will need the basic facts I have established up till now. I will draw upon the concept of descriptive complexity, and the constraint and cost principles described in Chapter 1, and apply these to the descriptive and conceptual inadequacy claims defended in Chapter 2. I have clarified what I will mean by "physicalism" using the theory I call "strong physicalism," a form of physicalism that is falsifiable and not merely a stance, so that a denial of anti-physicalism will be a substantive position.

There are other arguments meant to show consciousness will not be explained by the sciences, but space requires that I limit myself to those that I consider most influential and substantial. These are the knowledge argument, the modal argument, the conceivability argument, and the superfunctionality claim.

4.2 The Knowledge Argument

The knowledge argument is now as familiar as it is influential: from the premise that phenomenal experience gives a kind of information or otherwise provides some kind of knowledge, and the premise that the relevant sciences cannot predict or do not entail this information or knowledge, appears to follow the conclusion that these sciences are incomplete with respect to phenomenal experience. The first explicit formulation, and the most intuitively compelling form, of the knowledge argument was given by Frank Jackson (Jackson 1982). Jackson illustrates the argument with a thought experiment:

> Mary is a brilliant scientist who is, for whatever reason, forced to investigate the world from a black and white room via a black and white television monitor. She specializes in the neurophysiology of vision and acquires, let us suppose, all the physical information there is to obtain about what goes on when we see ripe tomatoes, or the sky, and use terms like "red," "blue," and so on.

DOI: 10.4324/9781003320685-4

What will happen when Mary is released from her black and white room or is given a color television monitor? . . . It seems just obvious that she will learn something about the world and our visual experience of it. But then it is inescapable that her previous knowledge was incomplete. But she had all the physical information. Ergo there is more to have than that, and Physicalism is false.

(1982: 130)

This argument leaves ambiguous what Mary supposedly knows before she leaves the room. We might read "all the physical information" to mean at least three different things. First, it might mean complete physical omniscience. Mary knows all physical facts, including particular empirical facts about what was where and when. Since we might suppose that relations between natural kinds are an empirical fact, I'm going to eschew the usual ambiguous term "empirical" for particular empirical facts and call a description of these "historical physical information" or "contingent physical information" (I mean this to be the same use outlined in Section 1.7.2) to draw attention to the fact that these are particular events. Complete physical omniscience therefore includes the complete knowledge of all historical physical information. Second, we might take the knowledge argument to ascribe to Mary sufficient physical theory competence. This is the view that Mary knows all the relevant true physical theories (any knowledge about physical theory she lacks is not relevant to understanding consciousness). Third, we might take it to mean Mary has augmented physical theory competence—that she knows all relevant true physical theories and she knows all relevant historical physical information.

Jackson offered a strengthened form of the knowledge argument in a later paper, in which:

[Mary] knows all the physical facts about us and our environment, in a wide sense of "physical" which includes everything in completed physics, chemistry, and neurophysiology, and all there is to know about the causal and relational facts consequent upon all this, including of course functional roles.

(1986: 291)

Thus, it seems Jackson's intention was that Mary has complete physical omniscience. This formulation of the argument has two grave problems. The first is that it describes a physically impossible situation. Even if the historical or contingent physical information in the universe is finite, it is still going to be immense beyond imagining. Mary would need a brain billions, perhaps trillions, of times the size of a normal human brain in order to store this information, under even the most optimistic of assumptions. Thoughts might take eons to cross her brain, except for the fact that it would collapse into a black hole. We should have grave suspicions about whether intuitions about a physically impossible situation can be relied upon to illustrate the actual limits of physical theory.

Second, to grant Mary complete physical omniscience makes the knowledge argument valid but trivially question begging. The suppositions of the thought experiment include the assumption that the experience of color is not a physical fact, since it is by supposition not already known. The thought experiment amounts to:

Knowledge Argument, Physical Omniscience Form

Premise 1A: Mary has a sufficient description of all physical information.

Premise 2A: Mary does not have a sufficient description of a phenomenal experience (what it is like to see red).

Requirement A for Physicalism (about the phenomenal experience): If physicalism is true, then if anyone had a sufficient description of all physical information then she would have a sufficient description of each phenomenal experience.

Conclusion: Physicalism is false.

(In what follows, I use "sufficient description" and its cognates to match Jackson's notion of nothing being "left out." On that view, if there is a sufficient physicalist description of a phenomenal experience, then there is nothing relevant to be known about that experience that is not in that description already. But the kind of description that we require for the measure of descriptive complexity would by definition be sufficient.) This argument is unimpressive because the suppositions of the argument explicitly and directly assume that physicalism is false. It merely illustrates some trivial logic.

Thus, this version of the knowledge argument begs the question. The premises of the argument are simply a statement of anti-physicalism. It is indeed hard to know what lesson we should take from this argument and even more hard to know what we are supposed to conclude from the resulting revised or expanded thought experiment. Mary has powers now that go beyond godlike. Even Zeus overlooked events at Troy when Hera's seductions distracted him and then put him to sleep. But Mary, not even alive until eons after Troy fell, knows the mass of the toenails of Achilles and can count the breaths of every sparrow that passed over the field of that siege. Surely, any philosopher's intuitions about such knowledge are worse than useless; such wild speculations are a dangerous thing. We should deny tenure to folks who claim to know what such a god would know.

But I do not want to reject every version of the knowledge argument because of its final trivial formulation nor every version of the thought experiment because of the disastrously numinous final form. Rather, I want to argue that it is not this form of the argument that makes the argument famous and influential. There is a version of the knowledge argument—the version, I believe, that we most naturally deduce from the thought experiment as originally stated—that is compelling not because Jackson provided ultimately a version that was indisputably valid. The thought experiment is instead compelling in its most natural interpretation because it asks a basic question that we easily grasp and are inclined to answer: whether we think Mary, as someone like ourselves, could know what red is like, given the initial conditions of the thought experiment. We imagine ourselves reading a book and listening to lectures about red, but never seeing red, and we feel confident that we would never know what red is from these sources of information alone. But what would *that* tell us?

Thus, the relevant question is, why do so many of us find the knowledge argument compelling? Anyone who has taught the problem of consciousness in a classroom can attest that the knowledge argument is one of the most compelling thought experiments, if not the most compelling thought experiment, used to advocate for anti-physicalism about consciousness. But the thought experiment would lack any appeal at all if interpreted in the form I described earlier. Furthermore, we can confidently assume that no reader of the argument is omniscient with respect to all physical facts, and so the reader has to make crucial assumptions about what it means to be omniscient about all physical facts in order to be willing to accept anything like premises 1A and 2A.

The argument's appeal lies in that we read the argument quite naturally as concerning physical theory competence or augmented physical theory competence, but—because we tend to overlook that information comes in quantities—notice no problem when the argument's defenders shift the interpretation to complete physical omniscience. The problem with this, however, is that while the complete physical omniscience form of the argument begs the question and has no intuitive appeal, the other two forms of the argument are not sound. I will consider each in turn to show this.

If we read the argument as supposing that Mary has physical theory competence, we can give the argument as the following enthymeme:

Knowledge Argument, Physical Theory Competence Form

Premise 1B: Mary has a sufficient (standard, scientific) theory of color vision and other necessary relevant sciences; call this T.

Premise 2B: Mary does not have a sufficient description of color experience before she sees colors but when she knows T.

Premise 3B: If Mary does not have a sufficient description of color experience before she sees colors but when she knows T, then a sufficient description of color experience is not entailed by T.

Conclusion: Physicalism is false.

Here I am assuming that a standard scientific theory is one that describes at least both natural kinds and natural laws that relate to these kinds. This is meant to be a very general notion of scientific theory and is consistent with either a classical syntactic view of theory or the various richer semantic views (see Suppes 1972; Giere 1994). The notion that a theory that describes natural kinds and the laws that relate them deserves to be called "standard" might be challenged, but the arguments that follow will only require that some theories are like this to make the relevant points.

This argument has an implicit premise that physicalism is false about some domain if the physical theory does not entail all of the relevant information. This is a strong assumption of a kind of completeness for physicalism. Thus, to be valid, the argument needs an analog of Requirement A. This replacement for Requirement A is:

> **Requirement B for Physicalism**: physicalism is true of phenomenon *E* if and only if a sufficient description of *E* is entailed by our relevant sufficient physicalist theory *T*.

Most responses to the knowledge argument attack this notion of physicalism. One way to do this is to argue that the information or knowledge gained in phenomenal experience is somehow different from the information or knowledge gained or described through physical theory, but different in a way that should not be seen as problematic for physicalism, and so physicalism should not have to explain all of the phenomenal experience but physicalism can still be somehow sufficient. Thus, Churchland rejects the argument by using the distinction between knowledge by acquaintance and knowledge by description (Churchland 1985); Loar proposes that phenomenal experience is the knowledge that concerns objects under a different description than they are given in theory (Loar 1990); Lewis argues that phenomenal experience is a kind of knowing how, whereas theory is a knowing that (Lewis 1999). These arguments aim to show that there is an ambiguity in "information" or "knowledge" (or both) such that this stronger notion of physicalism is true for one notion of information (e.g., knowledge by description or knowing that) but not for another (e.g., knowledge by acquaintance or knowing how).

But we can assume that Jackson's notion of information is unproblematic and still show that there is a grave problem with the physical theory competence interpretation of the argument. It contradicts the contingent information principle and overlooks the cost described in the incompressibility cost principle.

An example can refresh our recollection of the contingent information principle. Imagine a thought experiment in which Sue knows the sufficient theory of dynamics but is locked in a closed environment where she never sees the moon and is never told about the moon. One day she is let out and sees the moon, and so learns that the Earth does have such a satellite. The analog to the first form of the knowledge argument would then be:

Dynamics Argument

> **Premise 1**: Sue has a sufficient (standard, scientific) theory of dynamics.
> **Premise 2**: Sue does not have a sufficient description of the Terran moon and its motion before she sees the moon but when she knows the theory of dynamics.

Premise 3: If Sue does not have a sufficient description of the Terran moon and its motion before she sees the moon but when she knows the theory of dynamics, then a sufficient description of the Terran moon is not entailed by the theory of dynamics.

Conclusion: The claim that dynamics is a sufficient scientific theory of motion is false.

But this is obviously unsound. We should not conclude that dynamics were insufficient as a theory of motion. Most standard scientific theories will not entail all the relevant historical physical information but will still be excellent physicalist accounts of the relevant phenomena. Dynamics does not entail what masses there are and where they are and how they are moving; chemistry does not entail how many kilograms of hydrogen there are or where and when various chemical reactions take place; limnology does not tell us how many lakes and streams there are and where they are; and so on. Most of our successful scientific theories tell us not all the relevant historical physical information but rather what one can derive from the relevant kind of historical physical information.

This distinction addresses one version of the knowledge argument offered by George Graham and Terrence Horgan (2000). They believe that their version of the knowledge argument escapes the standard objections to Jackson's formulations. In their argument, there is another Mary, whom they call Mary Mary, who in addition to having (at least) complete knowledge of physical theory and being for some years unable to see colors, is also devoted to some particular form of physicalism (they use as their example Tye's PANIC theory—see Tye 1995—although they presume their point should generalize). When Mary first sees colors, she is surprised. But Graham and Horgan argue that there should be nothing like surprise since this suggests that the theory left something out:

> But should Mary Mary, while still in her monochromatic situation, expect to be surprised by the new experiences and new knowledge she would acquire upon beginning to have color experiences? Should she expect unanticipated delight at the new experiences and new knowledge, over and above any anticipated delight that she might expect to arise purely from the acquisition of new discriminatory and recognitional capacities per se? No, she should not.

(2000: 71)

If we read this as a claim about physical theory competence, it well illustrates the potential confusion between the information of relations between natural kinds that compose a theory and the kinds of things that may be the subject of the theory itself. The argument then is equivalent to arguing that Sue, described in the Dynamics Argument, should not be surprised and delighted when she sees Earth's moon.

It is of interest, however, that we do not need to engage in dueling thought experiments. We can illustrate the problem with the consideration of any surprising discovery in science that does not contradict the existing theory. For an example, we can refer to a particularly delightful discovery: the reexamination of the Burgess Shale. It is true that Stephen Gould famously argued that the Burgess Shale required us to rethink some of our presuppositions about evolutionary theory (1990), but his view is a maverick one now and appears not to be shared by many paleontologists nor by those who worked on the Burgess Shale findings in recent decades (e.g., Conway Morris 1998). However, it does appear that everyone agrees that the Burgess Shale findings are delightful and surprising. For example, in defending the conservative interpretation of the Burgess Shale, Richard Fortey has written:

> It is now becoming clearer that velvet worms were much more varied and diverse in the Cambrian—they had more designs and were more disparate then than they are today. Spiky forms no longer survive, for example. This was no different from a discovery that Simon Conway Morris had made in 1980 about another obscure group of living "worms," the priapulids, which were much more varied in the Burgess Shale than in our seas now. This is an important and exciting finding: we could no more predict what kinds of velvet worms were living in the Cambrian than we could infer the shapes of dinosaurs from thought alone. Only fossils could chart the story.
> (1997: 97–98)

But this is *exactly* to assert the kind of distinction being made earlier: we can be delighted and surprised by historical facts alone, and furthermore, it would be a grave error to think that evolutionary theory should be able to predict specific historical facts without access to other relevant historical facts (that is, the relevant fossils). And so, if Mary Mary is surprised or delighted, this may be simply because she learns historical facts which cannot themselves be derived except from both the relevant theory combined with other historical facts. In the case of the surprising and delightful findings of organisms in the Burgess Shale, additional historical physical information, from sites of similar ecosystems but dating circa or from before the Burgess Shale organisms, would be required to allow that such forms would be predictable. If someone had found the Chengjiang Laggerstätte first, and gotten from it fossil specimens of the strange velvet-worm-like organisms found there, we could safely predict that specimens like these might be found in the Burgess Shale. But that did not happen, we lacked the relevant historical physical information, and it was a surprise and delight to get this information first from the Burgess Shale Laggerstätte. Graham and Horgan's version of the knowledge argument, interpreted as a claim about theory competence, thus serves to well illustrate the fundamental difference between theoretical and historical physical information but provides no additional reason to doubt physicalism.

The physical theory competence form of the knowledge argument assumes that Mary has a standard scientific theory about color vision, which I described as at least being a theory that describes natural kinds and natural laws. It is a reasonable hypothesis that some physical theories are sufficient if they describe only natural kinds and the laws that relate these. Dynamics appears, for example, to be like this. On such a view, to predict some particular physical state, we would need not only the relevant physical theory but also some relevant historical physical information. The knowledge argument could be read as recognizing this if we interpret it as giving Mary augmented theory competence. I give this interpretation also as an enthymeme:

Knowledge Argument, Augmented Physical Theory Competence Form

> **Premise 1C**: Mary has a sufficient (standard, scientific) theory of color vision and other necessary relevant sciences; and she has all the relevant historical physical information about any particular kind of visual experience she might have when she leaves the black and white room; call this *T*+.
>
> **Premise 2C**: Before Mary sees colors, but while she knew *T*+, she did not have a sufficient description of color experience.
>
> **Premise 3C**: If before Mary sees colors, but while she knew *T*+, she did not have a sufficient description of color experience, then a sufficient description of color experience is not entailed by *T*+.
>
> **Conclusion:** Physicalism is false.

Implicit here is a weaker notion of physicalism, to replace Requirement B:

> **Requirement C for Physicalism**: phenomenon *E* is explained by physical theory *T* if and only if a sufficient description of *E* is entailed by both *T* and the relevant historical physical information of events antecedent to *E*.

Suppose that *T* is a sufficient standard kind of physical theory of color vision; we now understand this to mean that if we have a sufficient relevant description of a historical situation of color vision H_{t1}, *T* and H_{t1} together entail all the relevant facts at some later time 2, H_{t2}. We do not need to explain what H_{t1} and H_{t2} are like, except to illustrate the concept: in the case of physicalism, for example, each H_{tn} might be a sufficient description at time t_n of what is happening in someone's visual cortex during a color vision experience. Many would deny that this is a sufficient description of a phenomenal experience, of course, but as the target of the knowledge argument is physicalism, we need to address the premises as they would be formulated for a charitable version of physicalism.

Note that theory *T* is a kind of information; it is the information of the physical theory that describes natural kinds and their relations through natural laws. H_{t1} is also physical information but of a particular phenomenon; that is, it is a description of the relevant visual color information that the agent experiences at time t_1. Only historical physical theories, such as, for example, one finds in some parts of paleontology, entail historical physical information about the environment at any time. There is then no *a priori* reason that a theory of color vision must entail any input to the theory. This was my point earlier, when I reiterated the contingent information principle using several examples: T alone may not entail any relevant H_{tn} for any time t_n, just as, say, dynamics alone (without any historical physical information) does not entail that there is a moon in such and such a position in the orbit of the Earth.

But one could argue that a sufficient theory of color vision should include some, but surely not all, historically contingent information. This is to endorse the augmented physical theory competence interpretation of the knowledge argument. A defender of the argument would then hold that the physical theory of color vision would include some historical physical information and be of the form described earlier as $T+$, and so Mary should be able to derive H_{t2} for that time t_2 when she finally sees colors. Some plausible arguments can be made that a theory of color vision should include at least some such information. After all, a theory of color vision must have significant connections to disciplines like ethology and paleontology and to the historical facts that are available in some work in these disciplines and garner much historical physical information through these. On this view, the theory of color vision is more like cosmology or paleontology than like dynamics. The color vision theory is explaining what particular organisms do and experience, and therefore must include historical physical information about particular kinds of organisms (that is, humans), just as cosmology combines dynamics and other sciences with information about the historical facts of our actual universe, and paleontology combines biology and evolutionary theory with historical facts about particular species of organisms and particular ecologies. Thus, the knowledge argument could be reformulated to explicitly endorse some version, perhaps a limited version, of premise 1C.

This is where the knowledge argument has bite. Since by supposition Mary cannot previously be given this knowledge by being given the relevant experiences (that is, she first learns the theory $T+$ without seeing colors), this historical physical information must instead be conveyed in some kind of historical theory that we presume she reads or is told about. But it remains a compelling and plausible conclusion that no matter how well we describe red to Mary, she will still learn something when she sees red for the first time at time t_2. This is compelling because we have a ready familiarity with the fact that there is a great deal of knowledge or information in some visual experiences that is difficult to convey in language alone.

I would contrast this point with Jackson's own analysis of the appeal of the knowledge argument. Jackson later argued (2004: 419) that our sensory experience is actually highly structured relational and functional information, some of which includes information that is not directly about the external sensory world (we might say that the information is partly processed). Sensory information, such as Mary's experience of red, therefore contains more information than just what is directly caused by a red stimulus. We then make the mistake, Jackson concludes, of thinking that this something more is therefore not physical because not directly caused by the stimulus, but, Jackson argues, that information is caused by other physical things, and therefore not nonphysical.

I think that Jackson is right here about the nature of red experience, but I do not believe that he has explained the central problem for the knowledge argument. The argument's primary appeal lies in that we understand it is hard—in fact, often practically impossible—to convey the information in a sensory experience in words. This is equivalent to the *description inadequacy claim* (DI), defended in Chapter 2.

Thus, before we reflect on Jackson's interpretation, the thought experiment seems compelling, and it is compelling for the right reason (that is, DI is true). As noted in Chapter 1, we know that it would be very hard to describe to someone who never saw a Pollock or any of Pollock's imitators what *Lucifer* looks like; it would be very hard to tell someone sufficiently well for her to be able to recreate *Lucifer* or to distinguish it from Pollock's *Full Fathom Five*. Given this intuitive understanding, it seems at first that physicalism, even when a hypothetically sufficient theory is coupled with historical physical information, is false. The knowledge argument, in the clarified augmented physical theory competence interpretation, appears to work.

Herein lies the intuitive appeal of the knowledge argument. Clarified so that the premises are explicit, the complete physical omniscience interpretation of the argument is blatantly question begging. The theory competence form is clearly inadequate in its characterization of physicalism and physical theories. But when we imagine ourselves in Mary's shoes, we imagine learning theories like the other theories that we have learned, we imagine that these theories we learned are true, and then we imagine that we have not seen color before but that someone or some text has described them for us before we see them for the first time. We put ourselves, in other words, in the very situation described by the augmented theory competence form of the argument.

In sum, the central intuition that makes the knowledge argument compelling is that there is something in certain phenomenal experiences that is not captured in our everyday experience of texts and conversation and theory. This would be true if physicalism were false, and these texts and conversation and theory were just physicalist descriptions. But this intuition could be true for other reasons. For example, those phenomenal experiences could be more complex than our everyday texts and conversations and theories and even more complex than can be grasped by us (given our contingent biological abilities to hold and manipulate such linguistic information) through these channels.

The knowledge argument under the augmented physical theory competence interpretation contains an implicit and very dubious empirical assumption. This implicit assumption is that if physicalism is true, then the kind of physical information that we can recognize and manipulate must be sufficient to encompass all kinds of information. But the thought experiment is compelling because of the description of Mary, in her room, reading books and watching television. This means that Mary is told about red experience in books, through conversations, and in black-and-white television shows. And this in turn means that if Mary is to in this way learn a sufficient description of a red experience, then:

- Something like our current descriptions of a red experience must be adequate to this task;
- Something like our current theories of red experience must be adequate to the task;
- Mary must be able to grasp and manipulate that information with her theoretical understanding.

But each of these implicit assumptions is profoundly dubious; the reader is right to doubt that anything like this is (practically) possible. And, in fact, these implicit assumptions deny DI and CI, respectively (see Section 2.1 and following). But if either of these inadequacy claims defended in Chapter 2 is true, then this interpretation of Jackson's argument cannot be sound.

Recall that CI is the hypothesis that humans are *incapable* of grasping with their theoretical reasoning capabilities the information required to explain a phenomenal experience like color vision. Let's review the reasoning. We know that human individuals have at least the following two capabilities: they can understand, use, and manipulate theories, and they can see colored objects and respond to them or otherwise deal with them in various ways. I make no claim about whether these are ultimately the same kind of capabilities (that is, whether knowing how and knowing that are ultimately interreducible). But we cannot assume that these capabilities are the same token capability in Mary or in anyone attending to Jackson's thought experiment, nor that they are fully integrated with each other so that the information in one can be freely and fully manipulated by the other.

Recall also that the kind of description that we might measure with descriptive complexity could be a theory, such as the sufficient standard theory of color vision T, or it could be a historical description (perhaps incomplete) of the functional state of an individual visual cortex at time t_n, H_{tn}. Note that $T+$, the richer historical version of a theory of vision, is T plus some historical physical information of the same kind as H_{tn}. Review then an instance of the incompressibility argument. Let $C(T)$ be the descriptive complexity of T. If the phenomenal experience has essential properties that are very complex, then the subject may be unable to grasp (all of) T. This is a consequence of the fact that we presume that essential properties are described in our theories. Let H_{tl} be a description of all the relevant features of the state of the brain (presumably, the visual cortex) of Mary at time t_l that are required to fully describe the relevant (physical features of the) color experience at time t_l. Let $C(H_{tl})$ be the descriptive complexity of H_{tl}. Finally, call the upper limit of the information that can be manipulated by theoretical understanding L (in this case, L can be the storage capacity of the theoretical understanding of Mary).

Given these definitions, note that there is no reason to believe that $C(H_{t1}) \leq C(T)$, nor that $C(H_{t1}) + C(T) \leq L$, nor even that $C(H_{t1}) \leq L$ or that $C(T) \leq L$. CI is the claim that for paradigmatically mysterious phenomenal experiences, $C(H_{t1})$ is significantly greater, perhaps vastly greater, than L, and $C(T)$ could be significantly greater, perhaps vastly greater, than L. But what CI tells us then is that it could be that (1) T and H_{t1} are a fully sufficient physical account of color vision because together these entail the relevant subsequent state of the agent in question (T and H_{t1} entail H_{t2}) and (2) T and H_{t1} explain H_{t2} in such a way that if we did have a theoretical grasp of both T and H_{t1}, we would find no reason to believe that something was "left out" of the theory (that is, we would not accept the conclusion of the knowledge argument), but (3) L $\ll C(T)$ and $L \ll C(H_{t1})$, and $L \ll C(T+)$. In such a case, the agent could have available (perhaps in a computer model) a complete standard theory of color vision T, but the agent could lack the theoretical form of the information that constitutes the actual having of the experience of color vision (namely, descriptions of essential properties as given in T and also the information in H_{t1}) because, in practice, she cannot manipulate this information with her theoretical understanding.

Thus, each of DI and CI is consistent with the claim that Mary can herself experience color vision and thereby learn something new (that is, gain new information), since being aware of some information, being able to recognize it, being able to act in particular ways with that information, and so on, do not require that the agent's ability to theorize is sufficient to be able to grasp that visual information as part of a theory. This is not to deny that phenomenal information and scientific information might be the same kind of information ("physical information") but rather just to deny that every description has the same amount of information or that every system of the mind has the same mental capacity, and to deny that all information that enters the mind is available to every system of the mind.

This form or interpretation of Jackson's thought experiment is the compelling form or interpretation, but this interpretation is now unsound. An analogy may help make this very explicit. The descriptive complexity of Peano arithmetic is obviously small enough for human beings to memorize and work with this theory, but there are large numbers that are Chaitin random that a mathematician will not be able to memorize or practically manipulate. Suppose now that Jane knows a version of Peano arithmetic, Zermelo–Fraenkel set theory with the Axiom of Choice, and how to construct the natural numbers using set theory; let us call this combination of theories, basic arithmetic theory. A knowledge argument that arithmetic was not reducible to basic arithmetic theory would go something like this. There are very large Chaitin random numbers that Jane cannot memorize, recognize, or manipulate, even though she knows basic arithmetic theory; this follows simply from the facts that Jane must have a finite theoretical memory and that there are infinitely many numbers of descriptive complexity exceeding the information capacity of that memory. Let N be such a number. Even though Jane knows basic arithmetic theory, she cannot "in her head" add N to itself. Therefore, N and its properties are not expressible or derivable in basic arithmetic theory. Namely, basic arithmetic theory is incomplete with respect to addition with N. The analog of the augmented physical theory competence interpretation of the knowledge argument then is something like:

Basic Arithmetic Theory Argument

Premise 1: Jane knows basic arithmetic theory and she has the ability to store, recognize, and manipulate many numbers in which she may have an interest.

Premise 2: Jane cannot predict the relevant properties of N (e.g., $N+N$).

Premise 3: If Jane knows basic arithmetic theory and Jane cannot predict the relevant properties of some number N; then basic arithmetic theory is not a sufficient theory of numbers and their arithmetic properties.

Conclusion: Basic arithmetic theory is not a sufficient theory of numbers and their arithmetic properties.

This argument has obviously gone badly wrong. The problem is with premises 1 and 3, which mix human capabilities with the limitations of theory. All of the properties of N that interest us may be expressible or derivable in basic arithmetic theory. But N is just too large for Jane to handle, and so numbers she may have an interest in may be beyond her theoretical abilities to remember and manipulate. Just so, there is no reason to believe that the information in our visual systems, which we use effectively to guide ourselves through the world, can be compressed enough to be manipulated with those capabilities (a physicalist might suppose, with those brain modules) that enable theoretical reason, nor to be communicated in the bandwidth of human speech. But this does not show that this information is not the kind of information that could be fully expressed and used in predictions by a physical theory of color vision, just as Jane the mathematician's limitations show nothing about the relative completeness of basic arithmetic theory.

More explicitly, in the augmented physical theory competence interpretation of the knowledge argument, premise 1C allows for ambiguity about what Mary "has" and how she "has" it; premise 2C allows for ambiguity about what she "learns" and how and where she "learns" it; and Requirement C for physicalism addresses mere entailment, but the argument invites us to consider instead what Mary "knows"; and the notion of "knows" is ambiguous.

The mere possibility that DI or CI is true means that the historical physical information or relevant theoretical description of a particular visual experience may be beyond the theoretical scope of an individual working with a successful complete theory of vision. We should no more expect Mary to have all the information of a red experience than we should expect a great mathematician to be able to remember and divide "in her head" two incompressible (Chaitin random) numbers that are 10,000 numerals long.

This is a convenient place to respond to one objection to the position that I advocate. Peter Mandik has argued that my use of the hypothesis that phenomenal experiences are complex events to explain the knowledge argument intuition arises from a mistake. It will be necessary to quote his points at length:

> The mistake arises from treating phenomenal knowledge as a kind of occurrent thought. Phenomenal knowledge, like knowledge generally, is abeyant or standing. This fact about phenomenal knowledge is what allows us to retain our knowledge even under general anesthesia when we, presumably, have no occurrent mental states. Our standing conceptual knowledge, as argued above, is, from an information-theoretic point of view, enormously capacious, and more than adequate to the task of capturing the content of visual experience.
>
> (Swamp Mary Semantics 20–21)

Mandik also says that my argument compares "visual experiences to the wrongs sorts of mental entities: relatively impoverished occurrent states of working memory or language processing instead of the vastly more capacious states of standing knowledge" (SMS 20 footnote 4).

This is a valuable criticism because it forces clarifications of the complexity of consciousness claim, and of CI, but most importantly of the kinds of judgments that I aim to evaluate.

The claim that I make here, and in all the arguments that follow, is not that the information required to explain a phenomenal experience needs to be occurrent, ready for report, or some other similar claim. The important point is rather that, even if the brain has a huge information capacity, that capacity is not all dedicated to theoretical reason. When we make judgments about what we can know (in the case of the knowledge argument) or judgments about consistency (as I will discuss next for the case of the modal argument and zombie argument), it surely is not the entire brain that is making such a judgment. Much of the brain is dedicated to visual processing, or sound processing, or other sensory modalities; or to motor control; or to autonomic functions; and so on. One does not get to set aside a huge portion of the visual cortex and use it for a math problem, should the need arise. We simply are not wired that way. There will only be limited dedicated structures that we use for theoretical reasoning. Furthermore, the kinds of *judgments* that we are discussing in these arguments (e.g., our judgment that Mary learns something new) are not tacit. Such a judgment is a self-aware activity: I think about the Mary thought experiment, or Kripke's claims regarding Cartesian intuitions, or Chalmer's zombies in a version of Kripke's argument, and so on, and then I reason about whether I think it's possible and what follows from this. Such reasoning is not tacit, any more than, saying, thinking about how to complete a mathematical proof is tacit.

The intuitions that I aim to explain—that is, to explain away—are judgments that people make. They are not tacit knowledge that they can, if necessary, summon up. To make the judgments, they must consider the relevant kinds of information, such as the information in a color experience. They must consider it with whatever capabilities are used for such evaluations. Now, whether some knowledge is occurrent or tacit or standing or implicit or in any other form, the question is whether it is available to our theoretical reasoning abilities (that is, whether that information can be just copied over or otherwise properly manipulated by them) and whether it can fit into the structures enabling those abilities or the relevant operations on the information can fit into the structures enabling those abilities. My claim is that both of these expectations are dubious.

What about claiming the judgment can be made in the relevant brain regions that are already enabling the phenomenal experience? The word "judgment" might be vague enough to allow one to say that, say, stopping at a red light means that one judges the color is red. In one sense, I grant this, since I grant that we have visual experiences and other kinds of experiences, and that we are aware of them, and act accordingly. But the knowledge argument and the other arguments against physicalism require special modal claims about the information in these experiences. In particular, they require evaluation of whether the lack of that information would be consistent with something like known physical theory. And that is not the same thing as grasping that visual information in such a way that one can recognize what is, and is not, consistent with the existence of that information. This kind of modal judgment uniquely requires logical reasoning: the comparison of sets of claims. It seems unlikely that we do that with our visual cortex (or with our smell cortex if we run a Mary-never-smelled before argument, and so on).

Thus, the knowledge argument under the augmented theory competence interpretation does not show that phenomenal experience cannot be fully explained with a physical description. The plausibility of the augmented physical theory competence interpretation of the argument rests upon an unexamined and dubious empirical assumption about the mind: a naïve conception of a single, homogenous mental capability with unbounded storage capacity. It appears, however, that the mind is highly modular, and no physicalist can allow that any such module has unbounded storage capacity. We cannot then assume, as does the knowledge argument, that the information in one such module is available to or could even "fit" in another.

The claim that the relevant information in a phenomenal experience could be more complex than can be grasped by the relevant theoretical capabilities that we have should not be confused with the claim that a successful theory of phenomenal experience is, or could be, beyond our grasp. The latter claim is entertained in Nagel (1974). Nagel argued that we intuit that we cannot know what it is like to be a bat, and he recognizes that his intuition may have something to do with human limitations:

> My realism about the subjective domain in all its forms implies a belief in
> the existence of facts beyond the reach of human concepts. Certainly it is

possible for a human being to believe that there are facts which humans never will possess the requisite concepts to represent or comprehend.

(1974: 441)

The talk about concepts here is ambiguous. We can easily have a concept like that-which-humans-will-never-understand, and so have a concept of the phenomenon in question. Nagel seems to mean that the theory will contain laws or other kinds of theoretical descriptions that are beyond our capacity to comprehend. We can make more sense of such limitations if we recognize them as regarding theory and our abilities to hold and use such theories. To use the aforementioned notation, this would be to entertain that the information of a physicalist theory T of a kind of phenomenal experience, perhaps even if just a standard scientific theory without reference to historical states, may be greater than our theoretical grasp can handle: $L < C(T)$. This would not show us anything about whether T was an adequate theory of phenomenal experience; it would, however, explain perhaps some of our intuitions about the mysteriousness of phenomenal experience and might mean we would never fully grasp the physicalist theory about the phenomenal experience even if it were true. Thus, it could be that we cannot know what it is like to be a bat, but that there could be an adequate physical theory and physical description of this phenomenal experience.

Two final thoughts about the knowledge argument. First, we could make a very similar argument to the aforementioned one even if we take the position that the theory T of color vision will (or should) have as a theorem what a red experience is like. This is to say that some physical claims are theorems of physical theory, and maybe the relevant claims about red experience would be theorems of the relevant physical theory of color vision. But the incompressibility cost principle shows why this would be no help. If the amount of information in a red experience is very great, then even if the relevant theory entails the relevant claim H_{tl} as a theorem, the incompressibility cost principle tells us that it will require at least as much information as there is in the experience H_{tl} to identify this information as a theorem of T. So, the same kinds of considerations would arise in the same way.

Second, another revision of the thought experiment has been offered by Laurence BonJour. He cleverly reformulates the argument to avoid two common responses: that Mary doesn't learn some new fact but rather something else or that Mary acquires not knowledge but an ability. In BonJour's version, Mary is given two samples of color, one red and one green, but labeled only color A and color B. Then:

We now remind Mary of two specific cases that she has studied thoroughly and about which she knows all the physical/neurophysiological/functional facts. One of these is a case where a person was looking at newly mown grass, and the second is a case where a person was looking at a new painted fire engine. We tell Mary that one of these people had an experience predominately involving one of the colors with which she is now familiar and that the other person had an experience predominately involving the other color, but of course not which was which. If we call the colors presented by the samples *color A* and *color B,* Mary now knows that one of the following two pairs of claims is true:

(1) The experience of freshly mown grass predominately involves color A, and the experience of a newly painted fire engine predominately involves color B.

(2) The experience of freshly mown grass predominately involves color B, and the experience of a newly painted fire engine predominately involves color A.

(BonJour 2010: 12)

The importance of this formulation is that what's at stake is distinguishing between two propositions. If Mary can't decide between (1) and (2), then *prima facie* it seems implausible that this is not a fact that Mary now lacks, rather than some skill or non-factual knowledge.

Like the surprise argument, however, this revision is also either trivially valid, or it is unsound because the phenomenal experience may be extremely complex events. The trivial interpretation will be required if "she knows all the physical/neurophysiological/functional facts" is construed broadly enough to mean all the facts of physical theory and physical history. It would then be equivalent to the trivial but valid form that Jackson offered as the original interpretation of his revised thought experiment, and I have already responded to that. Instead, let us take this as the weaker interpretation (though I doubt that a single human can know all the relevant physical/neurophysiological/functional facts about vision, either). Mary, being in this interpretation mortal, and not the superior of Zeus, is in a situation not significantly different from the original thought experiment. That is, BonJour's formulation is not a significant alteration with respect to the argument here. Mary may not be able to distinguish between (1) and (2) because it may not be practical to acquire that kind of knowledge through linguistic channels like books and discussions. The reason is that the relevant knowledge may be more complex than the contents of most books or any conversations, and far more complex than, say, the short-term memory buffer we use to acquire the information in books and in conversations. Thus, if any of the inadequacy hypotheses is correct, we are right to conclude that Mary could not tell the difference between (1) and (2) from the paltry information available to her.

For what it's worth, note that Mary may actually be able to answer the question of which is correct, (1) or (2) (nothing in my arguments turns on this, but it is worth noting that the "anti-materialist" argument intended may fail). She will know that human color vision is poor or non-existent in weak light and also that green is more reflective of blues that we see more clearly in the dark, and therefore she could perform an experiment and turn off the lights and make an empirically guided judgment about the colors. Or, she'll know that certain configurations of Benham disks will cause her to see a very pale green and a brown, and she can make a Benham disk and compare her experiences. And so on.

4.3 The Modal Argument

Kripke provided one of the most influential and interesting arguments against physicalism with respect to consciousness. A brief summary of Kripke's argument (1972), slightly simplified,[1] will help identify where complexity considerations apply. According to Kripke:

(K1) There are only two relevant kinds of possibility, epistemic and metaphysical.[2]

(K2) Identity claims about phenomenal experiences and brain events are metaphysically necessary.

(K3) The Cartesian Intuitions include that any brain event B that we might believe identical with a phenomenal experience Q could be had without that phenomenal experience.

(K4) If the Cartesian Intuitions describe an epistemic possibility, then there is a way the world could be such that we could experience brain event B but experience it as appearing to be something other than Q.

(K5) Phenomenal experiences cannot appear as other than they are, because these experiences are their appearance.

(K6) Modus tollens of (K4) by (K5) tells us that the Cartesian Intuitions do not describe an epistemic possibility; therefore by (K1), we know the Cartesian Intuitions describe a metaphysical possibility.

(K7) Thus (by (K6) and (K2)) we know that either the Cartesian Intuitions are false or physicalism is false.

There is a hitherto unnoticed problem with this argument, occurring in step (K4).

From the perspective of the physicalist, the Cartesian Intuitions are like the claim that the Evening Star is not the Morning Star. In Kripke's account, it is metaphysically necessary that the Morning Star is the Evening Star, but it is epistemically possible that they are different. This means the appearances could underdetermine whether they are identical:

> Any necessary truth, whether a priori or a posteriori, could not have turned out otherwise. In the case of some necessary a posteriori truths, however, we can say that under appropriate qualitatively identical evidential situations, an appropriate corresponding qualitative statement might have been false.

> (1972: 142)

Suppose that we have two phenomenal experiences e_1 of kind E_1 and e_2 of kind E_2. These phenomenal experiences provide information to the agent—in what Kripke calls earlier a 'qualitative statement.' Call this information about the appearance of the phenomena, D_1 and D_2 (I assume that there is no distinction to be made between an instance of information and its kind and that all the descriptions D_n are descriptions pitched at the level of kinds—e.g., "this is a thing of kind K_n"). Finally, let O_1 be the Morning Star and O_2 be the Evening Star. Kripke's picture is something like this:

$$((O_1 c{\rightarrow} e_1) \ \& \ (e_1 i{\rightarrow} D_1))$$
$$((O_2 c{\rightarrow} e_2) \ \& \ (e_2 i{\rightarrow} D_2))$$

where "$c{\rightarrow}$" is a causal relation and "$i{\rightarrow}$" is an interpretive relation. Our description D_1 of the Morning Star is something like *the star seen near the sun at sunrise*, and our description D_2 of the Evening Star is something like *the star seen near the sun at sunset*. In this case, these descriptions differ because the causal chains that produce the relevant experiences differ. And because D_1 and D_2 both underdetermine O_1—that is, they don't provide sufficient information to determine that one object causes both the experience in the morning and the one we have in the evening—it appears to us possible (it is epistemically possible) that $O_1 \neq O_2$. And "this is so because we could have evidence qualitatively indistinguishable from the evidence we have and determine the reference of the two names by the positions of two planets in the sky, without the planets being the same" (1972: 104).

Using this apparatus, Kripke constructs a new twist on the Cartesian concept of privileged access to mental states. Kripke observes that a phenomenal experience is identical to one's experience of it. Phenomenal experiences therefore are quite different from objects like planets. If I have an experience, call it e_3, of kind E_3, and my goal is to understand it via a scientific theory that proposes it is an event of scientific kind K_3, then we presume that any instance of one is identical to some instance of the other, $k_3 = e_3$, and this of course because the kinds are identical, $K_3 = E_3$. To use the aforementioned schema:

$$((k_3 = e_3) \ \& \ (e_3 i{\rightarrow} D_3)).$$

This appears to result in a puzzle. As Kripke puts it, many share the Cartesian Intuitions that this or that phenomenal experience could exist without this or that brain event. But any identity claim would seem to lack the wiggle room that we have with the other natural kind claims since he explained the difference between epistemic possibility and metaphysical possibility in terms of causal chains that enable a successful reference. Here there are no such causal chains because the experience is identical to the phenomenon of the experience. So, the relevant kind is not identified via some phenomenal experience that could have been otherwise (an instance k_3 of K_3 cannot cause an instance of something other than e_3 of E_3, since their relation here is one of identity and not of causation). Kripke sees this as a heavy burden for physicalism. If A is some phenomenal experience and B is some body event, then:

> Someone who wishes to maintain an identity thesis cannot simply *accept* the Cartesian intuitions that A can exist without B, that B can exist without A, that the correlative presence of anything with mental properties is merely contingent to B, and that the correlative presence of any specific physical properties is merely contingent to A. He must explain these intuitions away, showing how they are illusory.
>
> (1972: 148)

But there is a very plausible way in which the physicalist could explain away the Cartesian Intuitions.

Kripke explains underdetermination through a deficiency in the causal chain from the thing to the relevant experience of it. But there is at least one other way that the "qualitative description" could have less information than is required to distinguish between, or identify, possible kinds. The interpretive relation between the experience and the description we form of the experience could also result in an underdetermination.

Kripke places no importance on the distinction between experiences and the descriptions of experiences, which he variously calls "epistemic situations," "sensory evidence," and "qualitative statements." But this distinction is crucial: phenomenal experiences cannot play any direct role in theories. In particular, they cannot be evaluated to determine their consistency with other claims since they are not sentences. But a truth value is necessary for a consistency evaluation, and in turn, a consistency evaluation is required for us to evaluate any modal claim. *All* modal evaluations—epistemic and metaphysical—compare not experiences or kinds of experiences but rather sentences that describe those experiences. (This is consistent with a causal theory of reference. Neither a claim about an experience nor a modal claim is a reference—or, at least, is not just a reference.)

In the case of a phenomenal experience, we have that a phenomenal experience e_3 (this pain here) of kind E_3 (pain experience) is an instance of the natural kind we want to study, K_3 (pain experience). On the other hand, we have some natural kind that the physicalist proposes is type identical to this phenomenal kind. It might be c-fibers firing or some other brain event. Call that kind K_4. The situation that Kripke describes is one in which it is given that:

$$K_3 = E_3,$$

While the physicalist proposes that:

$$K_4 = K_3,$$

The Cartesian Intuitions include that possibly $K_4 \neq E_3$. Kripke claims we have no room here for the epistemic possibility to arise since there is no causal connection between an instance of the kind to be explained and the experience of it. But one can only reason about what qualitative statement might be true or false, and what might be consistent with it, if one interprets the relevant experience in order to produce a relevant qualitative statement. The picture is rather that:

$$((k_3 = e_3) \ \& \ (e_3 \ i \rightarrow D_3)).$$

And what the physicalist is proposing is that:

$$((k_4 = e_3) \ \& \ (e_3 \ i \rightarrow D_4)).$$

What we must compare, what we must evaluate to determine consistency claims and so possibility claims, are D_3 and what we imagine D_4 must be like. The physicalist must not explain how two seemingly different experiences could be identical, but rather how two different descriptions could be interpretations of the same phenomenal experience.

Kripke could (and should) revise his argument to claim that the Cartesian Intuitions are concerned with descriptions (his "qualitative statements"). Then, the physicalist must explain how it could be that our descriptions of a phenomenal experience could seem so different from what we imagine the scientific account predicts, when it may seem reasonable to assume that my descriptions of my own experiences will not underdetermine them.

But this revised Kripkean argument is invalid. The Cartesian Intuitions depend on some essential features of the Cartesian mind: this mind is fully transparent to itself; every thought and perception is equally available and equally answerable to reason or other forms of mental manipulation. And, the Cartesian mind has boundless capacity: there is no concern that some information could be too complex for that mind, and there is no concern that some information in that mind might be too complex for some other parts of that mind.

No physicalist should grant these assumptions. Our inadequacy hypotheses are each inconsistent with Kripke's implicit assumptions. DI tells us that our current theories and our discourse that constitute our reasoning about possibility will be too simple, and CI tells us that our theoretical reasoning abilities are insufficient to represent the relevant information.[3]

If some aspect of phenomenal experience is very complex, then we may have an experience but be unable to articulate and express that experience in theoretical reason in a way that is sufficiently accurate to allow for correct interpretations into complete qualitative statements, which are required for correct inferences about what is possible with respect to the experience (as per the modal judgment constraint principle). And, if some phenomenal experiences were very complex, then it is impractical to expect that we can sufficiently capture their information content in a qualitative description of the kind we use to talk to each other about these matters, to draw up our philosophical theories, and consider possibilities. But if that is so, then any qualitative statement we produce about that phenomenal experience can underdetermine the experience (it can lack information that the experience includes) and as a result not be a reliable guide to what is possible with respect to the experience.

We should correct Kripke's argument with the following revision of step (K4):

(K4*) If the Cartesian Intuitions describe an epistemic possibility, then there is a way the world could be such that we could experience brain event B but describe that experience in a way that the description does not determine that B is identical with Q as we currently describe Q.

But now Kripke's argument is no longer valid. His claim that a phenomenal experience cannot appear other than it does (K5) does not allow for modus tollens with (K4*) since the consequent of the conditional is not a comparison of experiences but a comparison of descriptions of experiences. Modus tollens would require the additional assumption that our description of the experience was relevantly complete. And this defies DI and also common sense.

Thus, it could be the case that the phenomenal kind in question is identical to some physical kind, even though the descriptions we are forming of their relevant instances are different, and this is because we lose information about the phenomenal kind in order to discuss it in a practical way, or in order to reason about it. The Cartesian Intuitions are weaker than they appear: they amount to the claim that we intuit that there can be a possible world where certain physical states could be different from *what we are describing as* pain. But how we are describing pain can have less information than pain, and as a result, how we describe pain may seem possibly distinct from something from which pain (fully described) is not possibly distinct.

I can clarify this last point by demonstrating how the conceivability argument depends on eliding this distinction.

4.4 The Conceivability Arguments

Kripke's modal argument has a successor, in the conceivability arguments of Chalmers (2007, 2010c), where *P* is a large conjunction of the relevant physical facts and *Q* is something like the claim that there is a phenomenal experience or otherwise a conjunction of facts about phenomenal events:

(T1) *(P & ¬ Q)* is conceivable.
(T2) If *(P & ¬ Q)* is conceivable, then there is a possible world in which there are experiences consistent with *P* and with ¬ *Q*.
(T3) If there is a possible world in which there are experiences consistent with *P* and with ¬ *Q*, then it is metaphysically possible that *(P & ¬ Q)*.
(T4) If it is metaphysically possible that *(P & ¬ Q)*, then physicalism is false or Russellian Monism is true.

Modus ponens leads us to the conclusion that physicalism is false or Russellian Monism is true. As I've phrased the argument, step (T2) reads a bit awkwardly, but there being no experiences of the kinds referred to in "*Q*" can be taken to be the experience of $\neg\, Q$.

Steps (T2) and (T3) are the analog of Kripke's argument. Since I have shown that Kripke's argument is not sound and the properly revised version is not valid, this also then makes this conceivability argument invalid. But this conceivability argument further illustrates the importance of complexity considerations in that its additional premise—(T1)—hides a fatal ambiguity.

It is important to clarify two points. First, it cannot be that "metaphysically possible" and "conceivable" are synonyms. Chalmers argues that conceivability must be understood as *ideal* conceivability (2002). It's not clear how much information ideal rational reflection requires, but it cannot require omniscience since then no one alive can satisfy the first premise of the argument. Instead, I'll assume that "ideally conceivable" means at least that *nothing that the agent explicitly knows is inconsistent with the conceived claim*. Here, "inconsistent" is used in an absolute, realist way—not requiring reference to any procedure. We need only observe that even ideal conceivability must not be synonymous with metaphysical possibility. If it were, then the first premise of the argument from conceivability would be equivalent to:

(T1*)   *(P & $\neg$ Q)* is metaphysically possible.

And then steps (T2) and (T3) of the conceivability argument become irrelevant. Conceivability must be a kind of work; we must *conceive* to determine conceivability.[4]

This implies my second point. Although the description of the argument might suggest that we evaluate claims for their conceivability in isolation, this cannot be. We cannot evaluate "there could be no phenomenal experience" alone. We cannot even evaluate for their conceivability, "there could be no phenomenal experience," and all physical facts alone. Instead, we must bring to bear any number of background assumptions and additional information, and we must make inferences. Consider, for a simpler case, a sentence like "this thing could be a round square." Presumably, this is ideally inconceivable. But this cannot mean that the proposition "this thing could be a round square" is *alone* inconceivable. Rather, one must spend a moment and conceive of things like the definition of "round," the definition of "square," and what it means for one thing to satisfy both definitions; one must commit to various assumptions, like a two-dimensional geometry (we're not talking about two different perspectives on a cylinder here); and so on. Thus, even the trivial cases require a body of information to be considered and evaluated and many inferences to be drawn. Given this, it is not enough to insist that it is possible, *simpliciter,* that there could be a world physically identical to our own with no phenomenal experience. Rather, there has to be some work involved in conceiving a world with no phenomenal experience. And this work includes making use of background assumptions, unpacking the information referred to in the conception, and making inferences about what all this information entails.

The inadequacy theses (DI and CI), and the claim that paradigmatically mysterious phenomenal experiences are very complex events, entail that the amount of information that we use in our discourse, our current theories, and that we are able to manipulate with our theoretical capabilities are very much less than the amount of information in a paradigmatically mysterious phenomenal experience. From this, it follows that our working description of a phenomenal experience may be significantly simpler than the actual experience itself. But then the modal judgment constraint principle (see Section 1.7.1) tells us that our judgments about what is possible with respect to that experience are unreliable if we lack relevant information. It could be that if we had all the information in theoretical form about the phenomenal experience, then we would find inconceivable the claim that there could be a physically identical world without phenomenal experience, but with reduced information about phenomenal experiences, this appears conceivable.

Step (T1) of the conceivability argument trades on an ambiguity: we could accept the step based on less than a fully informative conception of Q, but then switch and suppose we have a fully adequate theory and description of Q for the other steps of the argument.

We can formulate a general claim about conceivability and information, where P and Q_i are conjunctions of sentences; let us call this the *conceivability requirements claim:*

(CRC) It is not the case that, for any Q_n and Q_m, if $(Q_n \rightarrow Q_m)$ but the information in Q_n is greater than the information in Q_m, then *(P & Q_m)* is conceivable only if *(P & Q_n)* is conceivable.

The point is that even if one's current description of a phenomenal experience (Q_m) is true, and even if it were entailed by an adequate complete theory and description of the experience (Q_n), it could well be that some other claim is consistent with Q_m but is not consistent with Q_n. That is, as noted in Section 1.7.1, if you had more information, your judgment about what is possible could change.

The defender of the conceivability argument has no good options here. She can deny (CRC), but (CRC) is rather easy to show. It is, for example, a consequence of the fact that if $(Q_n \rightarrow Q_m)$, it does not follow that *(P & Q_m)* is consistent only if *(P & Q_n)* is consistent.[5] So her best option is to claim that our current articulated theoretical (or pre-theoretical) conceptions of phenomenal experiences capture *all* the relevant information that there is to know about those phenomenal experiences and to claim that we can grasp and use this information when we sit in the armchair and reason about possibilities. But this is to deny DI and CI. This is an empirical claim and not to be settled with semantic and modal intuitions; it is enormously implausible given our best current understanding of mind; and it is not a claim that any physicalist should grant and so to assert it without evidence begs the question against physicalism.

The gap argument is closely related to the conceivability argument, and a similar response would be given to the gap argument. The gap argument is meant to show an epistemic, not an ontological, problem. However, the structure of the argument is similar. Here is an example—made, as so many arguments about phenomenal experience are made—again about color:

> Let's call the physical story for seeing red "R" and the physical story for seeing green "G." My claim is this. When we consider the qualitative character of our visual experience when looking at ripe McIntosh apples, as opposed to looking at ripe cucumbers, the difference is not explained by appeal to G and R. For R doesn't really explain why I have the one kind of qualitative experience—the kind I have when looking at McIntosh apples—and not the other. As evidence for this, note that it seems just as easy to imagine G as it is to imagine R underlying the qualitative experience that is in fact associated with R. The reverse, of course, also seems quite imaginable.
>
> (Levine 1983: 357–358)

My answer to this of course will be the same answer that I gave to the conceivability argument. What we believe is conceivable depends on what we know, *and* when we make these kinds of judgments, a complex phenomenon is one by definition about which we are more likely to know less or consider less than the full information in the phenomenon. One's fancy of what an explanation of G is like or R is like are not at all reliable guides to possibility if G and R are very complex. And, we might add, if R and G are complex and we erroneously assume that they are simple, then our intuitions are not only unreliable but are certain to be misleading.

4.5 The Superfunctionality Claim

One of the most widely used claims of those who are anti-physicalists concerning consciousness is also one of the least discussed and most rarely attacked. This is the claim—sometimes the conclusion of an argument but most often merely a bald assertion—that the nature of a phenomenal experience is not exhausted by its causal relations or any other objectively measurable relations. I will call this the *superfunctionality claim*. Here, the term "function" and cognate phrases like "structure" are meant in only the weakest possible teleofunctional sense: "functional" means having a significant causal role in the relevant behavioral system. The superfunctionality claim entails some form of anti-physicalism regarding consciousness if we also assume that science explains only causal relations or other objectively measurable relations. The claim is thus relevant to all the leading anti-physicalist arguments for consciousness.

My purpose in this part of the chapter is to clarify the nature of the superfunctionality claim, and the arguments that have been offered in its defense. After reviewing its history, I identify two arguments for the claim: a trivial (and question begging) one and an open question argument. Reading this latter argument as expressing an intuition that deserves explaining, I provide an alternative explanation, using fear as an example phenomenal event. In conclusion, I show that those who believe the superfunctionality claim are faced with a significant dilemma: either they must predict that the physical correlates of some phenomenal experiences are simple, or they must explain why the causal correlates of intense experiences are complex even though superfunctionality would make any such correlation arbitrary. This result is the first attempt to provide a direct refutation of the strongest argument for the superfunctionality claim.

The superfunctionality claim, and equivalent claims, appears repeatedly in papers defending an anti-physicalist view of consciousness. The basic sentiment was voiced by Thomas Nagel when he wrote that the subjective character of experience:

> is not analyzable in terms of any explanatory system of functional states, or intentional states, since these could be ascribed to robots or automata that behaved like people though they experienced nothing. It is not analyzable in terms of the causal role of experiences in relation to typical human behavior—for similar reasons.
>
> (1974: 436–437)

Frank Jackson expressed a similar view in writing that:

> Tell me everything physical that there is to tell about what is going on in a living brain, the kinds of states, their functional role, their relation to what goes on at other times in other brains, and so on and so forth, and be I as clever as can be in fitting it all together, you won't have told me about the hurtfulness of pains, the itchiness of itches, pangs of jealousy, or about the characteristic experience of tasting a lemon, smelling a rose, hearing a loud noise or seeing the sky.
>
> (1982: 127)

Joseph Levine has argued that "our concepts of qualitative character do not represent, at least in terms of their psychological contents, causal roles" (1993: 134).

In these seminal papers, the authors went on to offer thought experiments meant to motivate claims distinct from (but related to) the superfunctionality claim. David Chalmers has offered a clear and independent statement of the superfunctionality claim:

> What makes the hard problem hard and almost unique is that it goes *beyond* problems about the performance of functions. To see this, note that even when we have explained the performance of all the cognitive and behavioral functions in the vicinity of experience—perceptual discrimination,

> categorization, internal access, verbal report—a further unanswered question may remain: *why is the performance of these functions accompanied by experience?*

> (2010a: 8)

The claim expressed here and (sometimes implicitly) in many other anti-physicalist arguments is that phenomenal experiences have properties that go beyond their functional roles (though some go so far as to claim phenomenal experiences have no functional roles).[6]

The superfunctionality claim is typically coupled with the view sometimes called "structuralism": the claim that science only describes objective relations. Some minimal clarification about structuralism will thus be useful in placing superfunctionality in anti-physicalist arguments.

There are several forms of structuralism. The most relevant distinction here is between an *a priori* form, and an *a posteriori* form. *A priori* structuralism is the view that we can discern from the essential nature of science that it can only identify objective structural relations. Alternatively, *a priori* structuralism is sometimes the view that science *should* only identify objective structural relations. It is *a priori* structuralism that is coupled with the superfunctionality claim in contemporary arguments against physicalism about consciousness. The *a posteriori* form of structuralism is typified by contemporary structural realism (e.g., Ladyman et al. 2007) and is based on the idea that science gives us reason to believe that an ontology that is all structure is sufficient. This form of structuralism is not consistent with the superfunctionality claim since it typically includes an assumption of a naturalism in which unverifiable claims are rejected, and the superfunctionality claim would qualify as such an unverifiable claim (since by definition the properties supposed are not verifiable by third-person observations).

A priori structuralism has an auspicious ancestry. It has been proposed by not only philosophers but also scientists.[7] Carnap wrote in 1928 in *The Logical Structure of the World* that

> *each scientific statement can in principle be so transformed that it is nothing but a structure statement.* But this transformation is not only possible, it is imperative. For science wants to speak about what is objective, and whatever does not belong to the structure but to the material (i.e., anything that can be pointed out in a concrete ostensive definition) is, in the final analysis, subjective.

> (1969: 29)

A similar sentiment was expressed shortly after by A. S. Eddington in *The Nature of the Physical World*. Eddington writes that "The cleavage between the scientific and the extra-scientific domain of experience is, I believe, not a cleavage between the concrete and the transcendental but between the metrical and the non-metrical" (1933: 275). Eddington is explicit that science discovers *only* objective relations:

Whenever we state the properties of a body in terms of physical quantities we are imparting knowledge as to the response of various metrical indicators to its presence, *and nothing more*. . . . In relativity theory we accept this as full knowledge, the nature of an object in so far as it is ascertainable by scientific inquiry being the abstraction of its relations to all surrounding objects.

(1933: 257)

And coupled then with the superfunctionality claim, this entails that science cannot explain consciousness. In a passage typical of countless others written by philosophers about consciousness since his time, Eddington illustrates this incompleteness of a science consistent with *a priori* structuralism:

The physicist brings his tools and commences systematic exploration. All that he discovers is a collection of atoms and electrons and fields of force arrange in space and time, apparently similar to those found in inorganic objects. He may trace other physical characteristics, energy, temperature, entropy. None of these is identical with thought.

(1933: 258)

In psychology, a version of *a priori* structuralism and superfunctionality were both endorsed by J. B. Watson in his early formulations of behaviorism, as he allowed that there might be a way to study consciousness as an "object of observation" but psychology as the study of behavior was not that discipline (1913: 174). And in recent years, examples include not only those discussed in the following but also Jaegwon Kim (1998), who argues that any physicalist account requires a "functionalization" of mental states, which is essentially a definition of those states as functional relations. *A priori* structuralism also seems to be equivalent to the view of some philosophers that science discovers dispositions, and "science finds only dispositions all the way down" (Blackburn 1990: 63; a similar view is found in Armstrong 1968).

When it arises in the philosophy of mind, *a priori* structuralism is typically offered without defense, but rather as a kind of purported generalization about scientific claims. *A priori* structuralism is not, however, obvious. Since my concern here is with the superfunctionality claim, I will set aside my own doubts[8] about *a priori* structuralism, and the doubts of others,[9] and simply grant it when it is required for the sake of the arguments that follow. The relevant point here is that it is *a priori* structuralism, and not *a posteriori* structuralism, that is assumed in these arguments.

I do want to note two related worries with both *a priori* structuralism and the superfunctionality claim. The first and immediate worry is related to one discussed already in Chapter 3 (where we evaluated a priori notions of the "physical"). The issue here is that the notion of "function"—and cognates like "structure" or "structure and dynamics"—is a moving target, largely because what counts as a cause has been a moving target. For early atomists and mechanists, causes were the impacts of rigid bodies and perhaps a few other things (like the abhorrence of vacuum). Fields would not have counted as proper causes for the atomist. Now, of course, they do. Just so, if "function" or cognates like "structure and dynamics" mean something like *plays a causal role in the relevant kind of system,* then what is a function can change, and indeed is almost certain to change. The question then becomes, who gets to determine what is a function, and what is not? Applications of the superfunctionality claim routinely are coupled with the assumption that it is obvious what will count as a causal relation in the very distant future, or at least that it is obvious what kind of equivalence class being an objective relation is. But we cannot predict that any more than the early atomist could have predicted fields or quantum entanglement. This is to recognize that structuralism is problematic because it is an *a priori* doctrine. (It might seem that this problem can be set aside if we adopt constructive physicalism and if we then also agree that contemporary physical sciences are structuralist. But it is not clear that every conservative extension, as I defined these in Chapter 3, would preserve such structuralism.)

The second and related worry is that this vagueness in the notion of "function" forces taxonomies that we should not accept and which lead to unfalsifiable or at least trivial conclusions. The superfunctionality claim, when coupled with *a priori* structuralism, can act as the universal acid that dissolves all denials of dualism by defining any current shortfall in explanation as an essential oversight. When Chalmers offers a six-place taxonomy of ontological theories about consciousness and calls the claim that we might ultimately find a physical explanation of phenomenal experience "type-C materialism," he promptly argues that this view is "unstable," because:

> Some type-C materialists hold that we do not yet have a complete physics, so we cannot know what such a physics might explain. But here we do not need to have a complete physics. We simply need the claim that physical descriptions are in terms of structure and dynamics. This point is general across physical theories. Novel theories such a relativity and quantum mechanics may introduce new structures and new dynamics over those structures, but the general point (and the gap with consciousness) remains.
> (2010b: 120)

Thus, the superfunctionality claim is used to deny the possibility of type-C materialism. Chalmers concludes that type-C materialism collapses into neutral monism or "type-A materialism." Type-A materialism, it turns out, is the denial that phenomenal experiences are anything other than functions—that is, it is the denial of the superfunctionality claim. Similar arguments end up revealing that the salient taxonomy that Chalmers offers is not six-place but two: there are those theories consistent with, and those inconsistent with, the superfunctionality claim. But here is the problem: if we are to sort all theories into these two buckets and if we are to be arbiters of what counts as a cause and as structure and as dynamics now and forever into the future, we are simply treating "physicalism" as a synonym for *a priori* structuralism. If we do this, then the assumption of the superfunctionality claim makes any "physicalist" theory trivially inadequate. However, as always is the case with perniciously unfalsifiable claims, a term has shifting meaning: many physicalists will not want to identify physicalism with *a priori* structuralism. Thus, the denial of "physicalism" being made here is not a denial of what many of us mean by "physicalism."[10]

We could settle such worries if there were some substantive ways to establish both that (1) a priori structuralism was true and (2) the superfunctionality claim was true. My focus here is the superfunctionality claim, so I'll consider attempts at the latter task.

As noted earlier, most examples of the superfunctionality claim are offered as purported observations, or as conceptual truths, and not as the conclusion of an argument. We might call this the *obviousness justification* (using "obvious" as a gloss for observation, conceptual truth, or any other route to justification not requiring an argument or third-person verification to justify the claim). In (2010a), Chalmers at times evokes an explicit formulation of the obviousness justification. For example, he writes that "The key instead is the *conceptual* point that the explanation of functions does not suffice for the explanation of consciousness" (16). Thus, scientific methods (as construed by *a priori* structuralism) "are simply the wrong sort of methods" (13).

It does seem that there are appropriate cases of similar kinds of obviousness justifications. If Smith asks Jones why the toast is burnt, and Jones begins to offer some pure number theory proofs in response, it is quite right for Smith to tell Jones that she obviously is not offering the right kind of theory. That is, it is obvious that talking about number theory is not going to (alone) tell you about why the toast is burnt. And, furthermore, it may well be a conceptual point that Jones is wholly in the wrong ball park for offering an appropriate explanation. So, obviousness justifications are not inherently inappropriate.

However, the difficulty is that the obviousness justification can do nothing to settle a dispute. And there is a dispute here. Daniel Dennett (2005), Paul Churchland (1996), Patricia Churchland (1997), Peter Mandik (2010, ms), and others have explicitly denied the superfunctionality claim (and many other scholars are committed to a view inconsistent with the claim). This is sufficient evidence to show that it is not an observation, or a conceptual truth, or otherwise obvious that phenomenal experiences are more than functional relations.

Nor should the superfunctionality claim be seen as corroborated by other arguments for anti-physicalism about consciousness. The conclusion of conceivability arguments (e.g., Kirk 1974a, 1974b), the modal argument (Kripke 1972), and the knowledge argument (Jackson 1982) is a claim that phenomenal events will not be explained by (anything like contemporary) physical science. Some anti-physicalist claims would be true if the superfunctionality claim and *a priori* structuralism were true. But an anti-physicalist claim is at least potentially independent: one might hold that phenomenal events are entirely functional; only their functional role is not of a kind that anything like contemporary science will capture. Furthermore, it would be a mistake to allow any of these arguments to act as corroboration of the superfunctionality claim since it is often the case that the superfunctionality claim is taken as corroborating these arguments. Mutual corroboration is fine in observations, but as noted earlier, these conclusions are controversial, and not everyone believes that they are observations, so such mutual appeals will be perniciously circular.

We need some non-question-begging argument for the claim that phenomenal experiences are more than any possible objective relation. There is at least one such argument, given by Chalmers and by Levine. Here is Chalmers's account:

> *[W]hy is the performance of these functions accompanied by experience?* A simple explanation of the functions leaves this question open. . . [I] f someone says, "I can see that you have explained how information is discriminated, integrated, and reported, but you have not explained how it is experienced," they are not making a conceptual mistake. This is a nontrivial further question.
>
> (2010a: 8)

Levine famously reformulates claims about a metaphysical gap into an epistemic gap, but for our purposes, his argument is otherwise relevantly similar:

> By the "open question" argument, I have in mind the following. Suppose we are confronted with an alien species or an advanced robot. We know everything there is to know about its internal workings. It turns out that its functional organization is, down to a fairly low level of implementation, very much like our own, though the physical mechanisms are different. Now we ask, is it conscious? And, if so, is what it is like for this creature to see red the same as what it is like for us?
>
> (2007: 148)

If an open question argument like these is to have any bite, it must not be leading. No open question would give us reason to believe we have not explained consciousness if it were of the form, "Why haven't you explained consciousness?" That is more a claim than a question. Questions of this form and also of the form "But why is that conscious?" also contain a subtle but misleading presupposition. The sleight of hand is that phrasing the question in this way suggests that phenomenal experience is one thing, if not a simple (see Dennett 2005: 72ff). Most physicalists will be inclined to think that there are many phenomena of experience, requiring complex and diverse theories and explanations. We invite a classic Rylean category mistake (Ryle 1949) when we expect a single narrow explanation of a range of diverse phenomena.

With a very slight clarification, the open question can be made to neither lead nor mislead. We should rephrase it not as asking, "Why haven't you explained consciousness?" but rather as asking, "Why haven't you explained *all* the features of phenomenal experience?" Then, the implicit claim underlying the (modified) open question is that the speaker believes that the account given or the account that we imagine a science will provide *leaves something out*. She asks the question because she wants to know more before she feels she has been given a sufficiently complete theory.

I offer the following, slightly more formal version of the argument, which respects this avoidance of leading and misleading questions. I give it here as a general argument schema and will refer to it henceforth as *the open question argument*:

(1) Any scientific theory T about phenomenal experience E is successful if and only if T and the relevant historical information will provide a sufficiently complete description of all the objective relations F_T of E.

(2) For any phenomenal experience E, and for any scientific theory T and relevant historical information about phenomenal experience E that provides a sufficiently complete description of all the objective relations F_T of E, we can still ask relevant questions about E that T and the relevant data do not explain.

(3) If we can ask relevant questions about E that T and the relevant data do not explain, then E is more than the objective relations F_T.

(4) For any scientific theory T of E, E is more than the objective relations F_T.

Even granting for the sake of the argument the assumption of *a priori* structuralism in premise (1), this argument could be unsound and we could be unable to tell. Presumably, premise (2) is meant to describe some kind of in-principle failure in explanation, but the open question argument makes it clear that we determine whether (2) is justified by appealing to our own sense of whether an open question seems appropriate. But our own inability to identify how a theory T answers a question is not proof that T does not answer the question. We can make mistakes in asking questions. Any time we learn something new, for example, there may be a period where the theory we are learning is unintuitive, and we may be inclined to ask "But why?" questions that are in fact easily answered. For example, when learning new mathematical propositions we often ask "But why?" questions about decidable and accessible *a priori* truths. And so it must be said that an open question argument only shows that some of us share an intuition that there is something left out of what we imagine the relevant scientific attempts at explanation of consciousness will be like. Furthermore, in the *a posteriori* realm, many theories are complex and probably undecidable—I mean, there is likely for many scientific theories no effective procedure such that for any arbitrary question Q, there is a way to find an answer to Q even if T does provide an answer for Q.

However, I do grant that the failure to find an explanation of some features of E using T, given significant toil, is some corroboration for the claim that T appears inadequate with respect to (that feature of) E.[11] Many people are inclined, it seems, to accept particular instances of premise (2). This inclination expresses an intuition that, even if it is fallible, deserves some consideration. The intuition is that an explanation of a phenomenal experience using a scientific theory T will leave something about the phenomenal experience unexplained, even if T is true, and as a result, we predict that it will be reasonable to ask again relevant questions about E given our best understanding and application of T. In that case, the fact that the question is pertinent would be a kind of corroboration for the claim that T is inadequate.

However, we can identify at least two reasons why, even if a theory were true and adequate with respect to some phenomenal experience, we should expect that we will be inclined to ask relevant questions after we sample some of the explanations of the theory. If that is so, then the open question cannot be corroboration for the superfunctionality claim unless this alternative explanation for the intuition is ruled out. My claim then is a rejection of premise (2) of the open question argument: there is a difference between what we will typically offer as an explanation in light of a theory T, and the total or maximal explanation that can in principle be generated by a theory T coupled with numerous particular historical facts.

We are inclined to believe that something will be left out of our functional explanations because something like this is our nearly universal experience with ordinary functional explanations when they are offered regarding *complex* phenomena. Here, by "ordinary" functional explanations, I mean the kinds of explanations that we offer each other in everyday discourse about physical events, and which we use in almost all situations, even in most (but not all) specialized scientific endeavors. When we are given an ordinary functional explanation of a complex natural phenomenon, we are typically given an explanation that is in rather obvious ways *apparently incomplete*. We are quite accustomed, therefore, to the kind of apparent incompleteness that might lead us to conclude that something like premise (2) will be true of any theory T of consciousness—at least, we should be inclined to predict that something like premise (2) will be true of many instances of the kind of things that we will typically be given as examples of explanations for a theory T. But this apparent incompleteness of the ordinary functional explanation does not entail that T is itself incomplete.

This explanation requires the complexity of the consciousness claim. We can understand the apparent incompleteness of ordinary explanations of complex phenomena in two distinct ways. First, the generalizations that characterize our functional theories are primarily tools for organizing, rather than predicting, events, and our experience with such generalizations reveals how they can grossly simplify complex phenomena. If what matters to us about phenomenal experiences are the particular details, then we will expect such generalizations to be unsatisfactory—even to seem simplistic and so incomplete. Second, the contingent information principle reminds us there is a difference between theories and the particular historical facts that theories relate to; many aspects of phenomenal experience that we consider salient may indeed be these kinds of historical facts.

An example of a phenomenal experience will help to illustrate each of these two points. The ability to experience fear is an inherited pancultural human trait. Most people have felt afraid, including very afraid, on various occasions in their lives. We are familiar with what an intense experience of strong fear is. Let us suppose that Smith is very afraid, perhaps even terrified. Consider again the partial list of features of fear discussed in Chapter 2. What happens to Smith when he is experiencing this fear? A very great many things, including that Smith's:

- Heart rate increases;
- Body temperature increases;
- Blood pressure increases;
- Skin begins to sweat;
- Muscles become tense;
- Eyes dilate;
- Body posture changes;
- Breathing becomes fast and shallow;
- Pituitary releases norepinephrine;
- Digestion is slowed or suspended;
- Memory formation becomes highly active;
- Memory recall becomes selective of fear-relevant facts;
- Perception becomes acutely primed to fast motion and other fear-relevant stimuli.

As noted before, this is an incomplete list, and each item on the list is very complex.

In contrast to this list, consider how we would typically explain or describe the functions of fear. Biologically inclined psychologists—those who would adopt what philosophers call an affect program theory—typically offer ultimate theories that identify the purpose of the emotion in relation to a selection benefit of the structures that enable the emotion, and then explain the effects of the emotion in relation to that purpose. (Here I use "ultimate" in its standard sense in the biological sciences to mean explanation in terms of selection benefit and "proximate" in contrast means an explanation in terms of local cause and effects.) Thus, for example, the psychologist Richard Lazarus claimed that each emotion had a core relational theme; for fear, this core relational theme is "Facing an immediate, concrete, and overwhelming physical danger" (1991: 122). The kinds of effects seen earlier would then be explained by reference to adaptations that in ancestors of Smith succeeded in generating a beneficial response to immediate, concrete, and overwhelming dangers. Muscle tone, adrenalin, and changes in digestion help prepare the agent for flight. Changes in memory formation help the agent remember the danger in the future, should it reoccur. Changes in recall draw upon information that may be relevant to coping with the danger. And so on. We can combine these insights and make some particular functional claims like

> F_I: Smith's fear reaction has as a function preparation for flight and other possibly beneficial strategies in response to danger.

I recognize that F_I is given in a teleofunctional form, but that's no problem. Although "function"—as the superfunctionality claim defenders use the term—is meant to be minimally teleofunctional,[12] F_I entails a set of functions in the thin causal sense of objective relations.

Now let us suppose that after his fear has ended, Smith reports to us that his phenomenal experience was very intense. The physicalist responds that she can explain this using F_I. We should expect, in light of this explanation, that Smith might be inclined to say, "Yes, but why doesn't that [F_I] explain *all* the features of phenomenal experience?" If this is taken as confirmation of (an instance of) premise (2) of the open question argument, it may well seem that Smith has reason to believe functional explanations of this kind—or at least F_I—are inadequate.

Human fear reactions are enormously complex events. They include a vast amount of physiological and autonomic and cognitive changes, many of which can alter in very complex and subtle ways the phenomenal experience of the agent. That means that only the most extensive and complex explanation is going to adequately describe all of what happens during Smith's fear. But then any practical explanation—I mean, any explanation that you could offer someone in conversation or write in a short article or even a fat book—is going to be inadequate in the sense that it's going to leave information out of the account. A claim like F_I is *true* but, if we aim for a *complete explanation* of the functions of this particular instance of Smith's fear, it is woefully inadequate. We should not mistake F_I for a fully complete scientific description of Smith's fear event. It is not. But it is true, and it is practically useful. We can expect, in fact, that any ordinary functional explanation will, out of practical necessity, leave out relevant details—most, nearly all, of the relevant details—about a complex phenomenon.

Here, as noted in Chapter 2, there is a distinction to be made between those physical events which constitute the fear experience (that is, that constitute some physiological change of which the subject is aware), and those events essential to the fear but of which the subject is not directly aware. The open question argument could presumably be targeting either or both, but my contention would be that either would be sufficient to satisfy my argument here. That is, either class of events is going to seem susceptible to the open question argument, but not because of any failure of physicalism.

I gave as an example of an explanation an ultimate explanation. The defender of the superfunctionality claim might argue that she believes the open question argument would apply to a proximate explanation also. But it is also necessary to offer broad generalizations in proposing ordinary proximate explanations.

Consider an example at random. A standard advanced neural science textbook (Kandel et al. 2000) includes the following proximate claim:

> Many of the autonomic expressions of emotional states are mediated by the amygdala through its connections to the hypothalamus and the autonomic nervous system. The influence of the amygdala on conscious feeling is mediated by its projections to the cingulate gyrus and prefrontal cortex.
>
> (992)

Let us call this explanation F_2. This passage is noteworthy for several reasons. It is highly general, even though it is offering a proximate explanation of only one aspect of human emotions like fear. The reason it is highly general is that the actual facts to which it refers are enormously complex, and this explanation is written in the attempt to offer an abstract and general functional explanation true of those facts. Also, this explanation *explicitly refers to conscious feeling*. The defender of the superfunctionality claim is wrong in claiming that scientific explanations ignore consciousness; the defender of the superfunctionality claim must in fact offer an error theory and claim that these scientists are *wrong*, and do not mean conscious feelings when they say "conscious feelings."

Thus, ordinary proximate explanations are also going to be highly general, and because of their generality, leave out the details of phenomenal experience that make it the rich experience it is. They will be apparently incomplete. This is true even of proximate explanations that explicitly refer to phenomenal experiences. That is, the superfunctionality claim would suggest that a proximate explanation that included also phenomenal events in its explanation would no longer be in principle incomplete, but such an explanation (as given earlier) is just as susceptible to the open question argument. And it is susceptible not because it leaves out experience, but because it leaves out details about a complex event.

Part of what is happening in these cases is that functional explanations—both ultimate and proximate—will make use of generalizations that are hierarchically arranged in a way that means higher-level descriptions leave out lower-level details. F_1 entails few—almost none—of the additional functional details of how fear actually succeeds in preparing us to cope with dangers. Typically, we understand that an explanation like this is merely offering an insightful generalization that is intended to be true of all the relevant lower level, and more fine-grained, functional explanations that would be required to fully explain fear. And thus, F_1 leaves out most (nearly all!) of the relevant information. The same can be said for the proximate explanations like F_2. These explanations primarily work as organizing principles for other knowledge. They tell us how, were we to proceed to study and describe this instance of fear, we could group all our findings. F_1 and F_2 can be appropriate in the sense that they are both true and that all the relevant kinds of explanations of fear will be subsumed under these explanations (that is, F_1 will be true of all and only the ultimate explanations for fear, and explanations like F_2 will be true of all and only the relevant proximate explanations for human fear expression). But in another sense, either is very obviously and woefully incomplete. Nearly all the relevant information about what actually happened when Smith was afraid is left out of claim F_1 or F_2. If one is a physicalist about the phenomenal experience, one claims that this is the very information that constitutes the variety and intensity of Smith's experience.

The second reason for the apparent incompleteness of any likely ordinary explanation arises from the contingent information principle (see Section 1.7.2). Let us review the point. Physicalist explanations typically leave out particular or historical details. This is a fact often overlooked in discussions of physicalism. We might call this the observation of *historical independence*. Theories relate what we can call historical facts. Ecology, for example, offers us generalizations that we can then apply to an ecosystem. But ecology alone cannot predict or locate or fully describe a particular ecosystem *without* the addition of the relevant historical facts (such as a complete physical description of that ecosystem at a previous moment in time). The same is true of any part of physics. Dynamics tell us generalizations about motion that we can apply to any particular motion. But some particular motion cannot be predicted by dynamics alone. A particular motion is a particular historical fact.

No serious candidate for a scientific theory of consciousness would be such that the theory *alone* was meant to entail all the facts about a particular phenomenal event. Theories must be combined with historical facts to entail a prediction or even offer a retrospective explanation. But if a phenomenal experience is very complex, then the inputs to the relevant theory will likely need to be very complex. And referring to the theory alone only tells us how we could relate that complex event to other (subsequent) complex events. The theory would not alone entail that event or any of its details. Thus, someone who is wondering about the richness of a fear experience, told even a very detailed theory about the relations that occur between kinds of physiological events that occur during fear, would have been told nearly nothing about what she had sought.

Consider F_2. What makes Smith's fear reaction a rich phenomenal experience, if physicalism is true, is going to be the particular historical facts about the many, many changes that occur in his body. Some of these will include—to quote again the aforementioned observation—autonomic expressions of emotional states mediated by the amygdala through its connections to the hypothalamus and the autonomic nervous system, and the influence of the amygdala mediated by its projections to the cingulate gyrus and prefrontal cortex. But these are complex neural structures, with tens of millions of distinct connections. The details of their interaction will be enormously complex. And none of this detail is captured by either an ordinary or even by a formal functional explanation. It requires reference to particular historical facts in the world (that is, identification and description of the details of Smith's body's state) which are then fed into the relevant theory.

Therefore, we can reliably predict that if given a true and adequate theory of consciousness, we will be inclined to also ask questions meant to elicit more information about functional details. And, it is perfectly reasonable to predict that if given a true theory of consciousness, one will be inclined to ask questions meant to elicit more information about the historical events that act as inputs to the theory. Both of these expectations are reasonable even if the theory in question is fully adequate. When the phenomenon in question is complex, in almost all contexts, our functional explanations will be apparently incomplete.

But the open question argument fails then to reveal any in-principle incompleteness to the functional account. We can see this because the very same kind of open question claim could be made about scientific accounts of phenomena having nothing to do with consciousness and about which there is no controversy regarding physicalism. Consider the following situation. A child asks, "Why does the plant grow towards the light?" You answer, "in order to get as much light as possible on its leaves." This is what I have called an ordinary functional explanation. It is pitched at a very high level of abstraction, but it is also true. You pitch the explanation at this level for the reasons recognized earlier: to be succinct, but also because you consider this brief claim as having identified the primary ultimate explanation of the phenomenon. But it is perfectly reasonable for the child to ask, "But why?" and then go on to argue you've not said enough. And of course you have not said enough. There is so much more to be said it is hard to know where one should then go next. An explanation of photosynthesis? Or of geometry and optics? Or of evolution and adaptation? Ultimately, of course, a full explanation would require going to all these places and more.

Also, even if you offered all these explanations, the child can be dissatisfied, and ask something like, "But why did it bend like this or that?" pointing at particular and notable twists in the stem. Here, the problem of historical facts comes into play. You have offered highly general claims about all relevant kinds of plants. She wants to know about this particular plant, and its particular structural features. You must now describe particular historical facts: this plant, its age, the quality of the light here, the size and shape of the pot, the way the pot has been moved several times, and so on.

Thus, although presumably there is no superfunctionality claim true of plants, for the same reasons we can ask for more information about a physicalist explanation of fear, we can ask for more information about a physicalist explanation of a true account of why a plant grows the way it does. The open question argument then does not distinguish between these cases.

This problem is even more acute for imagined sciences—or, perhaps we should say, for bets on future science. The physicalist does not have a successful theory of consciousness, which is a shame but makes her no less well off than the anti-physicalist who also has none to offer. So, when the contemporary physicalist says something like, "phenomenal experiences are representations," she is at best saying something pitched at a highly abstract level, like F_1

or F_2. Thus, the open question seems appropriate in this case—but only for the same reasons, it seemed appropriate in response to F_1 or F_2 and also seemed appropriate as a response to the claim that the plant grows toward the light in order to get as much light as possible on its leaves.

Remember the claim of Section 2.6: I am not claiming that people know that their phenomenal experiences are descriptively complex. Rather, they are familiar with this complexity through the vast range of capabilities that they have to discriminate and act in boundless and subtle ways using those phenomenal experiences, and they are also familiar with this complexity through the richness of their phenomenal experiences. Poets write verses about these complexities, after all. We might say that we are all *familiar* with the consequences and flavor of this complexity. And, as a result, we have a sense of when an explanation does not rise to explain or describe this complexity.

Our inclination to believe premise (2) of the open question argument arises from our intuition that the kinds of scientific explanations we typically hear will be unsatisfactory when applied to our rich phenomenal experience. One reason for this could be because science can't explain these phenomena, as is the consequence of the combination of the superfunctionality and *a priori* structuralist claims. But I have proposed a more conservative alternative: not that we need new kinds of things (e.g., irreducible qualia) to explain these phenomena but just a very great deal of the kinds of things we already have (that is, very complex theories and data). Fear was a good illustration of a complex phenomenal experience. Premise (2) of our argument earlier was false; our everyday experience shows that we often use brief and inadequate theoretical descriptions because they are practically necessary, but that same everyday experience does not show that any such theory must be inadequate.

But there is a predictable response to this claim. The anti-physicalist who wants to cling to the revised open-question argument could deny the complexity of the consciousness claim. She could argue that the philosophical explanation must account for the incompleteness intuition wherever it arises. And it arises not only for fear but also for, say, color experience. And, the anti-physicalist could say, isn't color experience simple? And so wouldn't an adequate physical theory of color experience, if such a thing were possible, be simple? If it were, this explanation of the intuition would fail, since—this anti-physicalist will claim—we intuit that an open question can be asked of such an explanation also.

The complexity of consciousness claim entails that color experience is not simple, but it may be worthwhile here to review an important problem for the denial of the complexity of consciousness claim. If the claim is true, then all the kinds of phenomenal experiences about which we are inclined to ask the open question—that is, the paradigmatically mysterious phenomenal experiences—are complex, and if we are physicalists, this means that their adequate scientific explanations will be complex.

In light of this claim, we can demand of the adherent of the superfunctionality claim: why is it that fear is a paradigmatically mysterious phenomenal experience, but adding two small digits is not? There is very much something it is like to be terrified, but barely anything it is like at all to add 2 and 2. I have argued elsewhere (DeLancey 2002) that the reason is that fear is correlated with very significant bodily effects of which the agent is aware, and a simple math task is not. I turn the challenge back to the defender of the superfunctionality claim: how are we to explain the intensity and variety of phenomenal experiences if they are simple? When the bodily correlates of which the agent is aware are extensively and significantly altered, the agent has a diverse and intense phenomenal experience; for example, when she is terrified. And, when the bodily correlates of which the agent is aware are not extensively and significantly altered, the agent has a thin phenomenal experience. I don't feel much that could be called "intense" or "rich" when working on an easy math problem. But if the phenomenal experience were simple, there is no reason why these cases should differ; that is, it should not matter whether the body effects with which the phenomenal experience is correlated is complex or simple. If phenomenal experiences are superfunctional, then it should be possible, for example, that a single neuron firing, with the rest of the body remaining centered in the ranges of typical homeostatic norms, would be the physical correlate of overwhelming joy. Intensity and distinction should not be expected to correlate with the complexity of bodily effects, any more than the acceleration of a falling body should be changed by the complexity of the shape of the mass to which it is attracted.

I chose the term "superfunctionality" for its beneficent ambiguity: "super" could mean beyond, in the sense of "supererogatory," or it could mean an extreme example of, as in the sense of "superfine." The anti-physicalists committed to *a priori* structuralism are also committed to the former interpretation; for them, phenomenal experiences are beyond functions. In this section of the book, I have shown that the latter (the "extreme example" interpretation of superfunctionality) is a plausible claim about our phenomenal experiences; phenomenal experiences are very complex—that is, they are *very functional*—and therefore many of our functional platitudes about them, even if correct, will leave something out. This in turn explains why many share the intuition that the open question is an appropriate thing to ask.

The open question argument alone cannot deductively show that a theory is inadequate; the premises of the argument are too contentious. I have shown that if we take the argument as illustrating a perplexing intuition deserving some consideration, then we can equally well explain that perplexing intuition with the superfunctionality claim *or* with the claim that phenomenal experiences are very complex. Then, this incompleteness intuition corroborates either the superfunctionality claim or the claim that phenomenal experiences are very complex (including perhaps nothing more than very complex objective relations).

The proponent of the superfunctionality claim has one option: she can deny the claim that paradigmatically mysterious phenomenal experiences are complex. She can claim that some paradigmatically mysterious phenomenal experiences are simple or otherwise not very complex. Then, the defender of the superfunctionality claim can assert that the open question argument remains pertinent because it is asking why a physical theory has not explained a *simple* phenomenon, and no amount of additional historical facts or functional details should then matter (since, by definition of not being very complex, there should not be much more description of functional or historical details to be made). I have already shown how this challenge can be turned into a virtue for the physicalist. And, in Section 2.6, I have shown that this is not an observation or something that is *a priori* true, and so here it begs the question. In any case, this would be a very real kind of progress in our debates about consciousness. For the defender of superfunctionality who takes this path, the only option is (a) to stake the superfunctionality claim on a prediction that some of the physical correlates of some paradigmatically mysterious phenomenal experiences will be simple or not very complex, or (b) explain why these supposedly simple phenomenal quale correlate only with complex physical events. The first option has the pleasing result that it renders our debate empirical. The second option presents problems so demanding that it should cast doubt on the anti-physicalist project and the superfunctionality claim alike. On the other hand, the claim that paradigmatically mysterious phenomenal experiences are complex *predicts* that if physicalism is true, then we will always find very complex physical events correlating with the relevant kinds of paradigmatically mysterious qualitative experiences. This grants to the relevant physicalist claim the gold standard for theoretical honesty: the claim is falsifiable.

4.6 Conclusion

We have shown that the main arguments against physicalism with respect to paradigmatically mysterious phenomenal experiences all fail. If we have no good reason to abandon physicalism, and we have an explanation now of why paradigmatically mysterious phenomenal experiences are mysterious (it is because they are very complex), then physicalism about phenomenal experiences remains our best bet.

The next chapter is concerned with a prediction of the complexity of consciousness claim: simple phenomenal experiences will not appear mysterious. This is a surprising prediction but one that we can now confirm.

4.7 Appendix: Conceivability and Decidability

The argument of this section is independent of the arguments in the rest of this chapter. However, I believe it is worth drawing attention to the role that a certain view of physicalism implicitly plays in influential anti-physicalist arguments. This helps draw attention to the pernicious role of a view of physicalism as a completeness claim. However, my arguments here deal with subtleties that will make my claims quite contentious, so I am eager to reiterate that this section is independent of and not required by my primary arguments. Those not particularly interested in nuances of metaphysics are encouraged to skip ahead.

My concern here is with the application of certain views about physicalism, in the conceivability arguments. To review the basic form of such an argument: from the claim that, say, the conjunction of both all base physical facts and physical theory, *P*, and some other claim ¬ *R* (typically some denial of qualitative experience—so this is typically the claim that there are phenomenal zombies) are conjunctively conceivable, along with claims that *R* or ¬ *R* is known in a special way; we are to derive that physicalism about *R* is false.

Some scholars find these conceivability arguments very compelling. If I claim to conceive that *(P & ¬ R)* is possible, and you cannot show me that it is contradictory to so claim, then, the intuition goes, I have some evidence that *(P & ¬ R)* is possible. But people disagree about what is conceivable. Some claim zombies are conceivable, and some deny that they are conceivable. At first glance, these claims seem to rest entirely upon first-person authority. They are not verifiable and they are not reliably reproducible by others. If either were obvious or otherwise universally held, we might not worry about this lack of confirmation. But there is contention. So we need a way to evaluate opposing claims about what is conceivable.

It is worth noting in fact that contentious conceivability claims appear to be everywhere symmetric with their denial. If the conceivability argument were valid, the following argument would also be valid, if we grant the dual of the usual modal logic S5 axiom (that is, if we grant that for any sentence *S*, *(◊S → □◊S)*, and thus we would grant its dual *(◊□S→ □S)*; this is applied in the following at step 3).

1. □*(P→R)* is conceivable.
2. If □*(P→R)* is conceivable then □*(P→R)* is possible.
3. If □*(P→R)* is possible, then □*(P→R)*.
4. Physicalism about *R* is true.

The strategy remaining for those who adopt the conceivability argument to claim that *R* is not physical must be to either deny S5 or to claim that □*(P→R)* is inconceivable. Since a denial of S5 would be *ad hoc,* the latter is the most likely strategy. But then, were a conceivability argument against physicalism sound, one must deny that physicalism with respect to phenomenal experience is even conceivable, on pain of contradiction. The moral for our purposes here is that claims that conceivability tells us anything about possibility devolve directly into a melee over what is, and is not, conceivable; conceivability is doing *all* the work since similar arguments can be offered on all sides.

There is only one way that has ever been offered to settle a dispute about conceivability when we do not have a proof for or against the contrary (that is, with respect to the aforementioned case, when we lack a proof that *(P → ¬ R)* or that *(P → R)* or that *P* is independent of *R*). This is to claim that, for example, *(P & ¬ R)* is conceivable—or, if we want to generously weaken the case a little, *(P & ¬ R)* is defeasibly conceivable—if those who deny *(P & ¬ R)* is conceivable cannot demonstrate a contradiction with

(P & ¬ R). Call this *the contradiction criterion*. The justification is that *(P & ¬ R)* is ideally conceivable if and only if *(P & ¬ R)* is consistent. In the conceivability argument outlined in the last section, this criterion would entail that we should grant a claim that *(P & ¬ R)* is conceivable unless we can demonstrate a consequent contradiction. This is the *only* criterion we have on offer to settle debates about conceivability.

I have already shown that the contradiction criterion is inapplicable. It follows from the modal judgment constraint principle that if we are in any situation of limited information—and we are always in a situation of limited information—then we cannot know if our failure to find a contradiction is because we do not have the relevant (and contradictory) information. However, in this section, I will show another problem with the argument.

The problem arises because the application of the contradiction criterion assumes a strong decidability thesis. By a *decidability thesis,* I mean a claim like the following:

DT: If *P a priori* entails *Q*, then there is an effective procedure to determine that *(P → Q)*.

The problem lies with the contradiction criterion. We could try and fail to find a contradiction between *(P & ¬ R)* for three reasons. First, as noted earlier, it could be that we lack information about the contradicting facts. I will set this objection aside since I consider it well established now. Second, it could be that *P* is independent of *R* or that *P* entails *¬ R* (and so zombies are conceivable). Third, it could be that *P* entails *R*, but we have been unable to demonstrate this (so zombies are inconceivable, but we err in ignorance and assume that they are conceivable). If we cannot distinguish between independence and error, then we cannot tell whether we have, or don't have, evidence for the claim that *(P & ¬ R)* is conceivable, and so we cannot conclude whether we have any evidence that *(P & ¬ R)* is possible.

We could distinguish between these cases, however, if we defined conceivability in such a way that it must be (ideally, in principle) possible to derive the contradiction in question if it exists, so if we cannot derive the contradiction, then we know the claim is conceivable. Conceivability arguments are meant to be made, by human beings, *now. We* are supposed to discern *now,* from the supposed conceivability of zombies *now,* that zombies are possible. So the required demonstration cannot be infinitary.

Chalmers writes of arbitrary statement *S* that "S will be ideally conceivable when ideal rational reflection detects no contradiction in the hypothesis expressed by *S*; or equivalently, when ¬ *S* is not a priori" (2002: 147). Thus, if *S* is the claim that there are phenomenal zombies, then *S* is conceivable if I cannot derive a contradiction with *S* and the base physical facts. This criterion at least entails DT—for otherwise what would it mean to say we are assuming that rational ideal reflection can *detect* any contradictions in a false purportedly *a priori* claim? The operant factor is that we human metaphysicians (or, for that matter, an ideally reasoning metaphysician) can in principle *determine* if there is a contradiction. Thus,

> When **S** is ideally positively conceivable, it must be possible in principle to flesh out any missing details of an imagined situation that verifies **S**, such that these details are imagined clearly and distinctly and such that no contradiction is revealed.
>
> (2002: 153)

But if we can in principle "flesh out any missing details," then we can in principle determine whether those details are true. And, we can only in principle determine, flesh out, and identify some arbitrary *a priori* fact if there is an effective procedure to do so. Thus, it is assumed that: if a person knows the base physical facts, she will be able to identify a contradiction between a claim that some fact **R** is not entailed by the base physical facts if **R**. But this assumes that such an entailment relation exists and requires no additional information: it must be *a priori* entailed by the base physical facts. Thus, the agent, as Chalmers equivalently puts it (1996: 99), will "automatically" imagine the appropriate entailment of the fact **R** from the base physical facts if such an entailment exists.

The claim that *(P & ¬ R)* is (perhaps defeasibly) conceivable is then the claim that all the relevant facts that we know, and our best theory, **T**, will be enough to decide whether or not *(P & ¬ R)* is consistent (presumably by determining if **P** entails **R**). This is obviously problematic since what we know will not include all facts in **P**. Since this worry about omniscience is not my target here, let us idealize and assume the agent knows all the relevant facts $p \subseteq P$, where if **P** entails **R** or its contrary, then so does **p** and where **R** is independent of **P** only if **R** is independent of **p**. Then, the conceivability argument and the contradiction criterion require that for any arbitrary **P** and **R**:

> We can determine if *(P & ¬ R)* is conceivable iff it is decidable that it is not the case that $p \vdash_T R$

And, equivalently:

> We can determine if *(P & ¬ R)* is not conceivable iff it is decidable that $p \vdash_T R$.

(And, of course, given the earlier assumptions, we can determine if *(P & ¬ R)* is conceivable if it is decidable that $p \vdash_T \neg R$.) If the relevant entailment were not decidable, then there would be no point to the claim that a conceivability claim is corroborated by the lack of an identifiable contradiction. That is, the demand that those who deny that *(P & ¬ R)* is conceivable produce a contradiction with *(P & ¬ R)* *requires* that it be decidable that $p \vdash_T R$ if it is the case that **p** entails **R**. The demand is irrelevant otherwise because we cannot distinguish logical independence from error or ignorance. Thus, DT is essential to the conceivability arguments because the sole method we have to test a conceivability claim is to *decide* whether the base physical facts entail a contradiction with the conceivability claim.

It is of interest that Kripke's modal argument (1972) fits this pattern. Kripke claims both that we have Cartesian intuitions that phenomenal experiences are not necessarily brain states and also that we have special access to our phenomenal experiences such that we cannot be wrong about their phenomenal nature. From these claims, and the claim that physicalist identity claims must be necessary if true, he derives a dilemma: either we must explain away the Cartesian intuitions or we must deny physicalism. However, it does not follow from these claims alone that if physicalism is true we would be able to determine that the Cartesian intuitions are contradicted. The Cartesian intuitions could arise, even if the physical facts entail the phenomenal facts, because we are unable to derive the phenomenal facts we experience from the physical facts that we understand. This could happen even if we have special access granting us a kind of infallibility regarding our phenomenal experiences. To assume that a special access to our phenomenal facts *corroborates* the Cartesian intuitions suggests that we are assuming DT—that is, that we are assuming that we can effectively determine if the phenomenal facts as we experience them are entailed by the physical facts as we understand them. And, equivalently, by posing a dilemma between "explaining away" the Cartesian intuitions or abandoning physicalism, Kripke is implicitly suggesting that physicalists should be able to produce the contradiction with the Cartesian intuitions.

However, DT is highly improbable. The kind of mathematics required for mature sciences is almost certain to render the relevant theories undecidable. And, even if there were an *a priori* entailment from some privileged set of physical facts (the "base" facts) to all facts, then still (as the incompressibility cost principle shows) *finding* the relevant entailment will require additional information. Stated equivalently, *conceiving* that fact or its denial will require additional information. Facts of very great complexity, particularly facts of complexity exceeding that of our theory, can remain mysterious to us whether or not there exists an *a priori* entailment from some privileged set of physical facts to these other facts, and so we can only apply the contradiction criterion if we gather the relevant additional information. And this information is very unlikely to be available in the armchair; if the physicalist is right in her bet, it is likely going to require information that must be hard earned through long empirical research. Conceivability has nothing to offer here.

Notes

1. For Kripke, the Cartesian Intuitions include more than claim (K3). For example, they will also include the claim that we can have a phenomenal experience without a brain event. These additional claims would not alter my arguments but only require the consideration of some additional but not significantly different cases.

2. Some scholars recognize other kinds of possibility besides epistemic and metaphysical. However, for the arguments that follow, it is sufficient to simply divide all the kinds of possibility into these two broad groups. My arguments will apply to any of the alternative formulations that might be used in place of metaphysical possibility.

3. Remember that to deny that a phenomenal experience has information in it, or is the kind of thing that can have structure and so be complex, would beg the question. I am showing that Kripke's premise K4 is false; it is false because even if physicalism were true we could still have the Cartesian Intuitions, and this is because if the physical event which is identical with the phenomenal event were very complex, we may be unable to fully grasp a description of the event in order to properly evaluate it with respect to modal reduction claims.

4. Some philosophers have observed that claiming that one can conceive of zombies begs the question. I grant this point. As with the knowledge argument, my work here is meant to show why people find zombie arguments compelling, under the most charitable interpretation of the argument, and why the complexity of consciousness claim renders the implicit argument unsound.

5. For example, let R and S be independent sentences. Let Q_n be (R&S), let Q_m be R, and let P be ~S. Then $(Q_n \rightarrow Q_m)$ because $((R\&S) \rightarrow R)$; and $(P \& Q_n)$ is inconsistent because (~S & R & S) is inconsistent; but $(P \& Q_m)$ is consistent because (~S & R) is consistent.

6. This way of describing the superfunctionality claim allows that phenomenal experience can have structural features; I am reading the arguments that apply the superfunctionality claim as thus aiming to show that physicalist explanations are incomplete (and not that they will have nothing to say about phenomenal experiences). See Stoljar (2006: 146ff) for a valuable discussion of this distinction.

7. There is a challenge in that some scientists and philosophers state something that seems quite like structuralism but which may only be an endorsement of objectivity in observations. Thus C. I. Lewis cites Max Born as a structuralist (Lewis 1956: 393ff). But Born's position seems to be rather one of endorsing a move away from first person reports. Born does write about "invisible . . . light, inaudible sound" (1962: 2) but he goes on to explain that this is a matter of "*objectivization,* which aims at making observations as independent of the individual observer as possible" (2). His point then seems to be not that science cannot refer to particulars but rather that it must refer to things in the third person.

8. My concerns include that *a priori* structuralism may be motivated by a fallacious meta-induction. It is easy to find examples where science refers directly to particulars (e.g., *the* big bang, *the* Earth, *the* particular proton smashed in *this* collision, Lucy the australopithecine, etc.). If we ask of any of these particulars, *what kind of thing is that?*, the scientific answer will be relational—although other relata may be particulars. And, a similar observation can be made about kinds. But this is a very different thing from saying that science does not refer to or explain things with reference to properties or objects that are not solely relational (such things would presumably be something like a particular or kind that has properties posited as primitives in the science, and so assumed to exist in isolation and even in the absence of measuring relations). Even if it were the case that any particular that currently enters into scientific explanation will itself be explained by some set of relations, this does not entail that all scientific explanations entail no references to non-relational particulars. We could find ourselves in this position (where every particular we can find is ultimately explained away in terms of objective relations, but there are non-relational particulars), for example, if because of the progress of science, every present and past example of a posited particular or non-relational kind was ultimately explained by analysis, because science is revising

its understanding of its particulars and kinds. In other words, if some particular or kind is at first taken as a primitive and then ultimately analyzed into some relations, this may be theoretical progress, and not an implicit universal ontological commitment to relations.

9. Just as there are early examples of structuralists, there are good examples of responses from the last century to this coupling of structuralism with anti-physicalist positions in the philosophy of mind. Feigl, in his masterwork "The Mental and the Physical," offers two criticisms of the application of structuralism to the problem of consciousness (1958: 450–451). First, he notes that there is a fallacious move that occurs when these arguments slip from experiences to our knowledge about those experiences; if experiences are non-relational primitives, our knowledge about them is not. It is always our knowledge about phenomenal experience that is playing some role in an argument about conceivability or knowledge or modality. Second, there is no effective objection to calling some of the things identified through "triangulation" of scientific means qualitative and non-relational.

10. Other effective criticisms of this notion of functionless consciousness include (Weisberg 2011b).

11. I don't think that, in this discussion, much would turn on explaining the notion of theoretical adequacy in play here. But the standard I have used throughout this book is strong enough to avoid any objections on this ground; we can use the very strong notion that T is adequate to explain E if T can predict E and all the relevant features of E, given relevant information about the state of the physical situation a short while prior to the occurrence of E. E.g., "the physicalist theory is adequate" can mean, if you tell us about Smith's brain at time t_1, then we can in principle tell you E will occur (and tell you all the relevant features of E) at shortly later time t_2. Most importantly, an adequate theory must be able to describe the phenomena required to make such predictions.

12. It is, in fact, meant to be taken as not teleofunctional at all. I doubt that this is possible. One needs some criteria to distinguish the kind of relations that are relevant from the very many causal relations that are not relevant, and the only way to do this is to appeal to some sense that some causes play a role in some ongoing system. But nothing in these arguments turns on this observation.

5   Subjectivity and the Sample Bias

The complexity of consciousness claim is the claim that a phenomenal experience is paradigmatically mysterious if and only if that experience has distinguishing properties that are very complex. Coupled with the inadequacy claims, this entails an explanation of the apparent ineffability of phenomenal experiences. But the complexity claim also allows us to make a prediction: phenomenal experiences that are not very complex will not appear paradigmatically mysterious.

There is no better corroboration for a theory than confirmation of a surprising prediction, and we can now confirm this prediction. But the confirmation includes some additional surprises. Philosophers have developed and perpetuated biases in their observations and in their reasoning, in order to avoid the fact that simpler phenomenal experiences are not mysterious—or, at least, they are not mysterious in a way that makes any of the canonical arguments against physicalism seem remotely plausible.

This bias has manifested itself in two ways. The first is to claim that we can have subjectivity without a phenomenal experience. Obviously, the most parsimonious approach would be that if we were subjectively aware of a mental event, then we would have a phenomenal experience of the event. But this simplest assumption has been sometimes denied. The second bias, and much more significant in its practical effect, is to *always* pick the most complex phenomena as examples of phenomenal experiences, and then ignore, if not deny the existence of, other kinds of phenomenal experiences. There is no reason to adopt the latter bias, except in order to prejudiciously defend a theory. For example, one reason to ignore phenomenal experiences that are less mysterious is to protect the view that phenomenal experiences are ontologically distinct kinds.

5.1 The Consciousness Sample Bias

Consider the following (perhaps ordered) list of mental events. I will refer to this hereafter as "the list":

- Terror;
- Pain;

DOI: 10.4324/9781003320685-5

- Viewing a red tomato;
- Sensing that one's body is turning;
- Proprioception of the location of one's hands;
- Imagining the rotation of a geometric solid;
- Remembering your home address;
- Adding 17 and 12.

Each of these is a mental event of which human beings are capable and of which a human being can be aware. My own phenomenology reveals that there are instances of phenomenal experiences for each of these kinds of mental events (I will consider the denial of this claim later). I am not alone; some philosophers agree that there is a phenomenal experience for each of these kinds of mental events (for review, see Pitt 2004). But the canonical arguments that phenomenal experiences will not be explained by a physical theory all concern themselves with only some of these kinds of events. These arguments concern themselves only with those kinds of mental events near the top of the list—in fact, typically color experience is taken as fully representative of phenomenal experience.[1] These arguments ignore phenomenal experiences like those had for mental events of the kind found closer to the bottom of this list. This is a sample bias, which has distorted the debate about consciousness and resulted in errors in our evaluations of anti-physicalist claims.

Before we establish what, if anything, distinguishes the phenomenal experiences on this list, we can demonstrate that there is a significant difference in which of these phenomenal experiences we select when making anti-physicalist arguments about consciousness. The most influential arguments all rely upon taking examples like those near the top of the list. If we rephrase those arguments instead to make use of cases from the bottom of the list, the arguments lose all of their ability to compel. To see this, consider again three of the most influential arguments against physicalism about phenomenal experience: the knowledge argument, the conceivability argument, and applications of the superfunctionality claim.

Remember that Jackson's seminal form of the knowledge argument asks us to imagine a woman who knows all the relevant scientific facts (Jackson 1982)—or even all the physical facts (Jackson 1986)—but has never seen red; when she sees red, she supposedly learns something new; thus, what she learns must not be a relevant scientific or physical fact. But consider now a version of the argument using a different phenomenal state.

> Mary is raised in a controlled environment where she never is told about, nor hears mention of, numbers. She is taught all relevant logic[2] that one can learn without being taught about numbers (those who imprison her are cultish followers of Hartry Field's work). She is shown Arabic numbers, but not told to what they are meant to correspond. She is taught computer programming and can write and understand complex programs in a programming language that does not explicitly use numbers and which

does not have any Arabic numbers in its syntax. One day, she is let out of the room and shown a program for a computer that will do addition, and which expects input in Arabic numerals and prints its output in Arabic numerals. She studies the machine and discerns, as a first example, what it is to add seventeen and twelve. She performs this calculation then in her own head.

The question now is, does Mary learn something substantively new about the experience of arithmetic? Does she have a radically new kind of experience, one unavailable to her before? If we were to follow the analogy with the knowledge argument run for color and not arithmetic, we should say yes. Mary learns what it's like to add two numbers; before now, she knew all the other relevant logical facts except this; so adding two numbers must not be a logical fact. And so we would conclude that the experience of adding two numbers is an irreducible phenomenal experience that cannot be learned from knowing logic, computer programming, and any other skill other than explicit arithmetic.

But that's absurd: Mary will see the addition program as a familiar variant of many other kinds of operations that she has analyzed and produced before. It will be new but only trivially so. She will treat the Arabic numbers the way all logicians treat a new symbol being introduced, taking note of its use and moving on without a second thought. There is no plausibility to the claim that Mary learns some fundamentally new kind of phenomenal fact—that is, it is not plausible that she has a substantially new kind of experience—when she experiences arithmetic directly in this way for the first time.

In fact, it is hard to make the thought experiment sound even the slightest bit plausible. What would it be like to know all relevant logical facts but arithmetic, and not simply derive for yourself (at least some of) arithmetic long before? It seems this would happen inevitably. The anti-physicalist might claim that this is because arithmetic is different from physical facts, but I suggest the opposite is much more plausible: the axiomatic core of arithmetic is a much simpler thing than "all physical facts" or "all relevant physical facts," and so we see very clearly the implicit contradiction in the supposition of the thought experiment. This suggests that if we had as good a grasp of the theory of vision as we have of the theory of arithmetic, we would find it very hard to stomach a claim that one would know this theory of vision and not be able to explain what it was like to see red.

The conceivability arguments offer an extension of Kripke's modal argument (1972). Recall that Kripke's argument is meant to present a dilemma: either we must explain away the Cartesian intuitions shared by many people that phenomenal experiences are not identical to brain states, or we must reject physicalism. Kripke's argument rests on the Cartesian idea that we have special access to our mental states, such that our intuitions are especially insightful regarding phenomenal experience (and as such reveal metaphysical and not epistemic possibilities). The conceivability arguments present a variation: they ask us if we can imagine a "zombie" that does what we do but which lacks the phenomenal experience that accompanies these functional skills (Kirk 1974a, 1974b; Chalmers 1996). Kripke's modal argument made use of pain as his example of a phenomenal experience; typically the zombie arguments make use of color or some unspecified phenomenal experience as an example. Consider instead a conceivability argument using addition.

> One can conceive of an arithmetic zombie. This is an individual physically identical to you, that can add seventeen and twelve, *and which is aware of what it is doing when it adds seventeen and twelve,*[3] but which lacks the phenomenal experience that you and I have when adding seventeen and twelve.

According to those who believe conceivability reveals facts about metaphysical possibility, we should conclude then that the conceivability of an arithmetic zombie contradicts the necessity of any physicalism regarding arithmetic experiences and thus understand that the experience of adding 12 and 17 is not a physical fact. But regardless of whether one believes that conceivability is a guide to metaphysical possibility, the point is moot, because we cannot conceive of any such thing as the arithmetic zombie. Adding 12 and 17 and being aware of so doing is sufficient for the experience of adding 12 and 17. Nothing is left out, there is no mysterious residue to perplex us. It is enough to know what you are doing when adding to have the full experience of adding. And thus there cannot be an arithmetic zombie.

We have seen that those opposed to physicalism about consciousness will have a ready response: what the knowledge argument and the conceivability arguments show is that phenomenal experiences are not functional events— they don't have a causal role of the kind that science explains. This is the superfunctionality claim: the claim that phenomenal experiences are above or beyond or otherwise not constituted by objective causal relations. Combined with the claim that science only explains or refers to objective causal relations (itself a contentious claim), the superfunctionality claim renders consciousness non-physical.

Made baldly, the superfunctionality claim begs the question. It cannot convince us that phenomenal experiences are irreducible to causal relations; combined with the claim that science only explains objective causal relations, it amounts merely to the assertion that phenomenal experiences are not physical. But as we have seen, one kind of argument has been offered for the superfunctionality claim: an open question argument. If we demanded a specific example, we would be told that color experience or pain experience were sufficient examples.

But consider the argument with a specific example from farther down the list of mental events given earlier. In particular, imagine that we understand that Mary represents numbers in her mind and that she performs computations on them (for example, computations that are isomorphic to what we would expect from a computer program performing addition). Suppose furthermore that we all grant that Mary is aware of what she is doing. The open question asks, "Yes but why does Mary have the phenomenal experience of adding twelve and seventeen?" If the question is not superfluous, we are supposed to conclude that a physicalist account is incomplete (again, assuming we believe physicalism only allows reference to objective causal relations).

But the question *is* superfluous. To be aware while one adds 12 and 17, to be conscious of the steps taken, is sufficient to explain all there is to the phenomenal experience in question; or, at least, there is no added mystery beyond the ones we already have about how we actually represent numbers, perform operations on them, are aware of this, and so on.

5.2 Complexity Makes the Difference

Phenomenal experiences from near the top of the list appear mysterious and encourage us to allow leaps into mystery when they are the subject of various thought experiments. Phenomenal experiences from near the bottom of the list appear unmysterious, and render the canonical anti-physicalist arguments unconvincing—they can even render the thought experiments of these canonical arguments contradictory. What is the difference between those phenomenal experiences near the top, versus those near the bottom, of the list?

Of course, their phenomenal characters are different, but that is not sufficient to explain the issue here. The phenomenal characters of seeing red and seeing blue differ, but presumably people will find the canonical arguments no less convincing using red or blue as examples. So it is not phenomenal character *per se* that distinguishes an experience's place in the list.

One possibility is that this is a matter of some kind of access. Then, the difference between terror and color experience, on the one hand, and the experience of a simple addition problem, on the other, lie in some kind of architectural feature of our minds. This feature would make the former less accessible to our awareness. This appears consistent with a Fodorian modality theory (1983). Perception, including perception of things like the autonomic changes that occur during an emotion, appears to begin with and to rely upon modules that are domain-specific and partially information-encapsulated. If the information in a phenomenal experience were difficult to access, available only in limited ways to our cognitive awareness, it may have a seemingly mysterious otherness to it—it resists full understanding because we cannot fully acquire all the information in the mental event for cognitive consideration and analysis.

I believe that there is something to this idea, but it also appears insufficient to explain the difference we aim to explain. This is because there are perceptions that appear to be domain-specific and partially information encapsulated—just like vision—but which are less mysterious as phenomenal experiences. A good example is proprioception. There are illusions of proprioception, such as the Pinocchio illusion in which the subject feels her unmoving arm is actually pulling and stretching her nose (Lackner 1988). Such illusions provide as much evidence for the partial encapsulation of a proprioception module as we have for the encapsulation of other kinds of perception, like vision. And yet, the experience of proprioception is not very rich or mysterious. Someone who knows where his limbs are has proprioception in all its experiential glory. A proprioception zombie (a person who knows where his limbs are by way of proprioception but lacks the experience of proprioception) is contradictory.

An alternative hypothesis is that the complexity claim is true: the mysterious cases are mysterious because, and only because, they are complex. On this view, the important difference between items on the list of phenomenal experiences given earlier is that those near the top of the list are very complex, and those near the bottom of the list are relatively less complex.

We have already mounted a defense of the complexity claim, but let us review here the reasoning, in light of the list of phenomenal experiences given earlier in the list. Assume for a moment the physicalist's perspective. When we are terrified, a very great many alterations of which one is aware appear in the human body and in cognition: heart rate, muscle tension, blood pressure, and body temperature all increase; our focus of attention changes; there are significant changes in how we form memories; there are significant differences in how we recall memories; there are alterations in our perception; and many more effects occur. Each of these effects alone is enormously complex, but when they happen together, the specific details of the changes that occur in terror are absolutely immense. And, as noted in Chapter 2, when we have a visual experience, including a visual experience of a color, a huge portion of our neocortex is actively involved in generating this experience and in solving many cognitive visual problems like the shape of the colored thing; its distance; its spatial relation to other objects in the environment; the kind of object it is; the character of its motion, if any; and so on. The occipital lobe is the largest lobe of the neocortex; none of our other senses has so much neural machinery dedicated to it. The physical events that occur during a visual experience are of enormous complexity.

Contrast the very complex events of terror or vision with what happens in a brain when one adds 12 and 17. Assuming this is solely an isolated math problem (and not some problem needed to defuse a bomb on the table before you— that is, not part of a very exciting situation for which all kinds of other mental events like emotions will be occurring), there will be no appreciable change in one's heart rate, blood pressure, or any other autonomic feature. The other cognitive effects are minimal (that is, while we form memories more quickly and strongly when afraid, for example, there is no effect like this for doing math). The entire occipital lobe is not involved. Rather, a relatively small but distributed network in the neocortex—including such areas as the intraparietal sulcus—seems to be required for the representation of numbers (Dehaene et al. 1998; Wood et al. 2006) and a relatively small network of related parietal and frontal lobe regions appears to be involved in the performance and reporting of arithmetic (Fehr et al. 2007). The changes that occur of which one is aware are thus likely much more simple: one is merely tracking some representational tokens and performing actions on them. Relative to fear or color vision, the experience of addition is descriptively much simpler.

I would note a valuable corollary that helps corroborate these points. The complexity of the consciousness claim, combined with the capabilities inadequacy claim (CI), allows us to explain another overlooked feature of phenomenal experience. Some phenomenal experiences can be called up at will. Others cannot. We can remember a number, and it is the same as the first time we thought of the number. That is, my street address is 210. When I remember it is 210, the experience is the same as the last time I thought of the fact that it is 210. However, when I am afraid, and later when I remember being afraid, the experiences are different. CI tells us why this is so. Our declarative memory and our reasoning capabilities are just not capacious enough to store all the information that constituted the fear experience; also, it would be foolish for our memories to dedicate space to that information, given that our bodies are there to reproduce that information if need be.[4] But the information in a number like 210 does not exceed our reasoning capacity. We can have the experience at will, by reasoning about 210.

5.3 Why the Bias Is Pernicious

At first glance, it might seem that such a bias would be irrelevant. If all of these mental events have a qualitative nature, and what we aim to explain is the qualitative nature of consciousness, then should not any of these do as well as any other as an instance to be studied and explained? But a bias for the more complex cases would be highly pernicious to any attempt to develop a new theory. This is a general epistemic problem, not a metaphysical one.

To see why this is so, consider analogous cases from any successful scientific explanation. Suppose that the critical evaluations of early attempts at dynamics all demanded, of those early naturalists working to develop a theory of dynamics, that they first explain not the motion of a single falling object, but rather the motion of many interacting objects under various forces and moving through a viscous fluid. Dynamics would have stalled, as we marveled dumbly at the incomprehensibility of motion. Suppose that the scientific community demanded of Darwin not first his evidence for evolution but rather first the far more difficult task of explaining exactly how inheritable traits are encoded, and suppose that this scientific community then evaluated Darwin's theory on the basis of how completely it also explained these mechanisms of inheritance. Evolutionary theory would have died on the spot. Science, like many other epistemic endeavors, starts with the simpler cases, the cases that are first easiest to explain; it discovers hypothetical laws that cover those cases and only then turns to the difficult work of discovering how, and whether, those laws generalize to ever more complex cases, or how they can be revised or augmented to so apply. To start always with the most complex cases would render impotent each attempt at understanding. Demanding that a scientific endeavor starts with the most difficult cases is like demanding that a hiker cross a continent before taking a first step.

But in the study of consciousness, something analogous to these nightmare scenarios has become the norm. There are many kinds of phenomenal experiences. Some of them do not appear as mysterious as the others. A natural method, a method proved valuable by past successes, would be to attempt to explain the less mysterious cases first, with the expectations both that these will foster attempts to develop a theory and that one can then generalize that theory to the more complex cases. But this is not the approach that is the norm in philosophical discussions of physicalism regarding consciousness. We have instead discussed the most complex cases and ignored the less complex cases.

What makes the motion of many interacting bodies difficult to explain is that the resulting problem is complex; the required descriptive facts are great, and the computational demands of calculating outcomes are great. In contrast, the complexity of a two-body problem is correspondingly simpler. There is no fundamental ontological difference but rather just this difference in complexity. Just so, when we look at phenomenal experiences, some are vastly more complex than others. There may well be no relevant difference in the kinds involved, but rather just a difference in how complex the kinds are. We have allowed a pernicious sample bias to dominate all our discussions of consciousness, by allowing those who argue for anti-physicalism to pick the examples, and focus only upon the most complex cases, and then demand complete explanations of these most complex cases in all their complexity.

5.4 The Bias Has Corrupted Physicalism

One reason this sample bias has substantially hindered our understanding of phenomenal experience is that it has been accepted by those defending physicalist theories of consciousness. It occurs across the arguments against physicalism for phenomenal experience, but it has even infected some arguments for physicalism, creating as a result difficulties for those theories. If we start instead with events like addition, and not the most complex events like terror, we may find that we can develop theories that later can be extended to explain the more complex cases, and we may be able to simplify and improve the existing physical theories that have been adversely influenced by the sample bias.

To motivate this claim, consider an example of a philosophical theory of phenomenal experience—and one of the few positive theories of phenomenal experience that we have available: the representational theory of consciousness. This is an illustrative case because the prejudices of the sample bias have infected the discussion of the representational theory of consciousness. In particular, Tye's PANIC theory (Tye 1995; Tye 2000) has ceded the sample bias to the anti-physicalists, and as a result, this has rendered the PANIC theory less plausible. Correcting for the bias in our starting cases will produce a more elegant representational theory with better chances of success.

In the representational theory, phenomenal experiences are representations. The experiential content of these mental events is their representational content. This theory has the advantage of explaining certain puzzles about consciousness by showing that these puzzles are equivalent to puzzles about intentional (and intensional) content (see Tye 1995: 133ff). But Tye's PANIC theory goes farther than just identifying phenomenal experiences with representations. It requires that these phenomenal representations be Poised Abstract Nonconceptual Intentional Contents. To say that these representations are "poised" is to say that they are ready and available to influence the formation of beliefs, but they are abstract and nonconceptual in that they are not themselves beliefs. Tye explicitly adopts this view because he accepts the sample bias in the study of phenomenal experience. Contrasting "feelings" with desires, and positing a desire to eat ice cream, he asks:

> Is there not something it is like for me to have this desire? If so, is not this state phenomenally conscious? And what about the belief that I am a very fine fellow? Or the memory that September 2 is the date on which I first fell in love? Is there not some phenomenal flavor to both of these states?
>
> (1995: 4)

Tye answers his own questions in the negative, claiming, "Take away the feelings and experiences that happen to be associated with the aforementioned states in particular cases, and there is no phenomenal consciousness left" (1995: 4). He makes similar claims about things like memory recall and beliefs in general.

If a physicalist representational theory of phenomenal experience were true; and if one wrongly accepted the sample bias that characterizes contemporary discussion of phenomenal experience, then we should expect that any attempt to accommodate in theory the false difference illustrated in the sample bias will result in erroneous distinctions in the theories. Namely, we will be prone to posit an intrinsic, ontological difference where there is only a difference in complexity. And this is precisely what we find in Tye's theory. Criticisms of Tye's theory have rightly focused upon his concept of non-conceptual content. This notion primarily serves in his theory to accommodate the bias that informs the belief that, say, there is no phenomenal experience of addition, but there is one for pain or color. If this difference is only a matter of degree, and not of kind, we should expect any theoretical attempts to explain the nonexistent ontological difference will be refutable. And this is what we do find.

To pick just one example of a criticism[5] of Tye's PANIC theory: Uriah Kriegel has observed that Tye's claim entails that

> For any states S_1 and S_2, the fact (when it is a fact) that S_1 does and S_2 does not have phenomenal character at all is a fact about the representational properties of S_1 and S_2.
>
> (2002: 56)

In other words, if S_1 a pain state, and S_2 is an awareness that 17 and 12 are 29, then the claim that the former has phenomenal character and the latter lacks phenomenal character must be explained in Tye's theory by a difference in their representational character. Kriegel rightly notes that beliefs have abstract content (58). The example here, of addition, would seem quintessentially abstract. So this cannot account for the supposed difference in phenomenal character. The answer, as Tye claims, must lie in the non-conceptual nature of phenomenal contents. In response, Kriegel makes the following claims:

> A super-sentient creature is conceivable (and also possible, as far as I can tell), who would possess a concept for every shade of red. Any shade of red the creature can discriminate today it can recognize (among hundreds of samples) tomorrow, as well as next year. It would be odd to deny this creature phenomenal experiences of red on account of its augmented sensory and cognitive abilities. Surely it is not the limitations of our sensory and cognitive abilities that give rise to phenomenality.
>
> (59)

Conceivability claims have fully metastasized throughout the consciousness literature, but the point here can be made without talk of super-beings. We may agree that there is non-conceptual content and that many phenomenal experiences have non-conceptual content, but Tye has done nothing to explain or make plausible that *adding* conceptual content would neutralize a phenomenal experience and render it without phenomenal character. Indeed, it seems downright strange that the *addition* of cognitive categorization would render a phenomenal experience that had phenomenal character into a state of awareness that now lacked phenomenal character. Imagine some phenomenal and supposedly non-conceptual experience, like seeing red; Tye is saddled with the proposition that if for some reason, there were a concept always applied to this—if we then think, "that's red," when seeing red—we will have expunged the phenomenal character. Put in this way, Tye's claim is recognizably unmotivated and fails to explain the difference between representations with and without phenomenal character.

Presumably, the reply to Kriegel's point here is that it is not the addition of the concept, but rather the concept itself, that is without phenomenal character. Fair enough, but why is being conceptual—whatever that means[6]—sufficient to prevent a phenomenal experience? This is a supposition of the theory, not something for which he presents evidence. Other arguments for the bias have been offered, and they are singularly unsuccessful. For example, Carruthers and Veillet (2011) argue that "A property is phenomenal only if it contributes to the hard problem of consciousness, and in particular, only if it gives rise to an explanatory gap" (45). From this, they derive that there is no phenomenal experience of things like adding $2+2=4$. I hope it is obvious how pernicious such reasoning is; they *define* phenomenal experience in such a way that we explicitly forbid building our theories from the simpler, less difficult cases.

Again, on the analogy, imagine if the response to early developments in evolutionary theory was something like, "An explanation of evolution is sufficient only if it contributes to the hard problem of evolution, and in particular, only if it explains the transmission of genetic information and the origins of first life"; or imagine if the response to early developments in dynamics was something like, "An explanation of motion is sufficient only if it contributes to the hard problem of motion, and in particular, only if it can predict the motion of three or more bodies interacting while in motion in a viscous fluid." I hope it is obvious that Carruthers and Veillet's argument is antithetical to the scientific method.

An alternative explanation readily presents itself. The conceptual–nonconceptual divide may distinguish between beliefs and some pains, or—to use my examples—between addition and some color experiences (though I suspect that, concepts being mysterious, the very notion of conceptual versus nonconceptual is unhelpful in this debate). Presumably, this is why Tye and others have seized upon it. But when we recognize the sample bias (and therefore recognize that believing or adding have phenomenal character, only it is a very simple and thin phenomenal character), then we have spared the representational theory of consciousness the burden of trying to simultaneously equate phenomenal experiences with representations and also to divide between representations that have and that lack phenomenal character.

Belief and desire *do* have a phenomenal content. Only, that phenomenal content is very minor, because the states are relatively simple. On this view, then, there is no fundamental ontological difference between color and a belief. If color experience is non-conceptual, abstract, and poised, this is an accident, likely arising from the architectural demands of the mind. It is not intrinsic to the phenomenal character of color. Rather, the difference is that color experience has a lot of information in it, and a typical belief has very little information in it. A representational theory of phenomenal experience can allow that all of the representations of which we are aware are just those with phenomenal character. But then the representational theory of belief is greatly simplified; one need not explain what it is to be abstract or poised or non-conceptual and can focus upon developing a working theory of simpler cases (like an addition experience) and then working to scale the explanation up to the more complex cases (like color or emotion experience).[7] Tye's representational theory of mind thus serves as an example of how the sample bias can infect even physicalist theories and also serves as an example of how correcting for the bias can allow us to simplify and strengthen those theories.

My point here is not to mount a defense of the representational theory of consciousness, though I do consider it a promising positive program. Rather, it is to illustrate both how the sample bias is pernicious and how correcting for the sample bias renders some physicalist theories far more plausible and suggests productive ways to proceed with research. The morals should be obvious and uncontroversial: we should start with the simpler cases and work with the aspiration of developing a successful theory of those simpler cases until the theory is satisfactory, and only then strive to explain the more complex cases; and, we should not allow anyone to pick the most complex cases for explanation as sole representatives of the phenomena to be explained, nor even as good starting places for the development of any explanatory theory.

5.5 The Zombie Quarantine Problem

As shown earlier, the anti-physicalist arguments lack any bite when they are made for experiences near the bottom of the list of experiences given earlier. For any anti-physicalist who grants that there is an experience of addition, for example, this is an insurmountable problem. But another alternative would be to argue that there is some special ontological difference between those experiences at the top and bottom of the list. This can entail being an eliminativist about the experience for those mental events near the bottom of the list.

It is difficult to see how any claim that there is an ontological distinction between phenomenal experiences near the top and bottom of the list would not be question-begging. On this view, not just phenomenal character, but some additional phenomenal feature would distinguish, say, the experiences of terror and addition. But what would this feature be? As we saw earlier, the arguments for eliminativism are not only unconvincing, but they are antithetical to the scientific method; they essentially reify into an ontological claim, the observation that those experiences near the top of the list are more mysterious, and those near the bottom less mysterious. But an anti-physicalist argument cannot rest upon the posit of a property that is there only to add mysteriousness. That begs the question in a way that renders the relevant claims vacuous. This claim, then, should be rejected unless we are offered both some account or theory of what this supposed difference in intrinsic nature really is, and also are shown that the posit of the intrinsic difference does some theoretical work other than saving the claim there is some ontological difference here. It cannot be a wise epistemic move to propose that there is some intrinsic feature for these events without establishing on independent grounds that we cannot use the less-mysterious cases to develop our understanding. To return to the analogies given earlier, such reasoning would have us hypothesize that there is some special intrinsic difference between motions with many interacting bodies as opposed to the motion of one body or two interacting bodies. Furthermore, such a move would open the door to the strategy of offering only a perpetually moving target: each step of theoretical progress would be victim to the claim that we have not yet approached the missing intrinsic property, which could be claimed to inhere in whatever cases remain unexplained. Also, given that I have proposed an alternative explanation (that the complexity of the experience determines what distinguishes the top and bottom of the list), and this is a proposal for an objective and non-circular property, an alternative should at least rise to the standard of also being objective and non-circular.

But let us suppose that one adopts eliminativism about those items lower on the list; one could argue that they simply lack a phenomenal character. This is the move we saw Tye, and Carruthers and Veillet, make earlier. This eliminativism regarding the experience of some mental events will have a paradoxical consequence that undermines the anti-physicalist position. If we do not assume that all mental events of which we are aware include a phenomenal experience, we will have the very strange category of awareness without experience. This is what I called earlier "the subjectivity bias": we break subjective awareness away from the phenomenal experience. These may be distinct conceptually, but a conceptual difference is not proof that you can have subjective experience without phenomenal experience. It would seem *prima facie* reasonable, and also more parsimonious, to suppose that if we are aware of a mental event, then it has phenomenal quality. We break this link only to accommodate not our phenomenology but rather a theory. Some scholars are willing to bite this bullet, dividing mental events of which we are aware into those with and those without phenomenal character—as noted, even some physicalists adopt this view—but there is a damning consequence that has hitherto been overlooked.

The notion of the phenomenal zombie is meant to illustrate a metaphysical possibility that never actually occurs in our world. The thought experiment's role is solely to break metaphysical necessity from physical necessity; the phenomenal zombies exist in some possible world but not in our world. And what this means is that it could have been the case that our laws of physics but different metaphysical laws would result in a world like ours physically but without phenomenal experiences. It is a way of articulating a claim that a phenomenon is independent of a kind of theory. But the bias that we sometimes have subjective awareness without phenomenal quality makes us all partial zombies. That is, there is nothing otherworldly about the idea of the zombie for the subjectivity bias. Just like the zombie in another world, that sees blue and reacts appropriately except that it has no experience of blue; those who split subjectivity from phenomenal quality make us all zombies. We are, for example, mathematical zombies. We think of numbers and we react appropriately to numbers but we have no experience of numbers.

It gets worse. Daniel Dennett has repeatedly argued that most people who hear about phenomenal zombies and find the idea plausible don't understand what is meant by a zombie. I am convinced he is right. For the zombie is epistemically absurd. It claims it has phenomenal experiences; it writes poems about sunsets and love; it writes books about zombies and how strange they are and expresses its gladness that it is not one of them; it says things like "zombies exist in some possible world but they cannot and do not exist in this world"; it never makes an error in describing (as well as we humans can describe) its subjective states as having the kind of phenomenal feel we have when we are in that subjective state, but all these claims by the zombie are false. Worse, the zombie doesn't know they are false. Worser yet, no one can know if they are false—that is, no one (including the zombie) can know if the zombie is a zombie.

These ridiculous epistemic consequences are thought palatable because the zombie is off in a different hypothetical universe. The idea of a zombie is not meant to be that my neighbor could be a zombie. It's supposed to be that our physical laws don't rule out the zombies, and we therefore describe the zombies as "physically possible," and we use the wretchedly misleading philosophical terminology of saying then that "there is a zombie world," but we assume that things work out in this world such that there are no zombies. (The working out for the anti-physicalist occurs because, they assume, of some non-physical kind of linkages, some non-physical but metaphysical laws.) The zombies are quarantined in the zombie world, so the absurd consequences of the zombies are supposedly not refutations of the anti-physicalist position.

But now consider. All of us who do math are math zombies, according to the eliminativist who claims we lack experience for those mental events low on the list. We are aware of doing math, but we have no phenomenal experience of doing math. How is this different from reacting in all the appropriate ways to blue but lacking any experience of blue? And, those of us who claim to have an experience of doing math are like zombies writing sonnets about blue. We are describing what we cannot and do not experience. Why is this not an absurd consequence of the theory?

The answer, presumably, is that the difference lies in that we erroneously claim to have an experience of math while doing math. Many of us claim that we have an experience of adding 12 and 17. (I have an experience of adding two numbers. It is a very thin experience, very different from, and very much weaker than, the experience of color or an emotion, but it exists.) To claim that those of us who identify a phenomenal experience for those items lower on the list of mental events given earlier are wrong is to declare that we are partial zombies, having some mental events of which we are aware but about which we have no phenomenal experience, *and about which we claim to have phenomenal experience.* But now, our claim that we do have a phenomenal experience makes us like the absurd zombies of the canonical thought experiment.

One can of course claim that those who say they have an experience of math while doing math are sincere but wrong. That is, we are math zombies. And that then means that the zombies have broken quarantine. Remember, supposedly the zombie claims that are equivalent to anti-physicalism are not epistemically pernicious because we are not zombies, and zombies are not possible in this world. But if the *actual* world has partial zombies—namely, all of those who claim to experience addition are erring zombies with respect to addition—then in the *actual* world there can be no epistemic warrant to *any* phenomenological claims. We must deny that anyone can determine whether she, or anyone else, experiences anything. With the zombies out of quarantine, they will sweep the world, spreading their disease, and sully every phenomenal judgment. This renders all discussion of consciousness worthless.

But maybe that is too hasty. One could say that we are simply wrong for reasons other than being like zombies. For some reason, some of us claim to have an experience of math when we do math, but we're just wrong. This is peculiar because the error in question is systematic. It is not akin to other errors of phenomenology. For example, the failure to notice that we are colorblind in the periphery is not analogous. We can have a color experience in the center field, and we can have a color experience of what is in the periphery if we turn our heads, so the error is not in believing that we sometimes have a kind of experience, but rather the error lies in identifying when we have the experience. But to maintain the zombie quarantine, the error claim is radical: we who claim to experience addition erroneously believe we have a *kind* of experience.

If such an error is possible, we have established that phenomenal judgments are very fallible. And, it is worth noting now, none of the classical anti-physicalist arguments are likely to have a valid form if we allow for this kind of radical fallibility. What we think Mary might learn, where we think the gaps lie, our Cartesian intuitions, our thoughts about zombies, and our sense of which questions are open are all neutered, if we can be so systematically in error about our experiences as to claim to have experiences where we lack them.

But, in any case, what the anti-physicalist who wants to maintain this kind of break between phenomenal experience and subjectivity needs is an error theory: an explanation of why people like me make the error of believing they have a phenomenal experience when they do math. Furthermore, we want the explanation not to require that I am a zombie. The most likely answer—the only answer I can find plausible—is that I have a bias. This is certainly possible. Here I am, writing this book, and I want everything to fit together nicely. So I see my mathematical experience with a bias, unconsciously wanting it to be qualitative when it is not. It is not implausible that I suffer from such influences. And, it is important to recognize that in fact this is precisely *my* error theory for those who claim that they don't have an experience of adding two numbers; I claim that they have a bias in which they want to focus upon the complex cases and so they willfully ignore the simpler cases.[8] Their theoretical commitments lead them to claim that they have no experience of adding numbers.

We have now made the position of those who divide subjectivity from quality, and those who unite them, into symmetric positions. We both accuse the other of a theoretical bias. And this is very important because the anti-physicalists who make use of the split between subjectivity and phenomenal quality require that they are making *observations* about the nature of consciousness and are developing *a priori* arguments about the consequences of their observations and of their concepts. If we admit that those who unite subjectivity and phenomenal quality, and those who split them, are both making theoretical claims, equally supported by the available observational evidence, then other considerations must come into play. We must turn to other measures of theoretical virtue to decide between these theories. And the relevant theoretical virtues are the explanatory power and productivity of our respective theories.

The anti-physicalists have, quite literally, nothing at this time to offer in terms of explanatory power and productivity. The physicalists who are eliminativists about these simpler experiences are committed to maintaining mysterianism. Neither has a positive research program for the relevant cases. We should, on pragmatic grounds, and in response to the zombie quarantine problem, pursue the physicalist program that recognizes these simpler experiences as experiences and offers them as the starting place for developing an explanation of consciousness.

Notes

1. "In addressing the philosophical mysteries associated with conscious experience, a simple color sensation raises the problems as deeply as one's experience of a Bach chorale" (Chalmers 1996: 11). My contention is that neither the experience of color nor the experience of a Bach chorale are simple examples, and, as a result, they are in a sense not representative examples.
2. I cannot bring myself, in the name of parallelism with Jackson's argument, to suppose that Mary perhaps knows all logic. The idea that some human could learn all logic is baldly contradictory. For that matter, so is Jackson's claim that some human could know all physical facts (this is logically contradictory because nothing could be both recognizably human and have such information capacity). Fortunately, it's enough to suppose that Mary knows all relevant logical facts—such as all of contemporary logic less the elements referring to numbers—to demonstrate the failure of the argument.
3. This is crucial, and the zombie arguments would be allowed sleight of hand if we forget this: zombies are aware that they are seeing red things, being exposed to noxious stimuli, running from a bear with a beating heart; they just lack the experience of red, of pain, and of fear. They have awareness without experience.
4. This is another way to explain Damasio's somatic marker hypothesis (1994): if the body can act as a marker, carrying information, then use the body; memory space in the brain can be dedicated to other purposes.
5. Other criticisms concerning Tye's notion of non-conceptual content can be found in Byrne (2003).
6. I suspect that there is some fundamental confusion involved in these arguments when those defending the sample bias roll out their claims about "concepts" and "conceptual content." A thought is an event, but philosophers tend to think of concepts as nominalized predicates—that is, as abstract objects of logic. For this reason, such arguments open the door to confusions when we use terms like "conceptual content" and "abstract content" to think of the mental event of, say, doing addition. This event is not a nominalized predicate, it is not an abstracta, and the experience of the event is not an experience of an abstracta. Talking about such an event in terms of a static abstracta is surely a mistake.
7. The resulting approach sounds likely to be much closer to Lycan's representational theory of consciousness (Lycan 1996), which is not formulated to include the sample bias.
8. Again, see how explicit this is in the case of Carruthers and Veillet's argument: "A property is phenomenal only if it contributed to the hard problem of consciousness, and in particular, only if it gives rise to the explanatory gap" (2011: 45). Combine this with the complexity of consciousness claim, and you get that a mental event is phenomenal only if it is very complex. This literally rules out starting with the simpler cases.

Afterward

Consciousness as Complex Event

I have argued that some phenomenal experiences are very complex events and that this explains why they appear mysterious and continue to resist explanation. The result of my arguments is that our best bet at this time is to continue research under the assumption that physicalism about phenomenal experience is true. Future research may prove this wrong, but nothing in contemporary metaphysics gives us sufficient reason to doubt physicalism, and nothing in contemporary metaphysics offers an alternative research program of comparable productivity.

Some have called the march of scientific progress "the disenchantment of the world." On this view, science "reduces." Science makes the world—in some metaphorical sense—smaller.[1] The sentiment was expressed by Walt Whitman when he wrote,

> When I heard the learn'd astronomer,
> When the proofs, the figures, were ranged in columns before me,
> When I was shown the charts and diagrams, to add, divide, and measure them,
> When I sitting heard the astronomer where he lectured with much applause in the lecture-room,
> How soon unaccountable I became tired and sick,
> Till rising and gliding out I wander'd off by myself,
> In the mystical moist night-air, and from time to time,
> Look'd up in perfect silence at the stars.

Whitman seems to find the explanations of the astronomer take something away. They reduce his world. He feels compelled to turn away from such explanations and encounter the stars again without theory.

We can object to Whitman's sentiment. We can observe that the universe of the modern astronomer is astonishingly larger than anything conceived in ancient myths. But let us be sympathetic to him for a moment. He thought that stars were something beyond his imagination, something marvelous, and far from being explained. For him, stars were mysteries to remain unsolved but pleasantly beckoning us all to learn more about them. In this context, he feels

DOI: 10.4324/9781003320685-6

the astronomer has reduced all his expectations to some simplistic math and chemistry. Even if this sentiment of Whitman's is unfair, we can understand his reasoning.

I have argued that we should bet on physicalism with respect to consciousness. But, as explained in Section 3.4, this is not a simplistic, reductive physicalism. In the theory of descriptive complexity, we have the tools to understand how something can be both explained by a scientific theory, but also irreducibly complex. And consciousness, I have argued, is just such a phenomenon.

We have tended to think of the mind with mechanical analogies. The mind has been conceived as clockwork, as a switchboard, and as a computer. But perhaps the better metaphor is the mind as rain forest, a lush and enormously complex ecology of thoughts and experiences and abilities. Strangely shared, and more strangely solely one's own.

Consider the implications of the complexity of consciousness. Your phenomenal experience is of a kind unique to your species. No other system in the universe will have just those kinds of enormously complex events that constitute a human being seeing red, or feeling joy at listening to Beethoven, or knowing love for another human being. Furthermore, it is likely that many of your phenomenal experiences are unique to you because complex in the particulars of your own history. Your way of seeing the world, your emotional dispositions, your sense of purpose, and your practices of interacting with others—each of these is so complex as to be unique to you and unique in the universe.

Note

1. For the record, I believe the "disenchantment of the world" is largely the replacement of teleological explanations with causal ones, but some of it is also an objection to reductionism. While scientific progress has grown, in some ways, the mind has become more mysterious, in part because scientific progress has rested upon abandoning the kind of teleological explanations that, for a philosopher like Aristotle, gave us a unified account of both nature and mind.

Bibliography

Alexander, Samuel (1920) *Space, Time, and Deity*. London: Macmillan & Co.

Armstrong, D. M. (1968) *A Materialist Theory of Mind*. London: Routledge.

Baars, B. J. (1988) *A Cognitive Theory of Consciousness*. Cambridge: Cambridge University Press.

Ball, Derek (2008) "Why There Are No Phenomenal Concepts, and What Physicalists Should Do About It." Dissertation, University of Texas at Austin.

Balog, Katalin (2012) "In Defense of the Phenomenal Concepts Strategy." *Philosophy and Phenomenological Research* 84 (1): 1–23.

Bedau, Mark (1997) "Weak Emergence." In *Philosophical Perspectives: Mind, Causation, and World*, J. Tomberlin (ed.). Malden, MA: Blackwell.

Bekenstein, Jacob D. (1981) "Universal Upper Bound on the Entropy-to-Energy Ratio for Bounded Systems." *Physical Review D*. 23 (2): 287–298.

Blackburn, Simon (1990) "Filling in Space." *Analysis* 50: 60–65.

Block, Ned (1990) "Inverted Earth." *Philosophical Perspectives* 4: 53–79.

——— (1995) "On a Confusion About a Function of Consciousness." *The Behavioral and Brain Sciences* 18 (2).

——— (2011) "Perceptual Consciousness Overflows Access Consciousness." *Trends in Cognitive Science* 15 (12): 567–575.

Block, Ned and Cynthia MacDonald (2008) "Phenomenal and Access Consciousness." *Proceedings of the Aristotelian Society* cviii, Part 3.

Block, Ned and Robert Stalnaker (1999) "Conceptual Analysis, Dualism, and the Explanatory Gap." *The Philosophical Review* 108 (1): 1–46.

BonJour, Laurence (2010) "Against Materialism." In *The Waning of Materialism*, Robert C. Koons and George Bealer (eds.): 3–23. New York: Oxford University Press.

Born, Max (1962 [1924]) *Einstein's Theory of Relativity*. New York: Dover.

Bradley, Margaret and Peter Lang (2000) "Measuring Emotion: Behavior, Feeling, and Physiology." In *Cognitive Neuroscience of Emotion*, Richard Lane and Lynn Nadel (eds.): 242–276. New York: Oxford University Press.

Broad, C. D. (1925) *The Mind and Its Place in Nature*. London: Routledge Kegan Paul.

Brown, Robin and James Ladyman (2009) "Physicalism, Supervenience, and the Fundamental Level." *The Philosophical Quarterly* 59 (234): 20–38.

Burnett, D. Graham (2007) *Trying Leviathan*. Princeton, NJ: Princeton University Press.

Byrne, Alex (2003) "Consciousness and Nonconceptual Content." *Philosophical Studies* 113: 261–274.

Carnap, Rudolf (1969 [1928]) *The Logical Structure of the World and Psuedoproblems of Philosophy*. Translated by Rolf George. Berkeley and Los Angeles: University of California Press.

Carruthers, Peter (2006) *The Architecture of Mind*. New York: Oxford University Press.

Carruthers, Peter and Benedicte Veillet (2011) "The Case Against Cognitive Phenomenology." In *Cognitive Phenomenology*, Tim Bayne and Michelle Montague (eds.): 35–56. Oxford: Oxford University Press.

Chaitin, Gregory (1966) "On the Length of Programs for Computing Finite Binary Sequences." *Journal of the Association of Computing Machinery* 13: 547–569.

———— (1974) "Information-Theoretic Limitations of Formal Systems." *Journal of the Association of Computing Machinery* 21: 403–424.

———— (1982) "Gödel's Theorem and Information." *International Journal of Theoretical Physics* 22: 941–954.

———— (1990) "Randomness and Mathematical Proof." In *Information, Randomness, and Incompleteness: Papers on Algorithmic Information Theory, Second Edition:* 3–13. Singapore: World Scientific Publishing Co.

———— (2001) *Exploring Randomness (Discrete Mathematics and Theoretical Computer Science)*. New York: Springer.

———— (2003) *The Limits of Mathematics*. London: Springer-Verlag.

———— (2004) *Algorithmic Information Theory (Cambridge Tracts in Theoretical Computer Science)*. New York: Cambridge University Press.

Chalmers, David (1995) "Facing Up to the Hard Problem of Consciousness." *Journal of Consciousness Studies* 2 (3): 200–219.

———— (1996) *The Conscious Mind*. New York: Oxford University Press.

———— (2002) "Does Conceivability Entail Possibility?" In *Conceivability and Possibility,* T. Gendler and J. Hawthorne (eds.): 145–200. New York: Oxford University Press.

———— (2007) "Consciousness and Its Place in Nature." In *The Blackwell Guide to Philosophy of Mind*, S. P. Stich and T. A. Warfield (eds.): 102–141. Malden, MA: Blackwell Publishing Ltd.

———— (2010a) "Facing Up to the Problem of Consciousness." In *The Character of Consciousness*, David Chalmers (ed.): 3–34. New York: Oxford University Press.

———— (2010b) "Consciousness and Its Place in Nature." In *The Character of Consciousness*, David Chalmers (ed.): 103–139. New York: Oxford University Press.

———— (2010c) "The Two-Dimensional Argument Against Materialism." In *The Character of Consciousness:* 141–192. New York: Oxford University Press.

Chalmers, David and Frank Jackson (2001) "Conceptual Analysis and Reductive Explanation." *Philosophical Review* 110: 315–361.

Chemero, Anthony (2003) "Information for Perception and Information Processing." *Minds and Machines* 13: 577–588.

———— (2009) *Radical Embodied Cognitive Science*. Cambridge, MA: The MIT Press.

Churchland, Patricia (1997) "The Horswoggle Problem." In *Explaining Consciousness: The Hard Problem*, J. Shear (ed.). Cambridge, MA: MIT Press.

Churchland, Paul (1985) "Reduction, Qualia, and the Direct Introspection of Brain States." *Journal of Philosophy* 82 (1): 8–28.

———— (1988) "Perceptual Plasticity and Theoretical Neutrality: A Reply to Jerry Fodor." *Philosophy of Science* 55: 167–187.

———— (1996) "The Rediscovery of Light." *The Journal of Philosophy* 93: 211–228.

Clark, Andy (1997) *Being There*. Cambridge, MA: MIT Press.

Conway Morris, Simon (1998) *The Crucible of Creation: The Burgess Shale and the Rise of Animals*. New York: Oxford University Press.

Cosmides, Leda and John Tooby (1992) *The Adapted Mind*. New York: Oxford University Press.

Crane, T. and D. H. Mellor (1990) "There Is No Question of Physicalism." *Mind* 99 (394): 185–206.

Damasio, Antonio (1994) *Descartes Error*. New York: Putnam.

Dehaene, Stanilas, Ghislaine Dehaene-Lambertz and Laurent Cohen (1998) "Abstract Representations of Numbers in the Animal and Human Brain." *Trends in Neuroscience* 21: 355–361.

Dehaene, S. and L. Naccache (2001) "Towards a Cognitive Neuroscience of Consciousness." *Cognition* 79: 1–37.

DeLancey, Craig (2002) *Passionate Engines: What Emotions Reveal About Mind and Artificial Intelligence*. New York: Oxford University Press.

——— (2007a) "Phenomenal Experience and the Measure of Information." *Erkenntnis* 66 (3): 329–352.

——— (2007b) "Meaning Naturalism, Meaning Irrealism, and the Work of Language." *Synthese* 154 (2): 231–257.

——— (2011) "Does A Parsimony Principle Entail a Simple World?" *Metaphysica* 12 (2): 87–100.

Dennett, Daniel (2005) *Sweet Dreams: Philosophical Obstacles to a Science of Consciousness*. Cambridge, MA: MIT Press.

Dowell, J. L. (2008) "A Priori Entailment and Conceptual Analysis: Making Room for Type-C Physicalism." *Australasian Journal of Philosophy* 86: 93–111.

Eddington, A. S. (1933) *The Nature of the Physical World*. New York: The Macmillan Company.

Fama, Eugene (1965) "The Behavior of Stock Market Prices." *Journal of Business* 38: 34–105.

Fehr, Thorsten, Chris Code and Manfred Herrman (2007) "Common Brain Regions Underlying Different Arithmetic Operations as Revealed by Conjunct fMRI-BOLD Activation." *Brain Research* 1172: 93–102.

Feigl, Herbert (1958) "The 'Mental' and the 'Physical'." In *Minnesota Studies in the Philosophy of Science, Volume II: Concepts, Theories, and the Mind-Body Problem*, Herbert Feigl, Michael Scriven and Grover Maxwell (eds.): 370–497. Minnesota: University of Minnesota Press.

Felleman, D. J. and D. C. van Essen (1991) "Distributed Hierarchical Processing in Primate Cerebral Cortex." *Cerebral Cortex* 1: 1–47.

Fodor, Jerry (1983) *The Modularity of Mind*. Cambridge, MA: The MIT Press.

Fortey, Richard (1997) *Life: A Natural History of the First Four Billion Years of Life on Earth*. New York: Knopf.

Frankfurt, Harry (1971) "Freedom of the Will and the Concept of a Person." *Journal of Philosophy* 68 (1): 5–20.

Gibson, J. (1966) *The Senses Considered as Perceptual Systems*. Boston: Houghton Mifflin.

——— (1979) *The Ecological Approach to Visual Perception*. Boston: Houghton Mifflin.

Giere, Ronald N. (1994) "The Cognitive Structure of Scientific Theories." *Philosophy of Science* 61: 276–296.

Gocke, Benedikt (2009) "What Is Physicalism?" *Ratio* 22 (3): 291–307.

Goodstein, David (1989) "Richard P. Feynman, Teacher." *Physics Today* 42 (2): 70–75.

Gould, Stephen Jay (1990) *Wonderful Life: The Burgess Shale and the Nature of History*. New York: W. W. Norton & Company.

Goyal, R. K. and I. Hirano (1996) "The Enteric Nervous System." *The New England Journal of Medicine* 334: 1106–1115.

Graham, George and Terrence Horgan (2000) "Mary Mary, Quite Contrary." *Philosophical Studies* 99: 59–87.

Hempel, C. (1980) "Comments on Goodman's *Ways of Worldmaking*." *Synthese* 49: 139–199.

Horgan, Terrence (1984) "Supervenience and Cosmic Hermeneutics." *Southern Journal of Philosophy* 22 supplement: 19–38.

Howell, Robert (2009) "Emergentism and Supervenience Physicalism." *Australasian Journal of Philosophy* 87 (1): 83–98.

Jackson, Frank (1982) "Epiphenomenal Qualia." *The Philosophical Quarterly* 127 (32): 127–136.

———— (1986) "What Mary Didn't Know." *The Journal of Philosophy* 83: 291–295.

———— (1993) "Armchair Metaphysics." In *Philosophy in Mind*, M. Michael and John O'Leary-Hawthorne (eds.). Dordrecht: Kluwer.

———— (1998) *From Metaphysics to Ethics: A Defense of Conceptual Analysis*. New York: Oxford University Press.

———— (2004) "Postscript on Qualia." In *There's Something About Mary*, Frank Jackson, Peter Ludlow, Yujin Nagasawa, Daniel Stoljar (eds.): 417–421. Cambridge, MA: The MIT Press.

Joyce, James (1986) *Ulysses (the Corrected Text. First American Edition)*. New York: Random House.

Kandel, Eric R., James H. Schwartz and Thomas M. Jessel (eds.) (2000) *Principles of Neural Science, Fourth Edition*. New York: McGraw-Hill.

Kim, Jaegwon (1998) *Mind in a Physical World*. Cambridge, MA: MIT Press.

———— (1999) "Making Sense of Emergence." *Philosophical Studies* 95: 3–36.

———— (2009) " 'Supervenient and Yet Not Deducible': Is there a Coherent Concept of Ontological Emergence?" In *Reduction: Between the Mind and the Brain, (Austrian Ludwig Wittgenstein Society) (Volume 12)*, Alexander Hieke and Hannes Leitgeb (eds.). Edison, NJ: Transaction Publishers.

Kirk, R. (1974a) "Zombies v. Materialists." *Proceedings of the Aristotelian Society*, supplementary vol. 48: 135–152.

———— (1974b) "Sentience and Behaviour." *Mind* 83: 43–60.

Kolmogorov, A. N. (1965) "Three Approaches to the Quantitative Definition of Information." *Problems of Information Transmission* 1 (1): 1–7.

Koons, Robert C. and George Bealer (eds.) (2010) *The Waning of Materialism*. New York: Oxford University Press.

Kriegel, Uriah (2002) "PANIC Theory and the Prospects for a Representational Theory of Phenomenal Consciousness." *Philosophical Psychology* 15 (1): 55–64.

Kripke, Saul (1972) *Naming and Necessity*. Cambridge, MA: Harvard University Press.

Lackner, J. R. (1988) "Some Proprioceptive Influences on the Perceptual Representation of Body Shape and Orientation." *Brain* 111: 281–297.

Ladyman, James, Don Ross, David Spurrett and John Collier (2007) *Everything Must Go: Metaphysics Naturalized*. New York: Oxford University Press.

Laplace, Pierre Simon Marquis de (1902) *A Philosophical Essay on Probabilities*. New York: Wiley & Sons.

Lazarus, R. S. (1991) *Emotion and Adaptation*. New York: Oxford University Press.

Levine, Joseph (1983) "Materialism and Qualia: The Explanatory Gap." *Pacific Philosophical Quarterly* 64: 354–361.

———— (1993) "On Leaving Out What It's Like." In *Consciousness: Psychological and Philosophical Essays,* Martin Davies (ed.): 121–136. Cambridge: Blackwell.

———— (2001) *Purple Haze*. New York: Oxford University Press.

———— (2007) "Phenomenal Concepts and the Materialist Constraint." In *Phenomenal Concepts and Phenomenal Knowledge*, Torin Alter and Sven Walter (eds.). New York: Oxford University Press.

Lewis, C. I. (1956 [1929]) *Mind and the World Order: Outline of a Theory of Knowledge*. New York: Dover.

Lewis, David (1983a) "New Work for a Theory of Universals." *Australasian Journal of Philosophy* 61: 343–377.

———— (1983b) "Postscript to 'Mad Pain and Martian Pain'." In *Philosophical Papers, Volume I*. New York: Oxford.

———— (1986) *On the Plurality of Worlds*. New York: Blackwell.

———— (1999) "What Experience Teaches." In *Papers in Metaphysics and Epistemology, Volume 2*: 262–290. Cambridge, UK: Cambridge University Press.

Li, Ming and Paul Vitanyi (2008) *An Introduction to Kolmogorov Complexity and Its Applications, Third Edition*. New York: Springer.

Loar, Brian (1990) "Phenomenal States." In *Philosophical Perspectives 4, Action Theory and the Philosophy of Mind*, J. Tomberlin (ed.): 81–108. New York: Ridgeview Publishing Company.

Locke, J. (1975[1689]) *Essay Concerning Human Understanding*. Oxford: Oxford University Press.

Lycan, William G. (1996) *Consciousness and Experience*. Cambridge, MA: The MIT Press.

Mandik, Peter (2010) "Swamp Mary's Revenge: Deviant Phenomenal Knowledge and Physicalism." *Philosophical Studies* 148 (2): 231–247.

———— (ms.) "Swamp Mary Semantics: A Case for Physicalism Without Gaps."

Mehta, Ravi and Rui Juliet Zhu (2009) "Blue or Red? Exploring the Effect of Color on Cognitive Task Performances." *Science* 27, 323 (5918): 1226–1229.

Millikan, R. (1984) *Language, Thought, and Other Biological Categories*. Cambridge, MA: The MIT Press.

Montero, Barbara (1999) "The Body Problem." *Nous* 33 (2): 183–200.

Montero, Barbara and David Papineau (2005) "A Defence of the via Negativa Argument for Physicalism." *Analysis* 65 (287): 233–237.

Monti, M., D. Osherson, M. Martinze and L. Parsons (2007) "Functional Neuroanatomy of Deductive Inference: A Language-Independent Distributed Network." *Neuroimage* 37: 1005–1016.

Morgan, C. Llyod (1923) *Emergent Evolution*. London: Williams and Norgate.

Nagel, Thomas (1974) "What Is It Like to Be a Bat?" *The Philosophical Review* 83 (4): 435–450.

Neander, Karen (1991) "The Teleological Notion of 'Function'." *Australasian Journal of Philosophy* 69 (4): 454–468.

Nemirow, Laurence (1980) "Review of Thomas Nagel, *Mortal Questions*." *Philosophical Review* LXXXIX (3): 473–477.

Ney, Alyssa (2008) "Physicalism as an Attitude." *Philosophical Studies* 138: 1–15.

Niedenthal, Paula and Marc Setterlund (1994) "Emotion Congruence in Perception." *Personality and Social Psychology Bulletin* 20 (4): 401–411.

Noe, Alva (2004) *Action in Perception*. Cambridge, MA: The MIT Press.
——— (2009) *Out of Our Heads*. New York: Hill and Wang.
Oizumi, Masafumi, Larissa Albantakis and Giulio Tononi (2014) "From the Phenomenology to the Machines of Consciousness: Integrated Information Theory 3.0." *PLOS Computational Biology* 10 (5).
O'Regan, Kevin (2011) *Why Red Doesn't Sound Like a Bell*. New York: Oxford University Press.
O'Regan, Kevin, Heiner Deubel, James Clark and Ronald Resnick (2000) "Picture Changes During Blinks: Looking Without Seeing and Seeing Without Looking." *Visual Cognition* 7: 191–211.
Pettit, Philip (1994) "Microphysicalism Without Contingent Micro-Macro Laws." *Analysis* 54 (4): 253–257.
Pitt, David (2004) "The Phenomenology of Cognition, Or What Is It Like to Think That P?" *Philosophy and Phenomenological Research* 69 (1): 1–36.
Poland, Jeffrey (1994) *Physicalism*. New York: Oxford University Press.
Polger, Thomas (2008) "H_2O, 'Water,' and Transparent Reduction." *Erkenntnis* 69: 109–130.
Potochnik, Angela (2015) "The Diverse Aims of Science." *Studies in the History and Philosophy of Science* 53: 71–80.
Rissanen, J. J. (1978) "Modeling by the Shortest Data Description." *Automatica* 15: 465–471.
——— (1989) *Stochastical Complexity and Statistical Inquiry*. New York: World Scientific.
Robinson, William S. (2018) "Dualism." In *The Routledge Handbook of Consciousness,* Rocco J. Gennaro (ed.): 51–63. New York: Routledge.
Ryle, Gilbert (1949) *The Concept of Mind*. London: Hutchinson.
Sacks, Oliver and Robert Wasserman (1987) "The Case of the Colorblind Painter." *New York Review of Books,* November 19.
Samuels, Richard (1998) "Evolutionary Psychology and the Massive Modularity Hypothesis." *British Journal of the Philosophy of Science* 49: 575–602.
Samuelson, Paul (1965) "Proof That Properly Anticipated Prices Fluctuate Randomly." *Industrial Management Review* 6: 41–49.
Schaffer, Jonathan (2003) "Is There a Fundamental Level?" *Nous* 37 (3): 498–517.
Schiffer, Stephen (1990) "Physicalism." *Philosophical Perspectives 4: Action Theory and the Philosophy of Mind*: 153–185.
Schwitzgebel, Eric (2011) *Perplexities of Consciousness*. Cambridge, MA: The MIT Press.
Solomonoff, R. J. (1964) "A Formal Theory of Inductive Inference, Part 1 and Part 2." *Information and Control* 7: 1–22, 224–254.
Sperber, D. (1994) "The Modularity of Thought and the Epidemiology of Representations." In *Mapping the Mind*, L. A. Hirschfeld and S. A. Gelman (eds.): 39–67. Cambridge: Cambridge University Press.
Sperling, G. (1960) "The Information Available in Brief Visual Presentations." *Psychological Monographs* 74: 1–29.
Spurrett, David and D. Papineau (1999) "A Note on the Completeness of 'Physics'." *Analysis* 59: 25–29.
Stoljar, Daniel (2006) *Ignorance and Imagination*. New York: Oxford University Press.
——— (2010) *Physicalism*. New York: Routledge.

Stroud, Barry (1986) "The Physical World." *Proceedings of the Aristotelian Society* 87 (1): 263–277.

Suppes, F. (1972) "What's Wrong with the Received View on the Structure of Scientific Theories?" *Philosophy of Science* 39: 1–19.

Turing, Alan (1936) "On Computable Numbers, with an Application to the Entscheidungsproblem." *Proceedings of the London Mathematical Society* 2 (42): 230–265.

Tye, Michael (1995) *Ten Problems of Consciousness: A Representational Theory of the Phenomenal Mind.* Cambridge, MA: The MIT Press.

——— (2000) *Consciousness, Color, and Content.* Cambridge, MA: The MIT Press.

Tyndall, J. (1871) In *Fragments of Science (Volume 2).* New York: Appleton & Company.

Van Fraassen, B. (2002) *The Empirical Stance.* New Haven, CT: Yale University Press.

Watson, J. B. (1913) "Psychology as the Behaviorist Views It." *Psychological Review* 20: 158–177.

Weisberg, Josh (2011a) "Abusing the Notion of What-It's-Like-Ness: A Response to Block." *Analysis* 71 (3): 438–443.

——— (2011b) "The Zombie's Cogito: Meditations on Type-Q Materialism." *Philosophical Psychology* 24 (5): 585–605.

Weisberg, Michael (2007) "Three Kinds of Idealization." *Journal of Philosophy*, December 104 (12): 639–659.

Williford, Kenneth, David Rudrauf and Gregory Landini (2012) "The Paradoxes of Subjectivity and the Projective Structure of Consciousness." In *Consciousness and Subjectivity,* Sofia Miguens and Gerhard Preyer (eds.): 321–353. Frankfurt: Verlag.

Wilson, Jessica (2005) "Supervenience-Based Formulations of Physicalism." *Nous* 39 (3): 426–459.

——— (2013) "Nonlinearity and Metaphysical Emergence." In *Metaphysics and Science*, Stephen Mumford and Matthew Tugby (eds.). New York: Oxford University Press.

——— (2016) "Metaphysical Emergence: Weak and Strong." In *Metaphysics in Contemporary Physics*, Tomasz Bigaj and Christian Wuthrich (eds.). Boston, MA: Brill Rodopi.

Winsberg, Eric (2006) "Models of Success Versus the Success of Models." *Synthese* 152 (1): 1–19.

Wood, Guilherme, Hans-Christoph Nuerk and Klaus Willmes (2006) "Neural Representations of Two-Digit Numbers: A Parametric fMRI Study." *Neuroimage* 29: 358–367.

Index